Praise for *Mothers-in-law an~~~~~~~~~~~~~~~in-law*

"If you are a mother-in-law—or have ever been a daughter-in-law—you will find yourself in these pages. Susan Shapiro Barash, who is fast becoming America's resident expert on relationships, draws a layered picture of what may be the most fraught-with-danger relationship of all. The controversial mother-in-law/daughter-in-law scenarios are frankly confronted with clarity and candor... the results are original and thought-provoking."

> – Sherry Suib Cohen, journalist, contributing editor of *McCall's Magazine* and best-selling author of seventeen books including *Secrets of a Very Good Marriage*

"Susan Shapiro Barash's *Mothers-in-law and Daughters-in-law* sheds light on a familial relationship not many of us understand completely. Her book offers valuable insights that can improve one's relationship with her mother-in-law or daughter-in-law. Here is a newly presented exploration which explains this complex entity."

> – Lauren Lawrence, columnist and author of *Dream Keys for the Future: Unlocking the Secrets of Your Destiny*

"Whether you prefer mothers-in-law or daughters-in-law, this book will help you date both. Susan Shapiro Barash is a relationship whiz."

> – Lewis Burke Frumkes, humorist, radio personality and author of *How to Raise Your IQ by Eating Gifted Children*

"Filled with lots of great tips to look for the good in your mother-in-law or daughter-in-law, Susan Shapiro Barash brings comfort that we are not alone in mastering these challenging relationships. Love, hate, rivalry and reconciliation says it all! This book should be heralded as the definitive tool to remedy every possible situation."

> – Karen Gantz Zahler, literary agent, attorney and author of *Taste of New York*

Praise for Susan Shapiro Barash's *Second Wives*

"[Barash] combines her professional and personal insights to help women create solid bonds with their husbands and avoid feeling second-rate as Wife No. 2. Her helpful book...offers solid strategies for beating the statistics."

    — *Publishers Weekly*

"The book is for women thinking about becoming a second wife and those who have already taken the plunge."

    — *Tulsa World*

"Women who are thinking of marrying a man who is saying 'I do' again will find Barash's voice comforting."

    — *Library Journal*

"A thoughtful account...Barash does a commendable job of presenting an objective view. Readers are given the tools to make the marriage successful."

    — *Today's Librarian*

"If there's anything wrong with this book, it's the title. First wives, second wives, women marrying men who are either widowed or divorced and the men themselves would benefit from the insights and wise counsel from *Second Wives*."

    — *Stepfamilies* (Publication of the Stepfamily Association of America)

"Susan Shapiro Barash knows whereof she speaks—or in this case, writes. She's been there."

    — *Palm Beach Daily News*

"Barash brings her experience as an academic and, more importantly, a second wife to this useful book. The author's lucid reasoning and logical advice are a boon."

    — *ForeWord Magazine*

"Ironically, even though the number of second (and third) wives is at an all-time high, many feel there is nowhere to turn for advice and support. That makes this a particularly valuable book."

    — *Bookviews*

"Fascinating, informative reading...for any woman anticipating marriage to a widower or divorcee as well as second wives who have already taken the plunge."

    — *The Midwest Book Review*

Mothers-in-Law and Daughters-in-Law

Books by Susan Shapiro Barash

Second Wives:
The Pitfalls and Rewards of Marrying Widowers and Divorced Men

Sisters: Devoted or Divided

A Passion for More:
Wives Reveal the Affairs that Make or Break Their Marriages

The Men Out There: A Woman's Little Black Book

Reclaiming Ourselves: How Women Dispel a Legacy of Bad Choices

Inventing Savannah

Mothers-in-Law and Daughters-in-Law

Love, Hate, Rivalry and Reconciliation

by

Susan Shapiro Barash

New Horizon Press
Far Hills, NJ

Susan Shapiro Barash
    Mothers-in-law and Daughters-in-law: Love, Hate, Rivalry and Reconciliation

Cover Design: Robert Aulicino
Interior Design: Susan M. Sanderson
Author Photograph: Alonzo Boldin

Library of Congress Control Number: 00-132521

ISBN: 0-88282-206-3
New Horizon Press

Manufactured in the U.S.A.

2005   2004   2003   2002   2001   /   5   4   3   2   1

For my parents, Selma and Herbert L. Shapiro

*T*he mythological Venus, a goddess and the mother of Cupid, attempted to influence her son's choice of a wife. Cupid ignored his mother's suggestions and persuasions and married the young and beautiful Psyche, an earthly maiden. An immortal being, once Cupid married a mere mortal, he was doomed.

Recognizing Psyche's own ambiguous feelings about their marriage, he said to her: "...Is this how you repay my love? After having disobeyed my mother's command and taken you for my wife, I had so hoped that your faith would be as constant as my love...."

Venus was furious that her son had chosen a mortal for a wife, but she reserved her fiercest anger for Psyche, her daughter-in-law, for inflicting pain upon her beloved son. Instantly, we recognize in the immortal goddess very human emotions and attitudes, for Venus is being a protective mother who finds fault with her daughter-in-law's perceived unkindness and lack of love for her son.

The mother-child relationship is paradoxical and, in a sense, tragic. It requires the most intense love on the mother's side, yet this very love must help the child grow away from the mother and become fully independent.

Table of Contents

Author's Note x

Acknowledgements xi

Foreword xiii

Introduction 1

Chapter 1   Positives and Negatives of Mother-in-Law/ 7
             Daughter-in-Law Relationships

Chapter 2   Latest Complications/Divided Loyalties 33

Chapter 3   Mother Replacements/Shopping Excursions 53

Chapter 4   Mothers-in-Law and Their Daughters 73

Chapter 5   Religion, Race and Ethnicity 91

Chapter 6   Desperate Situations 109

Chapter 7   Shifting Patterns: Grandchildren, Careers,
             Mothering 127

Chapter 8   Endless Competition 153

Chapter 9   Holidays/Repeat Manipulations 169

Chapter 10   Resolutions/Mellowing With the Years 181

Epilogue 197

Mother-in-law/Daughter-in-law Questionnaire 201

References 205

Author's Note

This book is based on extensive personal interviews of mothers-in-law and daughters-in-law and experts in the fields of matrimonial law, psychology, sociology, family therapy and counseling. Names have been changed and recognizable characteristics disguised of all characters in this book except the contributing experts in order to protect privacy. Some characters are composites.

Acknowledgements

I am deeply grateful to my husband, Gary Barash, for his remarkable patience in the face of my commitment to this project, for his wisdom, unconditional love and amazing editorial skills.

I thank my three children, Jennie, Michael and Elizabeth Ripps, for their understanding, love and insights.

I also thank my family, especially my parents, Selma and Herbert L. Shapiro (my father for his impressive research ability) and my in-laws, Helene and Theodore Barash, for their constant support. I thank my dear friends who stand behind me.

The superb group at New Horizon Press, Joan Dunphy, Joseph Marron, Lynda Hatch, JoAnne Thomas and Rebecca Sheil, have been steadfast. At Marymount Manhattan College in New York City, I thank Suzanne M. Murphy, Carol Camper, Scott Rubin and Lewis Burke Frumkes. In publishing, I thank Cynthia Vartan and Lori Ames. I thank Robert Marcus, my attorney, for never letting me sign too quickly and for his guidance. Ryan Lonergan, my student researcher and computer expert, has been terrific.

The professionals who contributed their thoughts to this book are to be acknowledged: Brondi Borer, a New York City divorce attorney, specializes in mediation and nontraditional family law. Dr. Ronnie Burak is a clinical psychologist with a full time private practice in Jacksonville, Florida. Dr. Michaele Goodman works with individuals, couples and families as a clinical psychologist in private practice in New York City and Westchester County. Dr. Michele Kasson, a licensed psychologist practicing in New York City and Long Island, is a staff member of the Lifeline Center for Child Development. Alice Michaeli, sociologist, is a professor who teaches a course on marriage and family at the State University of New York. Antoinette Michaels, ACSW, is an ordained Interfaith Minister and founder and president of the Hope Counseling Center in Sayville, New York. Amy Reisen is a matrimonial lawyer practicing in Millburn, New Jersey and an advocate for non-contentious divorce. Brenda Szulman, CSW, maintains a full time private practice in the fields of Anxiety and Depressive Disorders and has a certification in marital therapy. Each contributor is, or has been, a daughter-in-law.

To those hundreds of mothers-in-law and daughters-in-law who have come forward to share their stories and deepest emotions, I extend a heartfelt thank you. Their experiences and feelings are the substance of this book.

Foreword
by
Dr. Michaele Goodman

We spend much of our lives physically and emotionally separating from our parents and more specifically from our mothers: We leave the womb; as babies, we cry with the awareness of separateness; we toddle away to explore the other sides of rooms; we say "no"; we hang out with friends instead of going home for our family dinners; we go away to colleges; we marry.

A son who marries introduces another woman into his family of origin. And she, as an outsider moving into this family, challenges the status quo of the family by her very existence. The potential for conflict between mother and wife is high as roles and expectations change within the family.

Critical to the success or failure of the mother-in-law/daughter-in-law relationship is the part the son and husband plays. For the man, one family has now become two: The family of origin in which his role is a son; the new family in which his role is a husband. How he negotiates between these two families is crucial to how the relationship develops between the two primary women in his life, his mother and his wife.

To understand how he will cope with these two women, we have to take a step back and behind present appearances to understand the family expectations. First, what were the family expectations about the son marrying? Was he supposed to marry at all? If so, most parents often anxiously wonder and fantasize about whom their child will date and marry. How close does this daughter-in-law match her mother-in-law's wishes for her son's wife? For example, is she, in the mother-in-law's expectations, the right age, religion, ethnicity? Will she blend into this family? Second, how crucial is it that family expectations be met? Is this a family that nurtures and respects independence or conformity in developing one's own family? Is it a family where compliance is valued and deviation from the family norm discouraged or even squashed? Are family expectations demands or merely wishes? To want a certain type of woman for one's son is different from demanding it.

The nature of the relationship between mother and son also influences family expectations. If the mother is secure in her place and has a solid relationship with her son, the son's autonomy may be encouraged and therefore the daughter-in-law poses no threat. But if the relationship is insecure, the mother may need to insist on her son's attention to prove to herself and perhaps to others that she is a loved and valued mother. In the latter case, a tremendous potential exists for power struggles and disruption in both families.

As alluded to before, the daughter-in-law is initially an outsider to her husband's family. Because she enters this family as a newcomer, she may notice and highlight what is dysfunctional within the family and/or within the mother-son relationship. The wife then has two roles: to join the family system and to disrupt it enough to facilitate needed separation between son and mother/family. She may encourage her husband to see his family in a new light and face aspects of his mother that have never before been articulated. The pitfall in all this, which I've seen in my work with couples, is the possibility of the daughter-in-law being overly critical of the mother which sometimes causes the man to defend his mother to the detriment of his relationship with his wife.

These are conflicts that revolve around the concept of loyalty. The man may feel torn as he tries to be both a good son and a good husband. This struggle is worsened if loyalty to one is seen as negating feelings for the other in a dichotomous fashion. If, as a husband, he tried to bond with his wife, his mother may interpret this as being disloyal or unloving toward her. If he supports his mother and retains too close a tie with her, the wife may feel similarly abandoned. Additionally, if this bond is too tight with the mother, it stymies the needed differentiation it takes to strengthen his relationship with his spouse and, therefore, undermines the power of the couple as a new entity, different from the family of origin and just beginning its own history. The man needs to move away from his role as son and into his new role as husband and potential father and to do so with a strong partner. In order for both families to grow, this needs to happen. Even a clinging mother may unconsciously wish her son to become autonomous, as seen by a mother who, when finally forced to deal with the reality of the daughter-in-law, backs down and adjusts to this new relationship. If this autonomy is not reached, it ultimately means the family has failed to negotiate this important stage of development from dependence to independence.

Whatever the script, the man's role in this triangular situation is pivotal. He has the power to establish boundaries and balance. In my work with couples, my efforts lie in strengthening the relatively new relationship of couple and encouraging the son-husband to take a stand and give primary attention to his wife. Only he has the potential to make the situation better, because only he has emotional leverage in both families. Despite fears, it is very rare that parents reject their child based on the spouse he chooses. As one mother finally said to her son, "I realize it is Daddy and I who will need to adjust. It's hard though." At the same time, the man needs to make efforts to maintain a secondary bond with his family of origin. This balance is best for growth and stability for the individual and in the marriage. As an example, this may mean that a husband needs to acknowledge his mother's disapproval of his wife and ask her all the same to be civil to her daughter-in-law. In reality, these two women do not have to like each other to make the relationship and the family work. Thus, in therapy it is often important to work towards shifting the expectations of oneself and of one's spouse and mother.

Just as the son is now in a new role as husband, so too is the mother in a new role as mother-in-law. She must find a way to include her daughter-in-law and share her son in a new manner. This means viewing him as an independent adult.

On the other hand, the mother may hold fears that she will be excluded from this new family and therefore might be critical of this independent choice her son has made. In response, aspects of competition between wife and mother may surface in a variety of ways. One generational difference and potential area for competition is that of career. Younger women, whether by choice or necessity, are often in the work force and sometimes in positions which pay as much as or more than their husband's position does. This may cause a different power dynamic in the couple than the one the mother-in-law has lived; her experience will be quite unlike her son's and daughter-in-law's. This mother might feel anxiety for her son's status in his marriage. Or she might feel envious of her daughter-in-law's economic freedom. And envy may exist for both these women: for a wife who works out of necessity, it may seem like a luxury to not work outside the home.

Another facet in these relationships is the fact that the mother-in-law has also been a daughter-in-law and her experiences may color how she approaches the mother-in-law role. Did she have a close or conflicting relationship with her own mother-in-law? How were things resolved? What has she learned from that experience?

Whether the mother-in-law includes the daughter-in-law or is included by her, they both must grapple with differences in family communication patterns. Every family has its own language, its own code. The daughter-in-law as outsider learns that code even as she and her husband develop their own unique way of communicating. Confronted by her mother-in-law and that family's language, the daughter-in-law may feel like she is on the outside looking in. I experience a version of this as therapist, as I too am initially an outsider to the couple. For example, in a couple, a man may see a look on his wife's face and avoid certain subjects, knowing she does not have the emotional capacity at that moment to deal with them. As one husband said, "We need very few words between us to know what we mean." I, as the outsider, the therapist in this case, won't necessarily know that he has just avoided something based on nonverbal communication. I may feel confused by what happened, because they have a code and language to which I am not as yet privy. As I learn to read them better and speak their language, things become clearer. Until a new wife learns this, she too may feel similarly confused when in the midst of her husband's family interactions.

When children are born, the dynamic shifts again. Having a baby in the family can facilitate reconciliation and/or heighten competitive issues. Because the wife is now a mother, as her mother-in-law has been a mother, it may be felt that she is treading on what until then was her mother-in-law's territory. This can provoke unsolicited advice and increase conflict between these two women. Of course, the opportunity also exists for something new and positive to happen. Advice may be given lovingly and taken in the same spirit. A child may provide a mutual focus of attention on a less conflicting third party and thus allow the mother-in-law and daughter-in-law to stand shoulder to shoulder in caring for the child.

Mothers-in-law do not as frequently utilize therapy. They, most commonly, use other resources for emotional support, such as friends and peers. Younger women, men, and couples do discuss issues with mothers and mothers-in-law as aspects of their therapy. According to them, the stresses of this relationship often begin much before the wedding. Family rituals, religious holidays, cultural differences and the wedding itself may intensify feelings of possessiveness and a fear of loss in the prospective mother-in-law, a worry that some aspect of the family relationship or perceived control may be lost.

Because conflict draws our attention inequitably, it is sometimes hard to keep in mind the potentially positive aspects and benefits of mother-in-law/daughter-in-law relationships. Here are two women who can relate as wives and potentially as mothers, sharing a common family. The relationship does not hold the kind of intensity and conflict that may have existed with one's own mother/daughter. Therefore, these two women may in time relate to each other in a way that is comfortable and comforting.

When positive relationships do develop between mothers-in-law and daughters-in-law, it opens up the opportunity for each to work out emotional issues with the other that are unfinished with their own mother/daughter relationships. A mother-in-law can function as a second, less conflicting mother and the daughter-in-law can give the mother a second chance to be a mother in a new relationship. This relationship, when successful, also provides deeper emotional bonds between husband and wife, son and mother.

Introduction

Mothers, throughout the ages, have frequently evidenced apprehension if not outright mistrust of their children's future partners. They can be strongly suspicious that the prospective spouses are not quite right and not quite good enough for their sons or daughters. While it may seem like a cliché or the worst kind of stereotypical thinking, many mothers' suspicions, sometimes with reason and sometimes without, harden into firm convictions. Certainly, fathers are not immune to a degree of skepticism regarding their children's intended spouses, but in terms of gender, the strongest difficulties are prone to exist between the mothers of sons and the sons' wives. The proverbial mother-in-law/daughter-in-law problem has provided the raw material for jokes throughout centuries and continues today to be the fodder of stand-up comedy, plays, films and television sitcoms. But are all mother-in-law/daughter-in-law relationships destined to be strained and painful? Are there any healthy, happy ones?

In writing this book, my intention is to put forth real examples of mother-in-law/daughter-in-law relationships, in the women's own words. These have been garnered through my interviews of hundreds of mothers-in-law and daughters-in-law. Additionally, I will provide a guide through both the negative and positive aspects and experiences associated with the complex bond between the mother of a son and the woman who loves him. I hope to show both mothers-in-law and daughters-in-law that there are remedies and solutions to the many problematic issues that exist between millions of women.

According to the United States Census Bureau, fifty-six percent (of almost 111 million people) of the population consists of married

1

adults. Thus, over fifty million women in America are wives. We can estimate that the great majority of these wives have mothers-in-law or step-
mothers-in-law, perhaps both. In this universal, age-old dilemma of the
mother-in-law/daughter-in-law situation, there is a plethora of kinds of
mothers-in-law, from those giving unsolicited advice to those who are
encouraging and helpful. For every variety of mother-in-law, there are
equally numerous sorts of daughters-in-law, ranging from those who are
resentful and negative toward their mothers-in-law to those who are
grateful and seek out close connections.

Years ago, I eavesdropped on two women in a diner talking about
their daughters-in-law. The first woman said, "Gail, you wouldn't believe
the disrespectful way my daughter-in-law, Jessie, treats me. She always
agrees with my suggestions and then, behind my back, does whatever she
wants anyway." At the time, I was a new daughter-in-law myself and I
remember thinking how clever this young wife must be, fully understanding why she chose to handle her mother-in-law in this manner. Yet, as I've
matured I've come to believe that for the thousands, perhaps millions of
daughters-in-law who find it difficult to respond to overbearing or authoritative mothers-in-law, handling them in a duplicitous fashion is not a
healthy solution. The truth of the matter is, while this approach might
keep the relationship between the two women from completely dissolving,
the issues between them will remain unresolved.

Resolving or avoiding conflict should be the goal of both of the
women who make up two thirds of the eternal triangle of mother/son-
husband/wife. While the literal "man in the middle," the son-husband,
can help to smooth the relationship, it really falls to the mother-in-law
and daughter-in-law to create the give and take of relating to one
another effectively and to define the relationship's parameters and
boundaries. Through all the activities and interactions of the extended
family, from births and graduations, holidays and celebrations to sibling
rivalries and financial disagreements, there needs to be an ongoing
search for recognition and mutual respect between mother-in-law and
daughter-in-law.

The reality, however, is that women, whether newly wedded or
ten year veterans, frequently complain about their mothers-in-law. In
turn, mothers-in-law seem to have many complaints about their daughters-in-law. When these daughters-in-law have babies and become mothers themselves, the intensity of the mother-in-law/daughter-in-law
issues may escalate. Some women, especially those who return to work,
are indebted to their mothers-in-law for helping out with the baby, but
they seem to be the exception and not the rule. Most daughters-in-law,
whatever life they lead, will at times find their mothers-in-law to be
intrusive and opinionated. How a daughter-in-law internalizes and then

acts on such intrusiveness will determine whether a battle of wills ensues or cordiality reigns.

A mother-in-law, of course, has a responsibility to encourage amity with her daughter-in-law. All too often, she may view her daughter-in-law as ungrateful and unmalleable, headstrong and too independent. Such mothers-in-law may be convinced that their sons are taken for granted and are being depleted both financially and emotionally by their wives. It is very possible that these mothers-in-law, who were once daughters-in-law themselves, had vowed to never impose themselves inappropriately on daughters-in-law of their own. Yet, suddenly finding themselves cast in the role of mother-in-law, rather than be non-judgmental and generous of spirit, they have transformed into the very stereotype they wanted to avoid. Ironically, many of my peers, most of whom are future mothers-in-law, already muse that whoever their sons marry one day will most likely not measure up to their standards. Already, in their minds, these faceless, future daughters-in-law are not entitled to be their sons' partners. And so, in a society where the family is at the center, compelling and complex, many mother-in-law/daughter-in-law conflicts are perpetuated, in varying degrees of toxicity, from generation to generation.

The passage of time can ameliorate strained relationships, although it may be years before the problems smooth out and the complaints quiet down. Daughters-in-law who once were vociferous about their mothers-in-law and dreaded family vacations and get-togethers, may change their tune. Over time, mothers-in-law also may begin to appreciate their daughters-in-law for what they do for their sons and grandchildren, even though the daughters-in-law's styles might not be theirs. The daughters-in-law, as their lives become busier with teenage children and the demands of work and scheduling, may come to better understand and appreciate their mothers-in-law's achievements. If this new attitude occurs on the part of both women, it will be based on experiences and emotions that transpire over the duration of the relationship.

When there is conflict for the daughter-in-law, it usually begins early in the marriage. A future mother-in-law who in the beginning seems supportive and nurturing may hold the woman once engaged to her son to another standard after the marriage has occurred. It could be that the mother-in-law does not realize her own change of attitude once her daughter-in-law has crossed the line from fiancee to wife. In response, the daughter-in-law feels affronted and negative toward her mother-in-law and begins to complain to her husband about his mother. The son-husband doesn't comprehend his wife's change of heart, because initially the two women seemed to get along. The tension mounts.

In the opposite case, a prospective mother-in-law who has been indifferent may now warm toward her son's "girlfriend" and find her endearing once the young woman is her daughter-in-law and a part of the family. These two women may visit often and go on outings together, developing and deepening their relationship. Possibly they find they share common interests or areas of expertise. They may learn from each other and experience each other as individuals, not just "in-laws."

Despite centuries of mother-in-law/daughter-in-law/son-husband triangles, new scenarios that impact modern relationships have come into play. These include greater geographic mobility, the increase in women working outside the home, rising divorce and remarriage rates, increased life expectancy and transformed lifestyles. The emergence of these relatively new issues sometimes skews people's understanding and expectations. For instance, in this fast-paced, mobile society of ours, more and more family members live great distances from each other. Yet in a long-distance mother-in-law/daughter-in-law relationship, expectations, both realistic and unreasonable, will still exist. This is true even if the two women only see each other on holidays and extended weekends.

To a new wife, the prospect of having a mother-in-law *and* a stepmother-in-law may seem daunting, but with the increase in divorce and remarriage, it is not an uncommon occurrence. As with all relationships between individuals, there may be numerous permutations of the traditional roles. A stepmother-in-law may be loving and eager to extend herself to her new stepdaughter-in-law. A mother-in-law may prefer an ex-daughter-in-law to the new one. For a number of the women I interviewed who are second time daughters-in-law, a seasoned approach to their mothers-in-law, has resulted in exceeded expectations. In a second marriage, too, both the mother-in-law and the daughter-in-law may be more tolerant and less anticipatory. The mother-in-law may be grateful to see her son settled in a new marriage; the daughter-in-law may be delighted to have a second chance at marriage. Neither woman wants to make the transition difficult for the son-husband, thus they make necessary efforts to keep their relationship on a steady course.

Keeping mother-in-law/daughter-in-law relationships healthy and grounded is especially important today, because longevity for women is higher now than it ever has been. The fact is that most mothers-in-law are going to be parts of their daughters-in-law's lives for more years than ever before.

Undoubtedly, the most significant influence that distinguishes marriages in the twenty-first century from marriages in the past is the blending of the traditional wife/husband and mother/father roles. In today's differing lifestyles, women often are immersed in careers, parenthood becomes a shared responsibility and the choice to not have children is an alternative. Despite the fact that many consider the acceptance of these changes to be positive, the dynamic within some families precludes acceptance of such new life choices. Frequently, a mother-in-law will hold fast to her traditional expectations and thus chronically complain: My daughter-in-law does not deserve my son, she is an inept wife, mother, money manager and so forth

Likewise, some daughters-in-law complain that their mothers-in-law are interfering and overbearing, divisive and controlling. The power play may heighten, with the son-husband in the midst of it. Or it may not be about the son at all, but about the two women and their differences in values and goals. Some marriages may grow stronger in the face of domineering mothers-in-law, with the couples joining forces against them. Frequently, however, marriages are unable to withstand the hindrances and fail. As Joelle, a daughter-in-law, explained to me, when she turned forty she could no longer abide her mother-in-law. After fourteen years of marriage, she divorced her husband over his continual defense of his mother. According to Amy Reisen, a divorce attorney, and Dr. Michele Kasson, a psychologist, mother-in-law problems are major factors in the issues arising in divorce, along with stepchildren and finances.

Mothers-in-law and daughters-in-law have been explored throughout history and literature, mythology, television and film for centuries. In such diverse forms as television programs like *The Honeymooners*, *I Love Lucy* and *The Flintstones*, the written word such as *I, Claudius*, the biography of Eleanor Roosevelt, the myth of Psyche and Cupid and the novel, *The Two Mrs. Grenvilles*, to the films *Guess Who's Coming to Dinner* and the recent *Hush*, starring Jessica Lange and Gwyneth Paltrow, evidence of the contention between mothers-in-law and daughters-in-law abounds.

Of all these representations, the most revered and benevolent mother-in-law/daughter-in-law relationship is that of Ruth and Naomi from the Book of Ruth in the Bible. Ruth was a Moabite woman who married an Israelite. She left her homeland to follow her mother-in-law, Naomi, into Bethlehem. Naomi, once Ruth was widowed, invited Ruth to remain with her and Ruth agreed, saying: "Whither thou goes, I will go. Thy people shall be my people, and thy God my God. Where thou diest I will die and there I will be buried."

This type of all encompassing love for a mother-in-law is not something that was often apparent in my interviews, but can be viewed as idyllic all the same. The arcs of our lives as daughters-in-law or mothers-in-law could encompass almost a half century and thus it behooves us to do our best to achieve successful, mutually beneficial relationships with the wives of our sons or the mothers of our husbands. Even if it begins with animosity, it can end with the mother-in-law and daughter-in-law deeply immersed in a meaningful connection.

The mother-in-law/daughter-in-law issue straddles all socio-economic levels and affects millions of marriages. When the rapport between the mother-in-law and daughter-in-law is strong, the relationship grows as time passes. When problems develop, there are no quick fixes, but there are means to allay the disruption and tension.

The professionals with whom I have sought to discuss the specifics on the dynamics of these relationships provide sound advice, objectivity and expertise. The interviewees themselves, mothers-in-law and daughters-in-law of all ages and varying backgrounds, have come to their own conclusions, which they share in these pages. I have purposely chosen women in many different stages of the relationship, from the beginning of marriage to marriage with small children to mature marriage, to compare their sensibilities. In writing this book, I have searched for the perceptions of both mothers-in-law and daughters-in-law, to better know why and how the relationships between the two women develop.

Regardless of the circumstances, the impact of a mother-in-law on a marriage and the influence of a daughter-in-law on the mother/son relationship is ongoing, evolving at distinct stages in the marriage. The roles often fluctuate and transform throughout the duration of the marriage; sometimes a battle of wills is enacted and at other times mutual understanding and harmony prevail. A future of compassionate mothers-in-law and enlightened daughters-in-law is the hope, one which benefits all three participants: Mother-in-law, daughter-in-law and son-husband.

1

Positives and Negatives of Mother-in-Law/Daughter-in-Law Relationships

Annabelle warned her son before he married his wife that it was not going to be an easy life. "My son, Tom, was in his early thirties when he married Tina, a woman with grown children. I knew he was in over his head, but she flattered and charmed him and he bought it. I doubt he is happy, but he doesn't really say. She is not good for him, because she isn't good for anyone. Though she has no children at home, she refuses to work. She has no interests. She has a volatile temper and screams at my son, her kids and her own mother. She won't speak to her sister and she has no friends. I think she is emotionally disturbed. She is very isolated and she has managed to isolate my son.

"She has taken my son away from our entire family. Despite my efforts, he is really lost to us and to his old friends. She has twisted everything that anyone from his past has ever done and poisoned it. I can't urge him if he isn't ready, but my fondest wish for my son is that he leaves his wife and finds a nice girl. He could have children with someone younger. He is cheating himself out of a fulfilling life and he doesn't even know it. I am so disappointed as a mother-in-law."

While Annabelle's attitude toward her daughter-in-law may seem like an extreme example of a toxic mother-in-law/daughter-in-law relationship, she is, unfortunately, by no means alone in her total disapproval of her son's choice of wife. All too often, there seems to be something about the relationship between mothers-in-law and daughters-in-law that creates difficulties and conflicts.

At a time when lifespans are increasing, the mother-in-law/daughter-in-law relationship frequently extends over a long period of time, perhaps as many as fifty years. A difficult relationship can seem never-ending, while an amicable one can be a long-term source of comfort to both women. Family culture has recast itself during the last half of the twentieth century and the extended family is no longer as common or as viable as it once was. Often, the traditional "nuclear family," consisting of a mother, father and children, will live great distances from other relatives. Yet, the ability of a mother-in-law and daughter-in-law, even at a distance, to interact in a beneficial manner or to engage in combat, persists. For many mothers-in-law, the concept of managing their families cannot be dispelled, despite our highly technological, long distance, fast paced world.

Most mothers-in-law view daughters-in-law in terms of their sons. If a son knows that his mother is difficult to get along with or that his wife is not interested in forming a connection with his mother, his life is more difficult. He wants to be loyal to both women and he feels he is in a no-win situation. "A mother-in-law who tries to control her son is common," according to psychotherapist Brenda Szulman, "because many mothers do not want to relinquish their children. It is only when the children are differentiated or individuated from their mothers that their marriages are more flexible. The key is how fully the son is differentiated from his mother."

Authors Gerald L. Kleiman and Myrna W. Weissman, in their essay, "Depressions Among Women," argue that "minor stresses associated particularly with the role of 'married women' deserve more attention." Since the 1980s, it has been documented that married women have higher rates of depression than men or unmarried women. Despite how far we have come in terms of career opportunities, reproductive freedom and a raised collective consciousness regarding the role of women, there still remain conflicts generated by the traditional labels for married women. This results in females who may exhibit dependency, passivity and helplessness, according to Kleiman and Weissman. If this is true, it is ironic that mothers-in-law and daughters-in-law do not band together more often since, despite their generational differences, they both experience similar deprivations and situations in which they cannot grow.

Dr. Ronnie Burak, a clinical psychologist, points out how the expectations of both the mother-in-law and daughter-in-law generate problems. "At the beginning of a marriage, a wife is very idealistic and expects to be treated fairly and with respect for her individuality. Her mother-in-law, too, is expecting respect and perhaps a bit of compliance. If both women don't understand the other's expectations, there could be angry blow-ups over their perceived shortcomings or intolerance. It becomes clear early on that it will not be an easy path for either of them."

One example of a woman with these misconceived expectations is Audrey, who believes that her mother-in-law is responsible for her husband's dysfunction. "My husband has personality flaws that I attribute to my mother-in law. Because she has always allowed him to do what he wants without considering others or learning how to perform independently, he can be very difficult. I have told my mother-in-law this and she just laughs. But I feel she is in large part to blame for his faults and problems. When he can't function, I think it's because of being raised in an insular, dysfunctional environment. What bothers me the most is her attitude toward life. She hasn't a global view, although she might know who is running for president during a campaign year. She does not read the newspaper and won't acknowledge there is a world out there any more than she'll acknowledge that my husband and I are people, adult people."

When a daughter-in-law like Audrey sees her mother-in-law's negative influence on her husband's behavior, it impacts the marriage. Her choice is to point out such flaws or to ignore the behavior and gradually try to wean him away from negative actions and thinking. Often times, her efforts are not effective and this causes her to resent her mother-in-law more.

MOTHER INFLUENCE
* **The daughter-in-law sees her husband as negatively influenced by his mother.**
* **She identifies poor traits in him that she feels have come about as a result of his upbringing.**
* **The mother-in-law's presence becomes a source of aggravation.**

Mothers-in-law may feel similar misgivings. Bea, who has been a mother-in-law for seventeen years and has three sons and three daughters-in-law, finds her role unfulfilling. "None of my daughters-in-law has filled the place of a daughter, which I desperately wanted, for me. I didn't like my first daughter-in-law from the moment I saw her. She was not my type or taste. Still, when my son introduced us, I gave him my wedding ring from my first marriage to give to her. Since their marriage, I have not lived nearby and I cannot really judge it, but my understanding is that this woman is good to my son. That is all that really matters.

"With my second daughter-in-law, the relationship is guarded. I love my son too much to be critical of this woman. I see it as emasculating to do that. She wasn't my choice and I have learned not to comment on this. I have done everything to welcome this daughter-in-law, but she is distant and excludes us. As for my third daughter-in-law, I have been dancing around her for years and she around me without successfully communicating. We are not totally natural or comfortable with each other and we do not connect. She would never pick up the telephone and call me and when I call to speak with my son, she never gets on the line to say hello. Because they are the same religion and same profession, I thought we would have a good relationship, but it isn't so. Then I remember that she adores my son and I try to accept her because of this."

Not only mothers-in-law, but daughters-in-law have hopes of good relationships which are sometimes thwarted. Sybil, a daughter-in-law, anticipated that her mother-in-law would be supportive and kind. Today, Sybil has negative feelings towards her mother-in-law. "My marriage lasted for ten years and then I was widowed with three small children. Due to the children, my connection to my mother-in-law is ongoing. During my husband's courtship, his mother was gracious and generous. We lived halfway across the country from her at the time. My husband was in medical school and we had our own lives. From the moment we were married and my husband joined his family's medical practice, my mother-in-law became domineering, difficult and demanding. We moved back to his hometown. My mother-in-law manipulated it so that we ended up seeing them socially every weekend. She was furious if we had a social life beyond the family. My husband saw his mother every day because she was the office manager. She and her husband controlled everything through money. Eventually, when my husband became very ill, I kept my complaints about his mother to myself. But my feelings that she was a negative influence never changed throughout his illness and death.

"Today, she still controls our family through money, but I exert control through the children. When her son died, she had to count on me to have a rapport with her grandchildren. I am keenly aware that she still is my mother-in-law. That is the part I cannot change. I continue to answer to her on some level and she infuriates me by asking too many questions about the girls, which are, in reality, criticisms at the way I am raising them. She judges every move I make, with work and friends. Had my husband lived, I think my complaints about his mother would have been ongoing. I wonder if the marriage could have survived with her interference."

Ideally, if a mother-in-law is able to place her son's feelings above hers and respect his choice of a wife, then the relationship between the mother-in-law and daughter-in-law may not be close, but it can be respectful and cordial. In this case, the mother-in-law realizes that the marriage may last for many years and the daughter-in-law recognizes that her mother-in-law could live for decades. The two women know they are linked together and must work at achieving harmony or at least minimizing conflict.

ROCKY BEGINNINGS
* **The son chooses a woman who is unlike his mother.**
* **If the mother-in-law is antagonistic, the daughter-in-law turns her back on the relationship.**
* **If the daughter-in-law is unresponsive, the mother-in-law may distance herself.**
* **Both need to adjust.**

"When the son-husband attempts to be loyal to both his wife and his mother, he puts himself in an untenable position," states Dr. Ronnie Burak. "Often, both the wife and the mother feel that he has pressed the OFF button and is ignoring both of them. In this case, he is trying to escape a no-win situation. It is advisable that both women make life more harmonious." The kind of attitude which Burak describes on the part of the mother-in-law and daughter-in-law is especially insightful when one considers "the nature of the male predicament," as described by author Susan Faludi in her book *Stiffed: The Betrayal of the American Male*. Faludi tells us that many men feel out of control while society expects them to be in control. In fact, such men are "boxed in," even if the box is of their own making. If this is the case, then a son-husband cannot readily deal with the ongoing friction between his mother and his wife because he is not equipped to be a referee.

"If the mother-in-law and daughter-in-law do not get along," according to Brenda Szulman, "it is a very stressful triangulation for the son-husband. What works all around is flexibility, elasticity and room to make mistakes. If the daughter-in-law is not individuated and separated from her own family, there are projections being reenacted into the new relationship. This applies to the mother-in-law as well. Not only is the mother-in-law struggling with the lack of autonomy over her son because of his marital status, but the daughter-in-law may be reenacting some conflict from her past with her new mother-in-law."

Just as mothers-in-law like Bea feel disappointed by their relationships with their daughters-in-law, many daughters-in-law feel similarly.

"After all these years, I would say that my relationship with my mother-in-law is disappointing but stable," says Kate, who has three children and has been married for twelve years. "But I know now to think before I say anything or do anything. I always know that whatever I say or do will have some kind of consequence. Deep down, I still consider my mother-in-law a difficult person. For example, she continues to give me her thoughts on everything. She tells me what to get for the house and what do with my kids. When I disagree with her, I never articulate it. At first, I was put off by not telling her what I think. Now, I respond by simply saying that it sounds like an idea to consider and I'll think about it. Then I do what I planned to do all along. It is frustrating at times, but it works.

"I have respect for her in some areas, and that's what I emphasize. I don't really care that I haven't a genuine connection to her. I know my mother-in-law wanted a good relationship with me despite her behavior. In the beginning, I, too, wanted a more positive adult relationship. I wanted to call my mother-in-law by her first name, but she insisted on being called 'mom.' Over the years, my expectations and realizations have changed for the worse. Now I'm more focused on what a chore it is to visit her. The visits are so intense and unnatural that they cannot possibly be pleasurable. I can't enjoy time spent with my mother-in-law. Who wouldn't be disappointed by such a situation?"

Alice Michaeli, sociologist, notes how far off track many mother-in-law/daughter-in-law relationships have become over the last thirty years. "Since everyone is socialized differently, a mother-in-law could, in theory, teach the norms, values and expectations of their particular family to her daughter-in-law. The family history, inside jokes, patterns, could be explained. This would be helpful to the daughter-in-law and has been successful in other countries. For example, in a traditional Japanese family, the job of the mother-in-law is to educate her daughter-in-law. She is the 'trainer,' the daughter-in-law is the 'trainee.'" Since this system rarely occurs in our culture, many marriages lack the structure an extended family offers.

Marjorie, who first knew her daughter-in-law when the younger woman was Marjorie's son's high school sweetheart, has been surprised by the lack of contact the two women have today. "When my son and daughter-in-law come home for holidays or a visit, they see her family, but I do not always get to see my son. Since I am only an in-law and since my daughter-in-law makes all the decisions for family events, I am pushed aside. She has had my son give up his entire family for her. When I tried to put a stop to this, my daughter-in-law cried out that my claim was untrue and unfair. I have reached a point where I don't want to hurt anyone's feelings or make life more difficult for my son. It took me years to see how it really is. I refused to believe our rift was happening, because it was so painful to me. One of the saddest parts is how cheated my husband and I are as grandparents. The grandchildren are cheated, too. Still, my son says nothing. I often wonder what he thinks. I tried to meet him alone several times, but he avoided such meetings. I know I can't talk to him, he doesn't want to discuss this problem. If we have plans with them, my daughter-in-law often cancels the appointment.

"I wish I knew why my son goes along with this and says nothing. My daughter-in-law's mother was a real matriarch and she called the shots for all occasions. When she died, her eldest daughter took over. My daughter-in-law listens to her sister now. Nothing has changed in her actions toward me. I expected to be the luckiest mother-in-law alive, because we all knew each other and were from the same kind of families and shared the same religion. I thought our relationship would prosper, but instead, her attitude after the marriage was okay, lady, disappear. After twenty-two years, I've quit trying."

Unlike Marjorie's daughter-in-law, who has made no effort to cultivate a relationship with her mother-in-law, Lisa, is a daughter-in-law who has tried to cultivate a relationship, but now realizes that her mother-in-law doesn't want one. Despite this, Lisa now accepts her mother-in-law.

"I thought when I first met my mother-in-law that she was reserved and undemonstrative. I saw no affection towards me, but noticed instant distrust. She accepted me as her son's girlfriend, yet, at the same time, she didn't want us to be married. She was alone and widowed and she didn't want him moving out of the house. She wanted him to stay with her, which was unreasonable and slightly twisted. In fact, she wanted us to live with her when we were first married, but I refused. I said, 'No, absolutely not.' I think she never forgave me for that.

"We have four children today and a busy life. I try to include my mother-in-law and to keep her busy with our lives, but it isn't always easy. My mother-in-law is so old-fashioned. It extends to every aspect of life. Her mentality is that I should not have exercised while I was pregnant. She believes that men must come first. I try very hard for my husband's sake, but there is this residual tension and she always acts the martyr. I think she is still jealous of my marriage to her son.

"I am sorry not to have had a better relationship with my mother-in-law. I had hoped for more. Instead, what I have is a mother-in-law who has added nothing to my life, in fact she has taken away. I am relieved she doesn't have more of an effect on our lives than she already has had. It took me a while to figure her out. Now I understand her totally. Today I can actually laugh about some of our problems."

A mother-in-law can be jealous or resentful of her daughter-in-law's relationship with her son. This is particularly so if the mother-in-law is widowed or divorced and she expects her son to care for her. Most daughters-in-law will resent this expectation and will fight to keep their mothers-in-law at bay. This only escalates the mother-in-law's jealousy and ill will. The daughter-in-law becomes jealous and territorial in return if her husband concedes to his mother's wishes. The daughter-in-law/wife asks why her needs don't count.

JEALOUSY
* **The mother-in-law is jealous of her daughter-in-law's place in her son's life.**
* **The daughter-in-law is jealous of her husband's sense of duty to and/or relationship with his mother.**
* **The son may vacillate between the two women.**

My research has indicated that when a daughter-in-law tolerates her mother-in-law for her husband's sake and there is a semblance of family harmony, the son-husband is grateful. The mother-in-law is also grateful, although she may not show it, and a more convivial relationship is established. Conversely, when mothers-in-law include daughters-in-law socially and extend themselves to the grandchildren, most daughters-in-law respond positively.

If this positive exchange does not transpire, most often a power struggle evolves between the mother-in-law and daughter-in-law. According to sociologist Alice Michaeli, such relationships are no longer functional. "The question becomes, 'Whose man is this?' which does not work to anyone's advantage. What our society needs is to reinvent itself in terms of the family and in-laws. We can no longer adhere to what has been accepted behavior. The old method does not work."

As early as 1949, Margaret Mead, renowned author and sociologist, described the American family 'norm' as consisting of a husband, wife and minor children. In her book, *Male and Female*, Mead noted the harshness toward elderly parents of married children, suggesting that they were not expected to live with their children or to be integral parts of their lives, unless "absolutely necessary" or only in the case of widow-hood, because of "the rigorousness of the American belief that in-laws, especially mothers-in-law, are ruinous to marriages."

When a mother-in-law is perceived as invasive and difficult, a daughter-in-law often will complain to her husband. It is up to the son to achieve a middle ground, but often he is too afraid of his mother to stand up to her. If a daughter-in-law is perceived as controlling and unkind to the mother-in-law, a mother-in-law may complain to her son, but the son will seldom intervene.

TRIANGULATED AT BEST
* **It is up to the son, early on in the relationship, to buffer both women and to establish boundaries.**
* **Both women view him as the common thread.**
* **Little else connects them.**

According to the people with whom I talked, daughters-in-law are skeptical of their mothers-in-law for myriad reasons. They may blame their husband's negative traits on his mother. There may be resentment toward his style and philosophy of life, which stems from his family's influence. If a husband is penurious, for instance, the wife may believe this is a family trait. If a husband is not helpful around the house or not supportive of her career, which are prevalent attitudes in some marriages, the wife will assume these attitudes come from his family of origin. Another complication is that the wife/daughter-in-law could have a family of origin which is opposite in approach.

"When the mother-in-law believes her way is best and is insistent," Dr. Ronnie Burak remarks, "the daughter-in-law may reject her out of hand, thinking: *Who is this woman to me? She only cares about her son. She wants me to do things this way because of her son.* Then the disgruntled daughter-in-law ignores her mother-in-law's advice."

"Being a mother-in-law is not something you learn in school," laments Barbara, who has three daughters-in-law and has been a mother-in-law for nine years.

"I always thought that I would enter my role in a positive way. I wanted each young woman my sons married to feel welcome and loved by us. Today's marriage and courtship styles have, in two cases, given me a long time to get acquainted with my future daughters-in-law before the marriages took place. Usually, I see each daughter-in-law at separate times. Each has a different schedule so I may spend more time with one or the other, depending on the circumstances. Other times, I'll see a daughter-in-law with her husband. It's hard to say how much time I have actually spent with any daughter-in-law on a one-on-one basis. But the relationships have definitely changed over the years, not necessarily for the better.

"I tread lightly now, with great caution. I just want to avoid trouble. My grandchildren are very dear to me and, if I have to walk on eggshells to keep that working, I will. I think of my sons as unique and these daughters-in-law as interchangeable. It is the nature of the relationship. I categorize these women although I know they are individuals. I view each of these women as a type and I see that each son chose a woman who represented a certain direction. I would have preferred someone different in each case, but I know that these wives share my sons' goals. I remind myself of this quite frequently."

Other mothers-in-law whose sons are unsuccessful or dysfunctional may hope their daughters-in-law will be cure-alls for their sons' problems or shortcomings. When this plan fails and a son chooses someone quite unlike the helpmate his mother had in mind, the result can be disturbing.

"There has always been hostility between my daughter-in-law and myself," remarks Shawna, who became a mother-in-law twenty years ago. "I was not particularly close with my son when he married her and our relationship was fraught with difficulty from then on. I had hoped, had believed, that his marriage would rectify all of his personal problems, but instead they exacerbated them. My daughter-in-law is what I would describe as 'pink collar,' meaning she was a waitress while our family is intellectual and educated. It really bothered me that she came from this background. I had a particular antipathy for her lack of education and culture. My son knew this. Their favorite sport was bowling together. This is not the kind of activity my son was raised to participate in.

"I suppose the better explanation for my son's choice of wife is to say that he made a terrible decision. She was crude and ill-bred. He married her to spite us. I know that. For my son's sake, I made an effort to get along with her anyway. In the beginning, we went shopping once or twice, but it never worked out. The relationship was no good. I don't recall that there was any outward animosity, but it was not always pleasant or agreeable. I have tried to consider my son in these situations. I never lose sight of how important our relationship is and I swallow a great deal for his sake."

Many mothers-in-law object to their daughters-in-law's styles and beliefs, finding them the antithesis of their own. Instead of considering these women as pleasing to their sons, possibly for the very differences they offer, mothers-in-law may view them as enemies who bring foreign, false values into their sons' lives. It would benefit everyone if both groups of women, the mothers and the wives, could be introspective and honest with themselves about their prejudices, personalities and methods of coping. If the husband has a poor relationship with his parents, siblings and extended family, and does not work through it, this will filter into the marriage. Therapy is one solution for those who are conscious they have lingering, unresolved problems.

FAMILY PATHOLOGY

* **When the family of origin functions at a low level and is consumed with problems, the new marriage inherits this.**
* **If problems exist in the husband's family, the wife/daughter-in-law may not be capable of or prepared to cope with dysfunctional in-laws.**
* **If the problems are severe, therapy is recommended.**

Dissimilar family backgrounds can be a source of misunderstanding and turmoil. Molly views her mother-in-law's attitude toward her as remote because she is not from the same background as her husband. "My mother-in-law has always been polite, but so cool that I sometimes wonder if I do enough, if I should make more of an effort. She and her husband are very social and she has never expressed much interest in our children. When they were really little it seemed important. Now I tell myself that my kids don't have a lot of extra time and they have other, more important issues and relationships. It just seems to matter less.

"My husband is accustomed to his mother's ways. She's not very warm to her own family and she doesn't pretend to be involved with us. I doubt she talks about us or our kids to her friends because we don't interest her. She likes to see us for dinner, my husband and me, with my father-in-law, in adult situations. Although my mother-in-law and I have never had an argument, we are not invited to her home and everything is kept at a distance. She set it up that way from the start. I thought at first it was just me; I see now that she is distant with her own children as well. Playing golf and being with her friends is more important to her than family.

"While I've never had a problem with my mother-in-law, as I get older, I realize there is no real relationship. My husband doesn't notice his mother's behavior the way that I do. He comes from this controlled, structured, unemotional environment and he doesn't expect anything more."

While Molly feels that her mother-in-law is distant and cool out of choice and style, Martha, a mother-in-law, has distanced herself to improve the relationship with her daughter-in-law.

"I always mind my own business," Martha explains, "because I want to see my daughter-in-law and son as much as possible. My son is grateful that I am like this. There has been only one confrontation in all these years. It occurred when they were buying a house. They showed the house to me and I was less than enthused. Apparently, my daughter-in-law had already fallen in love with it and my son had solicited my opinion. In the end, they didn't buy it, which angered her. That was when I learned to keep my mouth shut.

"I also handle things gingerly where child rearing hints are concerned. I used to talk with my son more freely, but I realize now that he would run back to his wife and tell her everything I said. I have become indifferent towards my daughter-in-law and as a result, I resist voicing my opinion. I joke with my friends that whatever I say to my son, he repeats it and then my daughter-in-law always says, 'Your mother thinks this, your mother thinks that.' I know now that in order to enjoy a harmonious relationship with my son and his family, I have to be quiet and calm, no matter what I feel."

In the best case scenario, both the mother-in-law and her daughter-in-law reap the rewards of a successful relationship. But this is not always the case. When it becomes a question of loyalty, the new family should take priority. If there is conflict between the mother-in-law and her son, the daughter-in-law suffers by association. "When the mother-in-law/daughter-in-law relationship does not succeed," Brenda Szulman, psychotherapist, offers, "the mother feels alienated from her son and this is a great loss for her. Not all mothers-in-law are good mothers originally. The daughter-in-law who sees that there are problems between her husband and his mother should stay clear of this. In these very negative cases, the daughter-in-law needs to protect herself and to work on her marriage. She should not try to develop a relationship with a problematic mother-in-law."

ENLIGHTENED HUSBANDS
* **The husband-son acknowledges his mother's shortcomings.**
* **The husband helps his wife understand and cope with any ill will from his mother.**
* **The husband puts his marriage first.**

As a mother-in-law for twenty-six years, Joyce has never had any rapport with Anne, her daughter-in-law. "When you have three daughters and one daughter-in-law, interacting has to be uneasy for her. She has to have a problem finding her place with us. Plus, Anne is an only child and sees our family unit as difficult to penetrate. To worsen matters, my daughter-in-law is a product of a divorce and she is accustomed to being alone in the midst of family turmoil. She never had the stability of growing up in a house with a solid marriage. She never had siblings to fall back on.

"In her defense, the family dynamic of someone marrying into a tribe such as ours is overwhelming. My son is spoiled, the most spoiled of my four children. On the other hand, Anne has done nothing to improve my relationship with my son and I am sorry about that. Basically, I find this daughter-in-law disappointing and unadventurous. If she enhanced my son somehow, I would feel differently, but she doesn't seem to add anything to his life."

The concept of a daughter-in-law enhancing the relationship between her husband and his mother can be misleading. While the mother-in-law expects that her new daughter-in-law is capable of such a feat, in reality she may not be. Young wives/daughters-in-law today do not necessarily feel responsible for the sole nurturing of their own families, let alone extended families. However, for a mother-in-law who was raised with the stereotypic notion that women are better caretakers than men, there is the anticipation that a daughter-in-law will "fix" what has gone wrong. Such a mother-in-law imagines her son transformed by his wife. The daughter-in-law, on the other hand, may not be so motivated and probably has not been influenced by such stereotypic of women's roles.

GENDER & GENERATIONS
* **The mother-in-law views her daughter-in-law as the stereotypical nurturer and healer.**
* **The mother-in-law counts on her daughter-in-law to sort out the poor connection the older woman has to her son.**
* **The daughter-in-law, a product of a different generation, may not view it as her responsibility to nurse her husband's and his mother's relationship back to health.**

Ruth is a woman who, nevertheless, believed in these old stereotypes. "My son," Ruth laments, "has always been distant. When he married, I thought somehow it would be different. I liked his choice of a wife, although I do believe that whoever your son marries, it is a shock. However, my daughter-in-law, Angie, has been a pleasure from the start. She has the energy and determination which my son lacks. She can get him to do things and to be less negative. I am appreciative of that. But I watch their life only from a distance. I know that they could invite me to be with them on occasions and they do not.

"I imagined that once they were married, my son would come to me and share his life more. He would confide in me about his job and his marriage, about his plans to start a family. None of that has happened. I am a widow and would welcome some closeness with both of them. Yet, I cannot fault my daughter-in-law. She is a kind woman and a good wife for my son. I see that my daughter-in-law holds their life together. I don't meddle by choice and since we live an hour away from each other, no one is really on top of the other. There has never been any confrontation of any kind. On the other hand, there is no real connection. I believe that families should be there for each other and that grown children should give back to their parents. That is not happening in our relationship."

Many times, it is up to the mother-in-law and/or the daughter-in-law to form a bond. Sometime afterward, the son comes around, back to the family fold, through the efforts of his wife. Often, as a result, the son is happy at last, because he has found a partner and the mother-in-law is very thankful that this woman is on the scene.

DAUGHTER-IN-LAW AS SAVIOR
* **Mother-in-law and daughter-in-law become close.**
* **The son no longer resists going to family events.**
* **The daughter-in-law feels altruistic.**
* **The mother-in-law feels grateful to her daughter-in-law.**

Another factor interview subjects reported was common to the problematic mother-in-law/daughter-in-law scenario is when the mother-in-law and her daughter-in-law are very different types of people. "What becomes important for an individual in a family," notes psychologist Dr. Michele Kasson, "doesn't always work for the entire family. A son might discover that he does not fit in with his family's emotional needs. The son's temperament might not mesh with his family's temperament. In this case, though he has spent his life with his family of origin, he feels out of place. When this son chooses a partner, she is more to his liking and fits with his personal style. She is most likely as dissimilar from the mother-in-law as she can be."

One case of dissimilar styles causing conflict between mother-in-law and daughter-in-law was Dorothy's. "I am the total opposite of my mother-in-law in looks and interests," says Dorothy. "I am very petite with blonde hair and she is tall and regal with very dark hair. I quit junior college after one semester, while my mother-in-law has a Ph.D. in art history. However, my mother-in-law is a snob and she wanted me to become one, too. She seemed to know everything about everything, from clothes to jewelry to art to theater. She has always tried to teach me things, but I had no interest in learning from her and felt very loyal to my own mother. She thought she would take me under her wing and that I would aspire to her values, but I never have. I wasn't even curious about her world.

"My family had very little money when I was growing up and both my parents worked two jobs to keep us going. My mother-in-law owned hats that cost more than my mother made in a week.

"When I met Jay, my future husband, my friends all told me to go for it. One of the perks was to live like my mother-in-law, but I couldn't do it because I just can't stand her. I know she thought of me as trailer trash. I felt it every time we were together. I know she tried to talk Jay out of marrying me, but we have lasted for fifteen years.

"Things have not improved over the years. My husband and I fight on an ongoing basis about spending time with his family. I succumb to his wishes to be with his family for some holidays and I suffer in silence. At Christmas dinners, for instance, I know that she is looking me up and down. I once heard her whisper to a friend that my new haircut made me look like I was a waitress at the local diner. I have told my husband I couldn't care less about his parents. I have told him I am tired of them. He never defends me or his mother, but I see him caught in the middle. Not that this manifests in any sort of battle, but it's always under the surface. I suppose his ultimate rebellion was to marry me."

In another case of a dissimilar daughter-in-law, Priscilla did not notice initially that Antoine, her husband, chose her because her style was so unlike his mother's. "When I first became involved with my husband, I spent a lot of time with his family. I thought highly of my mother-in-law and saw her as sophisticated and worldly, unlike anyone I knew. I admired her intelligence, but it was not long before I realized that all of her stories were repeats. In fact, she has a limited repertoire and it is all from her past. I heard nothing new from her after a very short period. Her children and the other in-laws already knew, but I was the naive hopeful one. I thought she was so different from me that I would learn from her to become more cultured and worldly.

"It took me some time to figure her out. I kept expecting her values to be similar to mine, but they were not. My opinion of her began to turn, but a sense of duty prevailed. We would invite my husband's family over and visit them as often as necessary. I always included my mother-in-law when it came to the children's events, scholastic and sports alike. Despite my efforts, she began to complain about me to my husband, to my parents and to her friends. With time, I have come to understand that my mother-in-law is an egotistical woman who probably should not have had children. I blame my mother-in-law for many of my husband's shortcomings. As the mother of three, I know all to well that moms tolerate a lot of nonsense from their kids and still get a bad rap if their children do anything wrong. Despite that, I still feel my mother-in-law was not a capable mother."

If a daughter-in-law does not like her mother-in-law, it is very stressful, even if their interaction is limited. Marriage involves more players than the husband and wife. When there is negative energy between a mother-in-law and daughter-in-law, it comes between the husband and wife and has a residual effect. Resentment intensifies once children are born into the family. Contentions over money, control of the son-husband and assumptions about family life and holidays may build up. Unless the mother-in-law and daughter-in-law are able to find a joint solution, it can be very destructive to the entire family.

HATRED AND TOLERANCE
* **The mother-in-law undermines her daughter-in-law.**
* **The daughter-in-law undermines her mother-in-law.**
* **Children/grandchildren raise the stakes.**
* **They battle for control of the husband-son.**

This battle for control is illustrated by the story Carmen tells us. "I have been more disappointed with my son than my daughter-in-law for the past ten years. I know that neither of them has long-term employment and money is tight, but I look at them as co-dependent. He quits a job and then she quits a job. On top of this, I really worry about how my daughter-in-law, Rosie, takes care of the children. Because of this, I make myself available to those children whenever I can. I always hoped my son would do better than he has. I pushed him hard to excel when he was in high school. His wife is not the type of woman I wanted for my son and she resents the attention he pays to me. I raised him that way. Rosie should be grateful that her husband is good to his mother, but instead she thinks it is a contest between us.

"I say nothing about their sporadic unemployment. But, as this family grows I see myself as a ring around it. My daughter-in-law can be angry and dismayed by me, but I won't stop caring for my son and the children and I won't be quiet about telling him he needs to keep a job."

Battles for control are fought in other ways, too. There are those mothers-in-law who might admire the fact that their sons put their wives first. In Helen's case, she views her son as an appropriate husband but still struggles with the result. "Although I believe it's the right thing to think of the wife and children ahead of the mother, I have to be quiet and not open my mouth. I am cautious and avoid being caught in the middle. The goal here is to stay close to my son. I see that he goes along with whatever my daughter-in-law wants and her thrust is to keep people apart. I believe that my daughter-in-law is a fine person except in family situations. Of course, what other situations are there that would bring us together?

"My daughter-in-law and son came to visit us several times this year. Each time, she had such a Cinderella attitude, as if she was being exploited. I found her very manipulative with my son. For instance, every Christmas Eve she invites us to dinner but deliberately excludes my other children. Because of this, we have to choose between seeing my son or my daughters. My husband and I are so anxious that our son's relationship works that we have given in. Despite this, I know my daughter-in-law's pattern is exclusionary and divisive. She purposely positions my son in this manner, but I also know she and my son are in collusion."

In a successful mother-in-law/daughter-in-law/son-husband relationship, it is the husband who must deal with his family and his issues. The daughter-in-law must deal with her family and her issues. This way conflicts are avoided in everyday life and in crisis situations as well. If necessary, the husband can be a buffer between his wife and mother with the intention of finding common ground. Brenda Szulman warns, however, that finding this road will not happen if the son and his mother have not established a healthy rapport. In such cases, the fallout effects all three of the players, mother-in-law, daughter-in-law and son. "So much of what transpires between mother and son has to do with how they separated and individuated. If the mother and son have not gone through this process successfully, then symptoms of this problem begin to manifest themselves. This is further complicated by the daughter-in-law's history. If she is not individuated and separated from her family either, then there are projections being acted out in the new relationship by both husband and wife."

CONTAMINATION

* If the son is not separated emotionally from his mother, it
  will contaminate the marriage.
* If the daughter-in-law/wife has not separated from her
  family, the result is the same.
* In both cases, the ability of the couple to create a
  wholesome marriage is stymied if they have not become
  fully developed, independent adults.

Overt dependency on one's family of origin rather than on the
family created by one's marriage can cause great pain. "During a critical
time in my mother-in-law's life," April confides, "I was there to do whatever she needed, but I didn't seem to count. My father-in-law was dying, so
I did my mother-in-law's bidding. I was never acknowledged, because I
wasn't part of the original family unit. To this day, my husband and his two
brothers believe that their parents and siblings come ahead of their wives
and children. I have tried very hard, as have my sisters-in-law, to convince
our husbands that as their wives, we and our children should come first.

"The tricky part is that my mother-in-law claims I'm like a daughter, but she still sees me as an outsider in her family. She does treat her
son, my husband, with the greatest respect. Sometimes he is very distant
and short-tempered with her. I suspect such behavior is a payback for
whatever she did to him when he was a child. He treats her as he was
taught by her to treat others or perhaps there is some kind of resentment
festering within him towards her that he has never revealed to me.

"I have learned what not to do as a mother-in-law from my
mother-in-law. I expected her to be dignified and agreeable. Instead, she
is demeaning. She expects me to be there when she needs me, but does
not offer her help when I need her. What I resent the most is how my
mother-in-law displays us and shows us off as a 'perfect family' to the
outside world. I would not care so much about my mother-in-law's
manipulations if my husband would not jump so high for her. He has
been raised to think she is too forceful to fight. Her selfish behavior and
bad attitude comes between us. I can't respect her demands."

Social scientist Erving Goffman, in his book, *The Presentation of
Self in Everyday Life*, discusses how we each present ourselves in terms of
theatrical performance. "Although our image may be altered by circumstances, we are each playing a part in life which we hope our observers
will take seriously. Certain behavior is expected in certain roles and relationships are played out as if onstage. To succeed, the individual needs

to perpetuate the defined role." In the case of mother-in-law, daughter-in-law and son-husband, it often seems the mother-in-law is the most invested of the three players in perpetuating appearances.

The traditionally designated roles for females and males, which were socially constructed, called for women to be caregivers and men to be protectors. For the last three decades, as women's efforts toward equality have gathered momentum, many women have expressed dissatisfaction with the conventional roles assigned to them, opting for more liberal parameters to the narrowly defined positions of wife and mother. When these women find themselves engaging with a traditional-minded mother-in-law, the drama is set to begin. The marriage thus becomes the stage on which three characters, the wife, the husband and the mother/mother-in-law, posture and perform as they work towards establishing a familial relationship that still allows them to remain true to their own needs and beliefs.

The pretense of the happy family, for all too many people, is one of the great modern fantasies. Most daughters-in-law of the past have bought into this fairy tale, thus perpetuating it. Today's daughter-in-law usually will not feign that all is well between her mother-in-law and herself if it is not. She prefers to put the facts on the table and work at correcting and improving the situation, if possible. In addition, in the new climate of disclosure, mothers-in-law also admit their discontent. The son-husband, however, frequently will opt for the easier route, meaning he ignores festering problems and stays clear of potential combat zones.

ALL THE WORLD'S A STAGE
* **In the past, many families pretended to be happy and well adjusted despite their pathology.**
* **Discontent was brushed aside.**
* **Today, it is often the daughter-in-law who finds this unacceptable.**
* **Husbands-sons may detach when there is contention between their wives and mothers.**

One mother-in-law who dispels the pretense of the true happy family myth states, "It isn't that Carrie, my daughter-in-law, is not nice enough but that she will never go out of her way for me. Often my son and the children will come visit me without her," Amelia complains. "The truth is I get very upset with her because she took away my son. I imagine that he would be a better son if he were not married at all. Then

I remind myself that he has these adorable children and that makes it worthwhile. That puts it into perspective.

"My own mother-in-law was a bright woman who was ill at ease. We lived in the same city and had very little to do with each other. I always thought our poor relationship would teach me what to hope for in a daughter-in-law and what to be in a mother-in-law. But I find myself resenting my daughter-in-law anyway. As I've matured, I learned to be fair not from my mother or my mother-in-law but from life itself. I know not to be too pushy or nosy, but also to express myself. My own mother was demanding and controlling and I couldn't handle her attitude. I suppose that I had no mother figures to emulate."

Alice, unlike Amelia, does not expect a great deal from her daughters-in-law and her sons' happiness is what counts. "My own mother-in-law taught me how to be a good mother-in-law. She always took my side in any conflict. During her visits, my husband would complain about our children's behavior as if suddenly when his mother was there he had to act like a disciplining father. She realized he was disingenuous because she understood her son. It was as if my mother-in-law and I spoke the same language. Because of her example, I have always avoided any confrontation with my daughter-in-law, Chloe.

"From the beginning, I decided that nothing was going to get to me enough to have a row. That is how I've managed to succeed in getting along with my daughter-in-law. I have a keen sense of my son's strengths and weaknesses. I worry about the marriage and not my daughter-in-law. She is not a daughter to me, but I make compromises and overlook any shortcomings. We had one incident about ten years ago when I had a momentous birthday and neither of my two daughters-in-law planned a party. Clearly, it was up to them and not my sons. I was very hurt and made my feelings known to them. After that my sons understood they ought to be thoughtful of me and so did their wives. Though I have lowered my expectations, I have learned to verbalize my needs."

When a mother-in-law depends upon her daughter-in-law, and vice versa, to give them accolades and appreciation, there can be disappointments ahead. Modified expectations, in both directions, are better in most instances. In traditional societies, the younger members of the extended family were expected to venerate the older members. Alice Michaeli, sociologist, tells us that in a traditional Japanese society, the wife/daughter-in-law is subservient to the mother-in-law. Although there were love-based marriages in the past, there were also arranged marriages in which spouses were chosen by the parents. Today, however, the ideal of a love-based marriage prevails in most countries. The wife/daughter-in-law may seek her mother-in-law out or she may determine not to be involved with this woman who seems to be her nemesis. For the mother-in-law, there is the hope that the daughter-in-law will enrich her sons' life and, at the same time, that the two women will have a satisfying relationship.

Unquestionably, those modern ideas of love and marriage endure, yet much of what transpires in a marriage, Margaret Mead notes in her book, *Male and Female,* is indicative of that family's history and "the individual pasts of two partners." Mead examines the difficulty in living a life one has not been prepared for by former experiences. She concludes that a marriage is an adjustment. This begins even before the demands and expectations of the mother-in-law's and daughter-in-law's visions of their roles are set in motion.

Mothers-in-law's and daughters-in-law's needs are similar and yet disparate in our modern era. The needs of the mother-in-law are to be respected and appreciated. At the same time, the daughter-in-law's need for respect must be taken into consideration also, but with her independence guaranteed and a sense of equality. She, too, needs to be appreciated.

MODERN MOTHER-IN-LAW NEEDS
* Attention
* Respect
* Time & Inclusion
* Input
* Appreciation

VS

MODERN DAUGHTER-IN-LAW NEEDS
* Attention
* Respect
* Freedom
* Equality
* Appreciation

Clara had the advantage of not being Joan's first daughter-in-law. "My mother-in-law, Joan, disliked her older son's wife, but was smart enough to realize the mistakes she had made in that relationship. Whatever went on with the other daughter-in-law, I suspect her caution with me is a result of her own remorse. My husband is amazingly good with his mother and that sets the stage for me. I have always looked at the way a man treats his mother. If he treats her well then he is likely to treat his wife well also. Instead of being threatened by their closeness, I recognize them both as independent people. I view my husband's relationship with his mother as a plus and not a problem. I am reassured by their attachment. To me it means that these same characteristics, those of patience, kindness and goodness, will spill over into my marriage.

"I am not truly attached to my mother-in-law, but I see us as having a working relationship. We don't have much in common except for our devotion to her son, my husband. I work full-time and I know she remarks about it to my husband because I never cook and I won't clean. My husband, I imagine, defends me and so he should. Because he is the favored son and he is on my side, I am always confident in the marriage and with my mother-in-law."

Another daughter-in-law who has an arms-length, successful relationship with her mother-in-law is Dana. "In the beginning, my mother-in-law wanted to be in control of my life. My husband recognized the problem, but he handled it poorly. That was the first stage. Over the years, the relationship has improved and my husband and I no longer argue over her. He finally was able to place me and our children first.

"The key is that my husband and I have always seen her in the same light. To me, the real test is how a husband and wife regard the mother-in-law. If the couple is in accord, then it becomes a workable relationship and the wife is motivated to be understanding, because she is confident of her husband's support. However, if the husband and wife do not agree on strategy, problems arise. At times, my mother-in-law has become very difficult. She is a mixed bag of qualities, a good generous person who never interferes and yet someone who has very strong opinions. Although she will not meddle, if asked, she will definitely state an opinion.

"We have grown closer over the years, but I don't think anything has changed in terms of trust. When I look at my mother-in-law today, I see the same strengths in her that my mother has and I disregard the faults. If my marriage was not so strong, this might not be so."

When a son-husband defends his wife and is responsible for his own conflicts with his mother, the daughter-in-law/wife feels safe. "In some relationships, a wife will complain about her mother-in-law and the husband will not intervene on his wife's behalf or on his own behalf," remarks Brenda Szulman. "It is much more beneficial when the husband is able to respond to his mother's behavior. In the same vein, the wife should be responsible for her own family's behavior." A wife who witnesses her husband's passivity toward his mother may become very resentful of him. She will see him as weak and will question his priorities.

HUSBANDS AS DEFENDERS
* **If required, the husband should help establish boundaries between his mother and his wife.**
* **The hope is that both women will be respectful and thoughtful of each other.**
* **A passive husband-son, who does not defend his wife, allows the issues to escalate.**

"Letting someone become a part of your family can be chock full of issues," laughs Juanita, who is a mother-in-law. "I know my daughter-in-law has a certain vision of how her life should be. This is a throw back to my generation. She is thankful for our family and our family life. Maybe this is because she was not married young and she was ready to settle down or because she had to make her own way. She is extremely appreciative of whatever we do for her. I show her things because she is so responsive. She is wonderful for my son and, frankly, my son is such a pain.

"We are not close, but friendly. She calls me often, but I do not stay with her when I go to Florida anymore. Instead, I stay with my sister. My daughter-in-law and I understand each other, because she has to work and I had to work. I feel she is raising her family in the same way that I had to.

"I never had a mother-in-law as a role model and my feelings on how to play the role are my own. I was very possessive of my husband when we were young and I resented his sister, because she seemed to come ahead of me. I want my son to feel his wife comes first so that history does not repeat itself. I bend over backwards to keep the proper distance."

If there has been no mother-in-law role model for a woman, then there is no precedent of what to do and not to do as a mother-in-law once she becomes one. In this case, the new mother-in-law cannot imitate an experience she never had. Instead, she will invent what she imagines her role as mother-in-law should be. "In general, we follow examples that we observed in our lives," says Dr. Michele Kasson. " We tend to do what we have had done to us because it is all that we know. To break free in thought and action as a mother-in-law is a conscious achievement."

For the mother-in-law who is able to chart her own course from the memory of successful mother-in-law/daughter-in-law relationships she has observed in others or simply by intuition, there are psychic rewards. She is on the verge of a new prototype, that of the accommodating mother-in-law who anticipates her daughter-in-law's needs. This woman anticipates problems that will arise and tries to avoid them. She is positive toward her son and his wife, supportive of their life choices. The mother-in-law who deserves praise is one who puts her son's marriage first and is not critical of her daughter-in-law. The best approach is to view the daughter-in-law as the woman her son has chosen, the one who makes him happy.

AN ACCOMMODATING MOTHER-IN-LAW
* **Accepts her son's choice of a wife.**
* **Does not engage in negative behavior.**
* **Makes herself available when she is needed.**
* **Is not critical of her daughter-in-law or her son's marriage.**

Being a good mother-in-law can be an acquired trait, as Judith has learned. "My father once predicted, long ago, that I'd be an awful mother-in-law because I'm so opinionated," Judith remarks. "I didn't want him to be right. I didn't want it to happen. And so, with two daughters-in-law, I've worked very hard to get along with each of them, to prove my father wrong. Melanie, my first daughter-in-law lives three hours away and calls often inviting us to visit. I have never had a fight with her nor have I ever objected to her decisions or actions even when there was reason to. I decided at the beginning it was more important to keep the doors open for my son and grandchildren, than to make waves. I don't see it as my place to argue with my daughters-in-law. I have shared this thought with my friends, when they complain about their daughters-in-law.

"Claire, my other daughter-in-law is materialistic, but I overlook it because it is not an inherent problem in the marriage. My form of comment is my silence. I keep quiet, but both my sons and daughters-in-law know when I am displeased. As dissimilar as my two daughters-in-law are, their goals are the same. They want comfortable lives and to raise healthy, well-behaved children. I suspect that they are each, in different ways, demanding of my sons. Neither daughter-in-law is career oriented, although they worked until they were married. Fortunately, in both cases, my sons make good livings.

"I feel close to my sons, but as they get older, I also feel less involved. They have their own lives and commitments and so do their father and I. I remind myself that what they do with themselves is their business. I look at the mother-in-law/daughter-in-law situation as one where everyone has to mature and honor each other's individuality, the mother-in-law, daughter-in-law and son."

When a mother-in-law is able to respect her son's direction rather than dictate her own wishes, the relationships prosper, that of mother/son and mother-in-law/daughter-in-law. Initially, this does not always seem an optimal plan for the mother-in-law, but in the long run, it succeeds.

"I knew when I married," Lindsay remarks, "that I wasn't really what my mother-in-law wanted for her son. At first, after we married, she resented the attention my husband lavished upon me. Her closeness with her other daughter-in-law seemed like a mother/daughter relationship, not a mother-in-law/daughter-in-law bond. I saw it almost as a reaction to my husband's marriage to me. This daughter-in-law was impressed with our mother-in-law. She and her husband became the favorites and they were invited everywhere and their children became the preferred grandchildren. I accepted this and I bowed out. I didn't want to compete and I didn't want to upset my husband. I suppose I was somewhat possessive of my husband, but I also resented how his mother had created these preferential ties, how unfair it was.

"Today, sixteen years later, we all seem to get along and the dynamic is less intense. My mother-in-law and I are avid gardeners and share this common interest. It seems as if my mother-in-law has grown in some ways and has stopped trying to pit us against each other. Today, she is older and more involved in her own life. She has friends and plays golf and bridge often. I know she would rather be with her friends than with either of her daughters-in-law at this stage. Maybe it got tiring, being a mother-in-law. I don't need to be close to her, but I'd like her to know my children and for them to know her. I remind myself that things have improved with the years, but they will never be perfect. I don't even know what the ideal mother-in-law would be. And it doesn't matter any more. Both my mother-in-law and I bring something positive to our relationship."

With time, many mothers-in-law find their daughters-in-law can enrich their extended families as well as nurture their sons and grandchildren. When the quality of life for a son is improved with the help of his new wife, a mother-in-law almost always will value the younger woman's influence. In return, the mother-in-law may feel more compassionate and become another mother figure for the daughter-in-law. Yet, in some cases, the daughter-in-law may have to fight a long, hard battle for her rights and to be treated as an equal by her mother-in-law. As her abilities as a wife and mother become evident to her mother-in-law, eventually, the daughter-in-law comes to feel appreciated. At this juncture, she is more inclined to feel positive emotions toward her mother-in-law.

Of the mothers-in-law interviewed for this chapter on the negative and positive qualities of mother-in-law/daughter-in-law relationships, over ninety percent were disappointed in their daughters-in-law, but half of those women anticipated improving the relationship. Of the daughters-in-law interviewed, seventy percent were either accepting of their mothers-in-law or felt the relationship between them was improving.

THE POSITIVES OUTWEIGH THE NEGATIVES
* **The daughter-in-law proves herself to her mother-in-law over time.**
* **The mother-in-law becomes a friend and/or mother figure to her daughter-in-law.**
* **The two women share common interests.**
* **An understanding is built up between the two women.**

The objective for both mothers-in-law and daughters-in-law, despite any negative aspects of the relationship, is a hope for a sense of connection, a commonality. It really becomes a circular interdependence: Good will and civility beget consideration and thoughtfulness. The longer this pattern of behavior continues, the more the age-old relationship between mother-in-law and daughter-in-law moves towards betterment.

2

Latest Complications/ Divided Loyalties

"My son chose a completely different kind of woman for his second wife," Lucy explains. "I find myself comparing the two women, because I deal with them both. My new daughter-in-law, Allison, is not as educated as the first one was and has a limited social sphere. On the other hand, Allison is bright and sure of herself. She is very attractive, much prettier than the first. She is not as career oriented as Robert's first wife, although she works. Allison is a bit older than Robert and I doubt they will have children together. I admire how she treats my son's children, who live with them, but I still consider my first daughter-in-law to be a decent mother, despite her lack of patience. While I don't forgive her for what she did to my son, she is not out of my life. Nor is she out of my son's life. That is what happens when there are children in a divorce.

"Just before they separated, Carol, my first daughter-in-law, wrote to me to say she still loved me, but she wasn't happy with my son and she hoped that I understood. Then Carol divorced him. Later, she sent the kids back to live with my son, out of the blue. It took him by surprise and upset his new marriage. After that, I didn't want to be in touch with her; it all became too mixed up. She tried to ruin my son. Then I saw her trying to confuse the children, my grandchildren. That was too much for me. I know I will remain in touch with her because of the grandchildren. It's as if I have two daughters-in-law, past and present, the way my son has two wives, past and present."

In the twenty-first century, as in the latter third of the previous century, there frequently are new scenarios springing up as a result of divorce and remarriage that complicate mother-in-law/daughter-in-law relationships. A mother-in-law may favor an ex-daughter-in-law over a present daughter-in-law. In a positive mother-in-law/daughter-in-law relationship, even after the divorce, the two women may remain in touch. Such women have genuine feelings for each other, which are independent of the son/ex-husband. This relationship is not about the man, but about the two women. Psychotherapist Brenda Szulman believes it is possible to keep the relationship between the two women intact after the divorce. "A connection forms between the two women, from years of shared history and common interests. This bond is separate from the marriage, although it formed because of the marriage. The divorce brings about feelings of loss for both women."

Especially if there are grandchildren from the first marriage, the mother-in-law may feel not only loyal to their mother, the ex-daughter-in-law, but attached to her on some level. Often, this causes the new daughter-in-law to feel like an outsider. If this prevents her from developing a relationship with her mother-in-law, it is advisable for her husband to step in and explain to his mother that she needs to have a rapport with his new wife as well as his former wife.

On the other hand, a woman who remarries may keep a close relationship with her ex-mother-in-law and not be interested in bonding with her new mother-in-law.

Further complications arise in situations where a stepmother enters the picture and becomes close with her stepdaughter-in-law, even though the son-husband may not welcome his father's new wife into the family. This happens more frequently when the son's mother has died, rather than in a divorce situation. In such a case, the son often remains faithful to the memory of his mother and establishes no connection with his stepmother.

FIRST WIVES/SECOND WIVES AND A SHARED MOTHER-IN-LAW

* **The mother-in-law may remain close to the first daughter-in-law, eliminating a chance to become close to the second daughter-in-law.**
* **The son-husband ought to intervene, asking his mother not to slight his new wife.**
* **The mother-in-law might remain aloof from her new daughter-in-law, because she did not want the divorce and second marriage to transpire.**

In Penny's case, both she and her mother-in-law are second wives. "As a second wife who has inherited an angry mother-in-law," says Penny,

"I feel I have a lot to deal with. My mother-in-law, Gladys, is also newly married for the second time. I keep waiting for some sensitivity to shine through as we're both second wives, but she is too old to have a mother-in-law. Evidently, it doesn't occur to her that she would not want to be treated the way she treats me. Gladys' approach is that I listen to her suggestions and then take them to heart. That is what her first daughter-in-law did. Instead, I do nothing with her suggestions. I am polite and I listen and nod my head. In my first marriage, my relationship was solid with Rachel, my mother-in-law. I was able to tell her exactly how I felt about things. We had free range of each other's homes and we never took advantage of each other. She never interfered in my life. My relationship with Rachel continues because of my child. We still see each other and live in nearby towns. In fact, she is very willing to baby-sit and I encourage it. She was heartbroken when her son and I got divorced. She cried for days.

"I look back on my first mother-in-law relationship and I realize we never had an unpleasant incident. Rachel never overstepped her bounds. I suspect that if she had objected to something, she would have complained to my husband at the time. He somehow found a balance between us and she and I remained steady in our regard for each other. Today, in my second marriage, it isn't like that. My new mother-in-law is pushier than my first. At the same time, Gladys acts as if we are friends and insists that I call her by her first name. She's generous with her time and gifts, but I know she wants things to go her way. Gladys is good to my child and I appreciate that. What I find fault with is my husband. I suppose my first husband knew how to handle his mother better than my second husband does, at least when it concerns me. Also, I suspect that my present mother-in-law misses her first daughter-in-law."

"If a mother-in-law feels that the first wife was superior to the second wife in a variety of ways," says Dr. Michele Kasson, "and allows these feelings to show, she creates hostility and hurts her new daughter-in-law. The bottom line is that the husband has chosen a new wife. The mother-in-law has to accept this as a reality."

Yet my research and interviews indicate that what often happens in such situations is that the mother-in-law resists the relationship on several levels when she is displeased by her new daughter-in-law. There may be cultural issues surrounding her husband's choice of a second wife. The mother-in-law may have been greatly saddened by the divorce from his first wife for a variety of reasons. Perhaps she is very close with her first daughter-in-law's parents and extended family. If there are grandchildren involved, a mother-in-law will hesitate before condoning a divorce in many instances. Divorce in general may be alien to her, despite the times we live in, because she is from an older, more conservative generation. Another factor may be that the mother-in-law suffered her own divorce and regrets it, therefore believing her son should have remained in his first marriage.

With the traditional extended family so often just a memory in today's society, the role of mother-in-law/daughter-in-law is shifting. In some instances, there is a camaraderie, a kind of sisterhood, instead of a more traditional mother/daughter hierarchy based on age and status. However, divorce changes everything between the two women. No matter how close they were, the role of mother-in-law and the relationship the women shared is diminished by divorce and its aftermath.

Even if the two women did not share an especially close relationship, it may be that as the years passed, an implicit acceptance of each other's style developed between the older and younger woman. Such a mutual understanding allows for consistent interactions that the two women come to rely upon. Divorce shakes the foundations of their tenuous relationship. In a subsequent marriage, the mother--in-law may have difficulty bonding with her new daughter-in-law regardless of positive or negatives feelings held toward her previous daughter-in-law. As Margaret Mead points out in her book, *Male and Female*, each marriage is different and has "contrasts between the partners." Mead describes the newcomer—the second wife—as having different patterns from both the first wife and the husband's mother. "The foreigner's hand is unsure, as it handles unfamiliar things," writes Mead. "...the old American's hand bears marks of former generations and may tremble or clench anew over contact with some newly arrived and little-understood stranger." For a family, and especially a mother-in-law, the new daughter-in-law is the "foreigner," particularly when the mother-in-law has already invested herself in forming a familiar, and perhaps caring, relationship with her first daughter-in-law.

Many women, like Anita, are shocked and hurt when their first daughters-in-law disappear from their lives because of divorce. "Although it took years, my daughter-in-law, Yvonne, became very close to our family," recalls Anita, "and then she dumped my son, Thomas, and left him with their little son. She and I knew each other well enough for her not to have left him the way she did. I know they had marital problems from the beginning, but because I took her under my wing, I thought it would not end this way. What hurts me most, besides how Thomas had to regroup and how alone he was raising his child for several years, is that Yvonne had finally come into our family. She had become a part of our clan.

"Then my son met another woman, Faith, and married her. I was happy for him because he had been so alone, but I knew that it wouldn't be the same for me. Though I believe this girl is very devoted to my son,

I have learned the hard way that connecting with a daughter-in-law is not easy. Trading family secrets and inviting someone into the intimate core of a family is a big step. I'm not quite ready for that yet. In the meantime, I learned from what happened with my first daughter-in-law to shift my concern from how my new daughter-in-law meshes with our family to how she gets along with my son."

Margaret Mead also wrote about a "code," or a kind of language found in most marriages. Mead views this as a result of the individual qualities of the two partners meshing "...into a language that each understands imperfectly." Families, too, create "codes." Once a "code" has been created over time between a mother-in-law and daughter-in-law, it is not easy to discard and create a new style of communication—a new "code"—with a subsequent mother-in-law or daughter-in-law.

FITTING IN
* Initially, some mothers-in-law will try to "train" their daughters-in-law in the ways of the family.
* They will share family recipes and attempt to teach them aspects of their families' lives.
* They may develop a particular style of communicating, a "code" that helps them relate to each other.
* In the best scenario, the desire for family unity and amity inspires the confidence and acceptance of familial traditions, despite any struggles which may exist between the two women.

Once a marriage fails, unless the two women have an extraordinarily close relationship the daughter-in-law will seem lost to her mother-in-law on many levels. The manner in which she supported and enabled the son-husband is no longer viable, nor can there be much trust remaining, since the primary relationship, that of the marriage, is dissolved. One of the two women may lament the end of their relationship, embellishing the good parts. Often, a daughter-in-law disparages her mother-in-law during and after a divorce, while the mother-in-law, independent of her personal feelings toward her daughter-in-law, wishes the younger woman had remained married to her son.

ABRUPT ENDINGS
* The marriage fails; the mother-in-law/daughter-in-law relationship is diminished, if not severed.
* The mother-in-law suffers her son's pain.

* **All the family connections and history of which the daughter-in-law was once a part is discarded.**
* **Both mother-in-law and daughter-in-law suffer a loss, regardless of how they interacted during the marriage.**

The recent film, *A Walk on the Moon*, explores the concept of infidelity in a marriage as seen through the eyes of the mother-in-law and her daughter-in-law. The story takes place in the late sixties, in the Catskills, where the daughter-in-law and wife, played by Diane Lane, summers with her mother, played by Tovah Feldshuh. Liev Schreiber plays the hardworking husband and Viggo Mortensen plays the lover. As the mother-in-law observes her daughter-in-law's discontent with her husband and her roving eye for the ' blouse man', a traveling salesman, she defends her son. Finally, the mother-in-law makes a telephone call to her son back in the city, imploring him to come up to the mountains at once to save his marriage and win his wife back. As a woman, it seems that the mother-in-law understands her daughter-in-law's unrest in the marriage. As a mother-in-law, she fiercely defends her son and the sanctity of the marriage. The daughter-in-law suffers extra guilt when she returns from stolen time with her lover and must face her mother-in-law. This tale reflects the complexity of living within the extended family with its high expectations and moral commitment. When a mother-in-law is unable to convince her daughter-in-law to preserve her marriage, as in *A Walk on the Moon*, the fallout affects everyone.

"I had an affair which broke up my first marriage," confesses Tatiana. "I think my relationship with my mother-in-law, Rose, contributed to the state of my marriage. I suppose the marriage was doomed from the start, but the rift in my marriage definitely grew because of my mother-in-law. Bob, my husband, confided his unhappiness to his mother and she undermined me.

"There were times when there were truces between us. I always suspected, however, that Rose put a wedge in the marriage. I never imagined I could be close with her, nor could I trust her. She and Bob were so close that I knew I couldn't tell him things without her hearing them, too. Thankfully, we had no children together and eventually I left. I would have left anyway, but meeting someone else at work really clinched it. Of course, that was when my mother-in-law begged me to stay and decided I was actually a good wife and a good daughter-in-law, but it was too little too late. I told her how I really felt, that I didn't believe a word she said that was positive about me. By the end of the marriage, I viewed my husband as being very much like his mother.

"Today, I have a second chance in a new marriage and with a new mother-in-law, Ginnie. I am very grateful for this mother-in-law, who is a benign and unmeddlesome woman. I never desired anything more, this is all that I ever wanted. She knows the marriage is a result of my affair with her son, who was divorced at the time, yet she does not judge me. She is simply happy that her son is so happy. Although she is not a strong force like my first mother-in-law, my present husband feels a great filial duty and a great respect for her. On the other hand, he also knows that this is a second marriage for both of us and he can't force me to love his mother."

In our society, infidelity, divorce and remarriage are all a part of the fabric of dismantled and reinvented lives. With the divorce rate at over fifty percent, according to the United States Census Bureau, and seventy percent of the divorced population remarrying, chances are that the divorcing son-husband and daughter-in-law will each find a new partner. Many times an affair is the symptom of an unhappy marriage and the cure is divorce. A mother-in-law who witnesses her son's pain due to his wife's affair cannot easily forgive her daughter-in-law. Despite such complications in the marriage, the mother-in-law often encourages them to repair the relationship. However, if a mother-in-law is vehemently opposed to her daughter-in-law, then she may advocate the end of the marriage, viewing it as a vehicle to freedom and the possibility of a happier second marriage for her son. In rare instances, a mother-in-law and daughter-in-law come to terms with the end of the marriage and whatever precipitated it. They share a more positive viewpoint—that the divorce is best for both the son-husband and daughter-in-law.

AFFAIRS AND DAUGHTERS-IN-LAW
* **The first marriage was unhappy.**
* **An affair brings about a divorce.**
* **The mother-in-law accepts this, albeit reluctantly.**
* **The possibility of a new marriage, a new mother-in-law and a new daughter-in-law appear on the horizon.**

Sometimes mothers-in-law can do nothing but swallow their frustration and watch events unfold, as Pearl was forced to do. "Five years into the marriage, Lizzie, my daughter-in-law, left my son for her lover," says Pearl. "Once she married her lover, she had an affair with a married man while she conducted her new marriage. She always had to have a lover and a husband at the same time. We all live in a small town and these stories came back to haunt me. There were no children, thankfully. I saw this daughter-in-law as artistic, dramatic and intellectual. I really did admire her. When I asked my son, Tony, questions about what happened he refused to tell me anything. He said I would probably hear things around town, but he had no intention of discussing anything with me. He was very defensive.

"I knew he should not have married Lizzie. As a mother-in-law, however, I see no evil, hear no evil and speak no evil. Theirs was a marriage that should never have happened, but I never spoke against it or Lizzie. When she left my son, I had no idea why or what she planned to do. I did notice that Tony wasn't exactly heartbroken after she left, so something must have happened that I didn't know about. What I did learn later was that my daughter-in-law had cared for me. Lizzie wrote me a note and told me this. While I liked her and recognized her strengths, I was not surprised she had an affair. I never passed judgment, I simply heard about it and saw it happening."

There are those mothers-in-law who recognize their daughters-in-law's frustrations in their marriages. Woman to woman, a mother-in-law may realize her son's shortcomings because she has struggled in her own marriage with the same conflicts as her daughter-in-law. Nonetheless, the mother-in-law's dedication and loyalty are first and foremost to her son and, therefore, she cannot always express her true feelings completely.

AFFAIRS AND MOTHERS-IN-LAW
* **The mother-in-law cannot stop the affair or keep the marriage from crumbling.**
* **She may secretly empathize with her daughter-in-law's frustrations.**
* **Her daughter-in-law's situation may even mirror a part of her own history.**
* **Her loyalty to her son may prevent her from being honest about identifying with his wife.**

Although a mother-in-law may understand why her daughter-in-law is unhappy in the marriage, her bond to her son will usually prevail. The mother-in-law's deep secret may be that she had an affair during her marriage which did or did not result in a divorce. Nonetheless, she will stand by her son. A large part of this decision is formed by how society views the family. Alice Michaeli has noted that it would be quite unusual for a mother-in-law to side with a daughter-in-law in a divorce situation. "Even if the son is abusive or an alcoholic or a drug addict, in most cases, this would not enable the mother-in-law to side with her daughter-in-law. Her place is with her son, for better or for worse."

Although Emmie's affair resulted in a divorce, she still wishes she could be close to her former mother-in-law, Geraldine. "I was so young when I married, she became a second mother to me. My husband and I lived with Geraldine at first and I saw her every day. When we moved an hour away, she was still a part of my life. I will never forget that my mother-in-law was supportive of me when we were first married.

"Having had a child so young and being so dependent on my mother-in-law helped us to become close. When I got older and became disillusioned in my marriage, she knew on some level how I felt. I always respected Geraldine and she never told me what to do. When she saw how the marriage was falling apart, she was there for me. If the marriage had ended differently and I had not had an affair, we would still be talking. Instead, I'm left with feelings for her, but no real contact. I am sure that she misses me, too. I remained married for a long time after I was unhappy, because I needed my mother-in-law and her attention."

Extended families represent closeness and safe havens for daughters-in-law who lack these things in their own immediate families. A daughter-in-law who is close to her mother-in-law finds it difficult to give up the bond and may actually postpone a much desired divorce. A mother-in-law or daughter-in-law can appeal to one another on several levels—socially, intellectually or in terms of achievement—and fill a void where there is no mother figure or daughter figure. Shere Hite, in *The Hite Report on Family and Marriage*, reports that a majority of women who have been raised in intact families have ambivalent feelings toward their mother. While seventy-three percent of these women love their mothers and feel connected to them, according to Hite, these women are also angry that their mothers are passive and their fathers are dominating. If a mother-in-law represents another kind of mother figure for their daughter-in-law and is not like her own mother, then the daughter-in-law feels blessed to have a mother figure in her life with a new and different view of the world.

May, as a mother-in-law, feels warmly toward her daughter-in-law. "Eva makes me happy as a daughter-in-law. What counts for me is that she pleases my son, especially since he's been divorced. If I had to choose a wife for my son, it would be difficult. I keep this in mind and see her pluses. I know how much he loved her from the beginning. Eva is several years older than my son and although I am very close to my own daughter, there is another feeling I have with Eva. We take excursions and spend time together in ways that I would not with anyone else. She calls me 'Mother' and I feel in some ways that I am her mother."

While many mother-in-law/daughter-in-law relationships are not as close as May's and Eva's, in Stephanie's case, as a daughter-in-law, her unsuccessful first mother-in-law relationship compelled her to succeed with her second. "My first mother-in-law, Leonora, was domineering and always right. Her opinion counted more than anyone else's view. Everything she had done was bigger, better and superior to anyone else's accomplishments. She was from a WASP pioneering family. Growing up in a respectable but modest environment, she was also tough-minded. Leonora married a wealthy man and worked in his business, eventually becoming the force behind the business. She had strong family values, but I found it ironic that she had learned nothing from her own domineering mother-in-law. My mother-in-law had several husbands and she flirted constantly. She even flirted with her sons-in-law. I was there at the family events and I saw it all. As far as she and I went, we mixed about as well as oil and water.

"In retrospect, I was not very nice to her. She actually held onto my arm as she delivered a warning never to marry again—and she meant it. Leonora viewed marriage in a negative manner. When I did remarry, I was forty and I had a broader view. I made a point to enjoy my new mother-in-law and to appreciate her for what she had to offer."

Because men and women experience marriage in unique ways and men are reported to be happier than women are while married, it is not surprising that most men remarry within three years of their divorce. Usually, women who choose to remarry do find the second marriage more rewarding and more peaceful. In most cases, by mid-life, both men and women have achieved a heightened self-awareness and their choice of partner is better suited to them. If there are any problematic similarities between the first and the second mother-in-law, the daughter-in-law's attained maturity can make all the difference in the mother-in-law/daughter-in-law relationship dynamic the second time around.

When Gail Sheehy writes in her book, *New Passages: Mapping Your Life Across Time*, of the post-patriarchal man, she is referring to a man who is coming to new awareness after forty. This man may be more in touch with himself, his feelings, and his goals. Additionally, he may better understand and adopt contemporary ideas about gender roles. However, if there are any problems between this man's new wife and his mother, he may not intercede. As Gail Sheehy describes it, men disconnect and do not like marital conflict. Men avoid explosive issues whether they are in a first, second or third marriage.

MARITAL CONFLICT
* Many men will avoid confrontations in their marriages, including those that extend to their mothers and wives.

* **Ultimately, such a stance forces the two women to achieve a rapport without his help.**
* **With second time mothers-in-law and daughters-in-law, a mature outlook is the deciding factor in building a successful relationship.**

As I discovered when interviewing Mallory, husbands can play a critical role in helping or hurting the mother-in-law/daughter-in-law relationship. "I am acutely aware of what works and what doesn't work with my mother-in-law," says Mallory. "My ex-mother-in-law wanted more from me than I was willing to provide. Nevertheless, I thought she was great and someone with a lot of style. She taught me things. For instance, she taught me how to wash asparagus. I know that sounds laughable, but I was young and I observed whatever she did. At that time, I was very open to learning. My own mother had died and I was looking for a mother figure.

"For the past thirteen years, I have had a very different kind of mother-in-law than my first one. My mother-in-law, Claire, has been widowed for many years and my husband, Charlie, feels guilty if she doesn't come to visit from France at least four times a year. The best story is when she came to watch my two sons when my daughter was born. I came home from the hospital and there she was smoking and drinking in the living room. I waved away the smoke, but she didn't get it. I realized she was going to sit there and continue. She provided zero help with my three young children, one an infant. On top of it, my kitchen hadn't been installed yet and we had to make do. She was careless and sloppy, dropping ashes in the kitchen while my baby wailed. Right there, as my husband was explaining to me that his mother *was* helping, I began my postpartum depression. I miss my first mother-in-law; maybe I miss my first husband, too.

"In these kinds of situations with Claire, Charlie begins by defending his mother, but ends up strongly encouraging her to shorten her visit. It's rare that my husband and I are on the same side about anything, let alone his mother."

A son will often gravitate toward his wife's family rather than remain close with his own. This is in part because in traditional marriages, it is the wife who plans family visits and frequently chooses her parents over her husband's parents. Yet, there are circumstances when the son is attached to his mother. If his mother was widowed or divorced and raised her children alone, the result may be an adult child dedicated to his or her mother. While the mother-in-law could seem controlling or selfish to her daughter-in-law, the son-husband, based on his childhood, sees his closeness with his mother as a positive force.

The mother of such a son will also see his attention and devotion as a positive force in her life, as Ethel does. "I have been a mother-in-law for twenty-five years," Ethel explains. "The first twelve years were devoted to my first daughter-in-law, Teri, and the last thirteen have been for Celia, my son's second wife. We see Todd and Celia twice a year since they moved halfway across the country. Because we see each other so infrequently, a wedge has formed in the relationship. I believe that my daughter-in-law has no energy for domestic life and that bothers me. I resent her attitude of working so hard that she has nothing left for children and homemaking. I suppose if you work all day, the last thing you want to do is go home and cook. However, my daughter works full time also and she cooks meals for her family. My feeling is that because I was divorced and alone for a lengthy period of time before I remarried, Todd and I really got each other through hard times. He has always been very attentive and caring towards me. Teri, my first daughter-in-law, understood this whereas Celia feels it was so long ago it has nothing to do with Todd's present life."

For the daughter-in-law who decides to make a go of it the second time around with her second mother-in-law, there are undeniable rewards. The two women usually are not in search of a mother/daughter relationship per se, nor are their expectations as high as they were in the first marriages. While the first wife was held to a certain scrutiny, the second wife frequently is not. It seems less important to the mother-in-law now that there has been a divorce and her son has had to recover and regroup. Hopefully, she will not regard the second wife as an outsider and will not exclude her from the clan, as she may have done in her son's first marriage. In response, the second wife, who may have had an arduous time of it as a daughter-in-law in her first marriage, may be energized to work harder to achieve an amiable relationship with her new mother-in-law.

SECOND GO ROUND
* **The mother-in-law knows the limits of the relationship.**
* **The daughter-in-law understands a mother-in-law is never ideal.**
* **Expectations are lower.**

With a second marriage, the new daughter-in-law often doesn't feel the need to push her new mother-in-law away, as she might have done the first time. Similarly, the mother-in-law will likely welcome her new daughter-in-law instead of keeping her at arms length. The mother-in-law and her daughter-in-law are committed to a successful, if not intimate, relationship.

As Dr. Michele Kasson remarks, "Some mothers-in-law, later in life, are relieved that their sons are married. They feel that their sons are on the right path, in control of their lives and therefore do not require motherly attention. They no longer worry as much as they once did about their sons and, by extension, do not fear losing their sons to the wives' families. Mothers-in-law become less competitive and this works in everyone's favor."

One such mother-in-law, Dorothea, regards her son's second marriage as a vast improvement over his first. "I have learned to appreciate my daughter-in-law, Samantha. After what my son endured in his first marriage, I approve of his second wife. My son says he married someone like me this time, and though that's flattering, I don't really see the resemblance. Regardless, I like Samantha. I do not view her as a daughter of my own, but I appreciate her as a daughter-in-law."

"What I respect is how she can get my son to do things that I was never able to get him to do, such as housekeeping. They have a child and she works full-time, too. My son has a flexible schedule and stays home with the baby. Maybe he always wanted to be domestic and I never gave him the opportunity. I don't think anyone else can evoke such a response in my son as she has. I really think he married her because he couldn't stand the dating scene, plus he found her soothing. Samantha does not get in the way of the relationship my son and I have. In fact, things have improved between us since he remarried. Now he is a marvelous son. I'm grateful to her for that."

Collette, as a second daughter-in-law for ten years, knows her mother-in-law, Marianne, has learned to keep her thoughts to herself this time around. Her mother-in-law's approach is similar to Dorothea's. "I believe," says Collette, "that Marianne must have been relentless with her first daughter-in-law, but she isn't that way with me. I think she does, however, resent that I have two college degrees and I've achieved a successful career. My mother-in-law is educated and smart but from a generation in which women usually gave up their careers when they married or had children. I know it is a constant conflict for her, the fact that she gave up her career. She has regrets about her life and my success bothers her. My husband's first wife was also successful in her career, which makes me think this is a trait my husband finds appealing in women. It's as if he wants someone who is fulfilled in a career, because his own mother wasn't.

"My mother-in-law watches me and regrets her lack of experience. I wouldn't call it envy exactly, but I think she is sorry she wasn't able to persevere. What seems to upset her most is that I can do both the mothering and my work. With Rich's first wife, she complained bitterly about how she put her work ahead of the marriage. In this marriage, she says nothing. If it is threatening to have a daughter-in-law who has it all or who wants it all, my mother-in-law has learned to hold her tongue."

Gail Sheehy describes a "Second Adulthood" as occurring for women between the ages of forty-five and eighty-five and this includes, of course, both daughters-in-law and mothers-in-law. According to Sheehy, both groups of women are asking themselves what they will make of the next stage and how they want to live their lives. In the "revolution in life cycle" which she describes, we live longer and leave childhood sooner, but grow up more slowly. Baby boomers do not always consider themselves to be adults until their forties. If today forty represents what thirty was in the past, we all have a chance to reinvent ourselves and chart out another course for the latter portions of our lives. This alternate course can last many years, since Sheehy's impressive prediction is that a woman who reaches fifty today without any cancer or heart disease, can expect to live another forty years.

Of course, life's circumstances, the small tragedies and the large, can be sobering, even while we work at improving and redefining our lives. The role of mother-in-law may be altered by a series of events. Perhaps the mother-in-law has experienced a failed marriage herself or the loss of her husband, circumstances that might render her less combative and critical and more empathetic. Although originally she may not have been accepting of her daughter-in-law, she may come to realize the daughter-in-law's worth in terms of her son's happiness and therefore will be less likely to vocalize or act on issues she finds disturbing.

SLOW ACCEPTANCE
* **The mother-in-law cuts her losses.**
* **The daughter-in-law cuts her losses.**
* **A sense of mortality sets in for the family members.**
* **Peace in the family becomes the goal.**

From my research, it is clear that the average daughter-in-law does not consider herself the originator or perpetrator of the uneasiness between herself and her mother-in-law. A daughter-in-law almost always believes that it is her mother-in-law's fault that the connection has failed. From her point of view, her mother-in-law seems harsh and unreasonable. On the other hand, the mother-in-law often believes it is her daughter-in-law who is lacking and inept. Repeatedly, these are the feelings expressed by each side. This may be because, as sociologist Alice Michaeli points out, the role of mother-in-law is not a well defined one for many women, particularly in our society. She explains how in a cross-cultural comparison of

Japanese and Chinese women, a mother-in-law is a dominant and attention demanding figure. This applies to Central and Latin American cultures as well. "The mother-in-law has an important role in other cultures. What occurs in our country is the result of the advances in education and technology. The lack of well-formulated relationships between mothers-in-law and daughters-in-law is a Western practice."

The lack of well-defined roles makes relationships especially difficult when children are involved. For example, a recent phenomenon that has transpired as a result of divorce, remarriage and multiple in-laws is the subject of grandparents' rights. In June 2000, headlines across the country announced the Supreme Court's decision, in a 6-3 ruling, that grandparents Gary and Jenifer Troxel of Mount Vernon, Washington were not entitled to spend more time with their granddaughters than the girls' mother, Tommie Wynn, deemed appropriate. After the Troxel's son and Wynn's husband died, Wynn remarried and sought to limit the visitation with the Troxels to one day a month. Her reason was that she wanted her new family, including six other children, to bond. The Troxels requested at least one weekend a month. For the sixty million grandparents in America, the court's ruling was shocking and deeply disturbing.

In cultures where mothers-in-law are accepted as prominent and respected figures, such disputes over seeing grandchildren are unlikely to arise. However, in a typical American family, wives tend to organize family events, including those that involve in-laws. After a divorce, it is up to the former daughter-in-law to arrange for the former mother-in-law to see her grandchildren. This applies despite an almost universal, undeniable tension between the two women after a divorce, whether it was a pleasant relationship beforehand or not. As a result, both sides must make a greater effort to at least maintain civility.

"There are very practical reasons why in-laws should maintain a good relationship with their daughter-in-law after a divorce," notes Brondi Borer, divorce mediator. "With the decision on the Troxel case, grandparents' rights are now diminished. For a mother-in-law who already has a poor relationship with her daughter-in-law, if a divorce occurs, the daughter-in-law might withhold access to the grandchildren. It is wise for a mother-in-law/grandmother to try to maintain a good relationship with her former daughter-in-law, especially if her son is the non-custodial parent, in order to maintain contact with her grandchildren.

GRANDPARENTS RIGHTS
* **In the future, courts may rule solely in favor of the custodial parent.**

* **The daughter-in-law is frequently the custodial parent.**
* **A mother-in-law/grandmother will benefit from a healthy involvement with her former daughter-in-law.**

Blanche is a mother-in-law who has experienced the loss of her grandchildren as a result of her son's divorce. "I cannot believe the turn of events," laments Blanche, a mother-in-law for eight years. "I have three sons and one daughter. I felt I was close to my oldest son's second wife, Mia. We got along very well. We would have coffee together and go shopping. Once they had children, I went to their house every Tuesday and baby-sat for the day so Mia could have some time off. Then they moved away. I was very close with the two children and I thought I had a good relationship with my daughter-in-law. I wondered why she stopped calling me and why I had few invitations to visit them and see my grandchildren.

"Suddenly, Jimmy, my son, called me and announced they were getting divorced. I was astonished, really saddened by the news. I am a widow and it made me feel somehow even more alone in the world. My daughter-in-law was the one to file for divorce although Jimmy told me the feeling was mutual. I was upset over it because of my grandchildren. I feel very badly that my son is not living with them. In fact, they now live half way across the country from one another which makes it worse. I do not see my grandchildren much.

"Of course, Mia became the custodial parent because she was a stay-at-home mother. Any time I tried to make plans to see the children, she found an excuse. My son, who hardly had enough time with his own kids, would travel to see me a few times a year, but not often. Then Mia remarried. She actually sent me a newspaper clipping announcing her second wedding. It was like a bad dream. The children became a part of her new life with her second husband. I feel my grandchildren were taken from me."

A daughter-in-law's story of her ex-mother-in-law's visitation complaints shows the situation from another point-of-view. "My mother-in-law, Arlene, and I had always been close," says Melinda, whose mother-in-law has accused her of being unfair about visitation with the grandchildren. "I see her once a month and let my kids have any relationship with her that is offered. The way I look at it, their relationship with their grandmother has nothing to do with my relationship with my former mother-in-law. My girls are seven and nine and I wish Arlene understood that they really can't be with her for an entire weekend, because they have sports and classes, birthday parties and other events with their friends to attend. Plus, weekends are really the only time the girls and I have together when we're not rushed and running to work or school. Since we live in the same town,

I've tried to keep my end of the bargain up after the divorce, but it is hard. I'm a single mother and work full time. I have no family here or friends who do not work so if there is a problem and one of the girls gets sick, I'm really in a quandary. I find it hard to believe and extremely annoying that Arlene asks to have the children only on the weekends, when she lives in the same town and could be of great assistance to me. I wish I could count on her to help me with them on weekdays or in an emergency.

"Deep down, I have always intensely disliked my former mother-in-law. So why should I give up precious time with my kids for her? The relationship began amiably enough and her son, my ex-husband, has always gotten along with her. The children do, too. But I have never used the divorce as a weapon when it comes to the children, despite my feelings."

Grandmothers, whether they are also ex-mother-in-laws or not, are pivotal players in maintaining a child's well-being and mental health during and after a divorce. The optimum situation is that the mother-in-law, in her role as grandmother, rises above the behavior of the divorced parents. Grandparents shouldn't become embroiled in the contention that a divorce brings. Brondi Borer advises her clients that for practical reasons former daughters-in-law, ex-husbands, and ex-in-laws should maintain an interaction. "A grandmother who distances herself from the emotional upheaval in order to sustain an equilibrium is doing her grand-children a great service." To insure visitation rights in the future for grandmothers/ex-mothers-in-law, neutrality throughout the divorce and civility toward the former daughter-in-law is advised.

BEST INTEREST OF THE CHILD
* **The grandparents and their ex-daughter-in-law have a decent relationship.**
* **A harmonious extended family continues even after the divorce.**
* **Children are not made participants in battle.**

Although she knew her son's marriage couldn't last, this mother-in-law concentrated on keeping her relationship with her grandchildren. "The courts told my daughter-in-law, Tess, to get help and to consider taking antidepressants," says Connie, a mother-in-law who advocated her son's divorce. "While I see her as a good person, not a run around or any-thing like that, she is unstable. For her sake and the sake of the children, I'd like her to marry someone stable. I feel terrible for my son, John. He says since the divorce he is never at ease about the children, who are in Tess's care, and thinks of them all the time.

"Tess will always be a daughter-in-law to me, because she is the mother of my grandchildren. I do not forgive her for some of her actions. As a mother-in-law, I might want to berate her, but as a mother, I understand that my son was not perfect. I forgive Tess for what she has done in the past. Although the divorce is final, there recently have been some upsetting phone calls between Tess and John. She claims she needs to separate completely and then she calls him again and again. She is confused. My hope is that she will become better with medication and counseling. I try to think of her good points: She was never lazy and we had our good times together. But that friction between John and Tess was always there, while she and I were fine.

"I defended Tess for a long time and I urged them to keep the marriage together, then I realized they had to separate. Today, I concentrate on what can work and I don't regret the past. I see my grandchildren and I keep peace with Tess."

There are some instances where the mother-in-law maintains contact with her daughter-in-law after a divorce, according to matrimonial lawyer, Amy Reisen. "I have seen cases in my practice," reports Reisen, "where a husband decides he wants a new life. He leaves his wife and children, claiming he has to find himself. When this happens, the mother-in-law typically is not disloyal to her son, but remains supportive of her daughter-in-law, who is now forced to start over. On the other hand, in the majority of the divorce cases that I take on, the mother-in-law sides with her son, even when she has had a strong connection to her daughter-in-law over the years. Whether it is a long standing marriage or one of short duration, the mother-in-law will probably find herself cut off from her daughter-in-law anyway."

DIVORCE AND MOTHERS-IN-LAW
* The mother-in-law and former daughter-in-law stay in touch in rare circumstances.
* When the son precipitates the divorce, a mother-in-law may remain supportive of her former daughter-in-law.
* Usually the mother-in-law sides with her son.

While divorce may seem to be about two people, the husband and the wife, it is also a case of broken promises and divided loyalties that filter down to in-laws and friends alike. All too often, our society seems to expect, if not encourage, a break between the mother-in-law and daughter-in-law. There are few mothers-in-law and daughters-in-law who are able to sustain some kind of healthy relationship outside the dissolved marriage. If there are grandchildren, however, the women will often make an effort to remain civil.

SPLIT LOYALTIES
* **A mother-in-law may have insights into the problems in her son's marriage.**
* **Yet, with so much at stake, many mother-in-laws are reluctant to take sides.**
* **Ultimately, a mother-in-law's interactions with her former daughter-in-law may depend on the presence or absence of children/grandchildren.**

Hostility and animosity are common feelings in a divorce. While life marches on, loyalties alter. Whatever sympathies the mother-in-law and daughter-in-law held for one another, they cannot always withstand the trials of divorce. Unfortunately, there are no guidelines for appropriate behavior in these instances. "It is common when a divorce is in progress," says Amy Reisen, "that a suddenly ill mother-in-law will not be tended to by her soon-to-be ex-daughter-in-law. The daughter-in-law could be upset about her ex-mother-in-law's illness, but she might hesitate to care for her. She cannot stop the divorce or reverse the future because of the sickness. The daughter-in-law is sympathetic, but not actively involved anymore."

"I have been able to remain close with my ex-daughter-in-law, Caitlin, for the past nine years," Victoria tells us. "I understood from the beginning why my son wanted the divorce. He and his first wife really were not compatible. I knew, however, that I not only had to stay close with my granddaughter, Becca, who is now nineteen, but with her mother, who had the ability to facilitate or block my visits with Becca. I also had to welcome my new daughter-in-law into my life. She is actually a much better match for my son. Nevertheless, I consider my first daughter-in-law worthy of my respect. I have been careful in this delicate situation from the beginning. It would have caused monumental problems if I had interfered with Caitlin on any subject."

"My son was not in favor of this initially, but I had to create a middle ground position for myself. I keep my eye on what counts most, which is getting to see Becca, my granddaughter."

In an ideal world, the maturity and open-mindedness required to succeed with second daughters-in-law and second mothers-in-law after divorces would be plentiful. It would be possible for the mother-in-law to have positive feelings toward both women, her first daughter-in-law and the second, and a daughter-in-law would be able to sustain a relationship with her first mother-in-law and her second. When everyone communicates and the relationships are kept separate, in theory, no ties have to be severed. It becomes a dilemma, however, for a former mother-in-law or former daughter-in-law if the divorce was acrimonious.

Almost fifty percent of the mothers-in-law interviewed for this chapter felt that after the divorces, ties with their former daughters-in-law remained; twenty-five percent were angry toward their first daughters-in-law for both the duration and aftermath of the marriages; the remaining twenty-five percent viewed their new daughters-in-law as better suited for their sons and were determined to establish positive relationships with them.

Of the daughters-in-law interviewed, approximately fifty percent maintained a rapport with their former mothers-in-law; thirty percent had decided to embrace their second mothers-in-law, having learned from their first experiences; twenty percent had issues with their mothers-in-law both during and after the marriages.

Concerning children/grandchildren, about sixty percent of the mothers-in-law were pleased with their ongoing relatiónships with the grandchildren after the divorces while forty percent were dissatisfied. The daughters-in-law were evenly divided in this area; half of them encouraged their former mothers-in-law to see their grandchildren and the other half resisted sharing their children with their former mothers-in-law.

Theoretically, there is no reason why former mothers-in-law and former daughters-in-law cannot remain close or at least amicable. After all, they did not divorce each other. At the same time, a former mother-in-law who prefers the first wife to the second must still extend herself to her new daughter-in-law, her son's second wife. If there are children in the second marriage from the previous marriages, the extended blended family can be one of opportunity and support. For this to happen, all the players—mother-in-law, daughter-in-law, son, ex-mother-in-law, ex-daughter-in-law, ex-husband, children and stepchildren—need to be prepared for the new "norm." As my interviewees and experts confirmed, however, this is not easily achieved and requires great fortitude.

3

Mother Replacements/ Shopping Excursions

"Sometimes I will ask my mother-in-law's opinion when I would not ask my mother," admits Hannah. "I would rather speak with her because she is a better listener. My mother does not hear what I have to say. My mother-in-law is very sharp and I hold her in high regard. I have gotten annoyed with her over the years, but basically I am fortunate to have her as my mother-in-law. I am more demonstrative, while she is not affectionate and doesn't show any emotion. We get along, though, and I'm not put off by her coolness anymore. I know that my mother-in-law considers me a good wife and good mother and she considers her son a good son. I see her as the opposite of my mother in many ways. My husband is independent and strong because his mother was ahead of her time in how she raised him."

A scenario that frequently leads to a salutary relationship between a mother-in-law and daughter-in-law is when the mother-in-law fills a void in her daughter-in-law's life, as in Hannah's case, and /or the daughter-in-law fills a void in her mother-in-law's life. What complicates this theme is how a mother-in-law interacts with her own daughter and how a daughter-in-law interacts with her own mother. If the daughter-in-law's mother has died, the mother-in-law may be a replacement mother figure. If the mother-in-law has no daughter of her own and her daughter-in-law seeks her out, she often feels rewarded.

If a daughter-in-law has a poor relationship with or is estranged from her own mother, she may devote her energy to her mother-in-law in order to feel fulfilled. On the other hand, a daughter-in-law who has a close relationship with her own mother may shun her mother-in-law's advances, feeling that it is disloyal to her own mother to become too close with her mother-in-law. Such a woman likely cannot treat anyone else as a mother figure, because she has been raised to believe that there can only be one mother and that her mother is special and unique. A competition can arise between the mother-in-law and mother for the daughter-in-law's attention and affection. This may occur when the daughter-in-law is young and both women expect something from her. "If a daughter-in-law wants to keep peace in her marriage, it requires spending time with her mother-in-law," says Antoinette Michaels, relationship expert. "If her own mother is still alive, she feels guilty she isn't with her. And when both the mother-in-law and mother are together for family gatherings, their demands for her loyalty may put the daughter-in-law in a difficult position."

"I have never expected my mother-in-law, Florence, to be my mother," Norma confides. "In the beginning, I was a bit icy toward her. I am very close to my own family and I have always put them first. I influenced my husband to be with my family more. I also thought at first that his mother was to blame for the way he acts sometimes. Mostly, I think, it was about my attachment to my own mother. As time passed, I realized that it is important to have a successful mother-in-law/daughter-in-law relationship. I wanted to be accepted by my mother-in-law as a 'good girl.' That acceptance part of it is important to me.

"Once I opened up to Florence and let her into my life, I realized it didn't take away from my relationship with my mother. In fact, my mother-in-law enriched my life. We go to the theater together, which is something I never do with my own mother. Florence respects my privacy, which I appreciate, but always I remember that my marriage has first priority and Florence comes afterward. It isn't like that with my mother, simply because she is my mother."

Mothers and their daughters have been intriguing subjects throughout history. Anne Boleyn, the second wife of Henry VIII, allowed herself to be beheaded for the sake of her daughter's legacy to the throne of England in 1536. Had she granted King Henry a divorce, her daughter, Elizabeth, would not have become Queen of England. In our own time, we have seen the example of the late Jacqueline Kennedy Onassis teaching her daughter, Caroline Kennedy Schlossberg, the skills and intricacies of social service.

The literary world showcases the examples of Erica Jong, author of several books including *Fear of Flying* and her daughter, Molly Jong

Fast, who has recently published her own first novel. Both Mary Higgins Clark and her daughter, Carol Higgins Clark are best-selling authors of mystery novels. Author Nancy Friday devoted an entire book to exploring the complex relationships between mothers and daughters in *My Mother My Self.*

The entertainment industry seems to be fertile ground for mother/daughter actresses and singers. There are sisters Ashley and Wynonna Judd and their mother, Naomi. Tony Award Winner Jennifer Ehle is the daughter of actress Rosemary Harris and Natasha Richardson is the daughter of Vanessa Redgrave. Oscar winner Gwyneth Paltrow claims the talented actress Blythe Danner as her mother and recently, Kate Hudson, daughter of actress Goldie Hawn, received a Golden Globe Award for her acting achievements.

In the popular television series of the 1960s, *Bewitched,* mother and daughter, both witches, constantly battled over a mere mortal husband/son-in-law. Needless to say, there was little room for the husband's mother in this television show. After all, the chance for a mother-in-law to forge a relationship with a daughter-in-law whose sorceress mother was always meddling in the daughter's and her husband's lives was slim.

Mothers and daughters-in-law are of another order. Because there is no family history and theirs is an assigned relationship, heartfelt devotion, while it may happen eventually, cannot be expected automatically. Yet, it is a successful relationship with one's own mother that often enables a woman to become close with another mother figure, in this case a mother-in-law. In *My Mother My Self,* Nancy Friday writes about young women who seek as much love as they can gather from as many sources as possible. Friday concludes that a selection of mother figures is beneficial for such "daughters."

Charlene was pleasantly surprised by the relationship that evolved between herself and her daughter-in-law. "I did not know what to expect from my daughter-in-law, Denise," says Charlene, a mother-in-law for fifteen years. "Ronnie is my only son. I saw that Denise and he believed in the same things and that she, like him, is not very materialistic. I see their marriage as very traditional and I'm relieved that they get along so well. She had worked for years and she now wants to travel, take courses and raise the children. My son works hard to sustain the family.

"In the beginning, Denise was not overly friendly to me nor was her family. I doubted that she liked me. I know that her mother is more demanding than I am. I, on the other hand, avoid injecting my opinions into Ronnie and Denise's lives. Over the years, Denise has become closer to me and now accepts me as a mother figure. I had anticipated that this relationship would be difficult. Instead, it works for us. A daughter-in-law has to handle the mother-in-law and the mother-in-law has to respect whatever her daughter-in-law does. I doubt that this kind of a healthy mother-in-law/daughter-in-law relationship takes place very often."

While Charlene had few expectations and was pleasantly surprised by the mothering role she has come to fill for her daughter-in-law, Sandra, a daughter-in-law, was unprepared for her mother-in-law's lack of interest in her.

"My mother-in-law," sighs Sandra, "has no generosity of spirit. She actually once said, 'Thankfully, I have two daughters since I'm losing my son.' I was very hurt by that. Having had only sisters growing up, I didn't know how a boy with two sisters, like my husband, had been treated. He was the king, the prince. Margaret, my mother-in-law was intimidated by me because her son loved me and she thought I was taking him away her.

"I became a wife and daughter-in-law when I was very young. Later on, when I had children, Margaret treated them differently than she treated her daughters' children. It seemed her daughters' children were her real grandchildren and then there were my kids. I didn't count very much for her. I made my peace with it because we lived in different places and didn't see each other very often. I eventually stopped expecting her to treat me as a mother would treat a daughter. I was very close with my mother and decided that our relationship would have to suffice. I learned that having another mother figure wasn't in the cards for me."

Both the mother-in-law and the daughter-in-law need to have similar requirements of each other for their relationship to succeed. The reasons for a mother-in-law and daughter-in-law to attach or not attach to each other are varied. If a daughter-in-law has a distant relationship with her own mother, as in the case of Denise, Charlene's daughter-in-law, the mother-in-law can fill the emptiness. The mother-in-law offers distinct possibilities: camaraderie, counseling, shopping excursions (which are emblematic of how women bond). If a daughter-in-law had a gratifying relationship with her own mother, she will most likely expect to be a complement to her mother-in-law's life. In this case, it comes as a great shock if her mother-in-law is not interested in having a relationship. Conversely, if the daughter-in-law has a poor relationship with her own mother, she may hope to fill the maternal void with her mother-in-law. The same expectations apply to mothers-in-law, who may have daughters they are not close with, daughters they are very close with or no daughters at all.

Each type of mother/daughter relationship has an impact on the new mother-in-law/daughter-in-law relationship.

Dr. Ronnie Burak notes that many of our actions and reactions are a result of what is missing in our lives. "We tend to try to plug the holes in our lives with spouses, friends or in-laws. We try to have these people provide us with what is lacking in our lives, be it money, social status, education, emotional needs or someone to talk to. What we didn't get before from our own families, we attempt to acquire in this way. What a daughter-in-law and mother-in-law may have in common and what can help to bond them, is what their own mother or daughter didn't do for them."

FILLING THE HOLES
* **The mother-in-law and daughter-in-law each seek out ways to complete themselves.**
* **If the daughter-in-law has missed a close relationship with her mother, she may look for one with her mother-in-law.**
* **If the mother-in-law doesn't have a daughter, she may attempt to create a mother/daughter dynamic with her daughter-in-law.**

Deborah explains how the relationship with each of her daughters-in-law is as different as the women themselves. "My first daughter-in-law, Gillian, who is married to my older son and has been in the family for fourteen years, is an absolute daughter to me," Deborah reveals. "I feel so close and so much love for her. She lives nearby and I see her once a week with my son and their children and once a week without the children and my son. We have always seen each other that way, even before the children were born. We have a communication that does not involve the others. Our common love for her children, however, incorporates and cements our relationship.

"Gillian is like a daughter to me although I am well aware that I am not her mother. I understand that she does not feel about me as she does about her mother. While nothing was articulated, I am keenly aware that she suits my need for a daughter while she already has a mother with whom she has a close bond. I try to be what her mother isn't—I once took her to a spa for a week because her mother would not do that. I know where I fit in, with my work schedule and lifestyle. I know already if ever my son and daughter-in-law move away, they'll move closer to her mother. Gillian comes from that kind of close family. I accept this and I don't try to compete. Her mother and I are always pleasant to each other.

"My second daughter-in-law, Ashley, lives in another state and we do not have a similar relationship. In fact, we are not close at all. When my husband and I visit, which is about once a year, she and I go shopping or to lunch. We have a very superficial, arm's-length sort of relationship. What I tell myself is that my first daughter-in-law means so much to me and Ashley just didn't work out. There isn't any animosity, but we do not really share anything either. Ashley is very close to her own mother and sisters. So I doubt she wants much to do with me anyway. My feeling is that when we visit, she is counting the hours until it is over. I am sure I get on her nerves, although we do not outwardly disagree on matters. I have observed Ashley with her own mother and she is a fabulous daughter. That doesn't leave much room for me. The grandchildren always go to her mother; she has the role of primary grandmother. I believe the mother of the wife, in a marriage, has the power and the mother of the husband has little control. It all falls to the wife's side of the family.

The societal expectation of the mother-in-law is that she links the family of origin to the family of procreation. Just as she was once a young girl who watched her own mother connect their family to both sets of grandparents, she too becomes a young woman, bride, mother and conduit to the extended family. Although mothers love their sons, most women with daughters assume that their daughters will always be there for them, emotionally and practically. The expectation is that they will follow the mothers' traditions in a more enduring, unwavering manner than will sons. In the best of circumstances, everyone in a family will get along with each other. They will share a similar family style or will respect a dissimilar style between the daughter-in-law's family and her husband's family. When there has been an unsuccessful mother-in-law/daughter-in-law relationship and the daughter-in-law becomes a mother-in-law herself, hopefully she will not make the same mistakes and, in fact, will be conciliatory toward her daughter-in-law.

Since it was well known that Eleanor Roosevelt had difficulties with her mother-in-law, Sara Delano Roosevelt, it is surprising that Eleanor did not welcome her first daughter-in-law, Betsy Cushing Roosevelt of the socially prominent Cushing sisters, into the inner sanctum of the family. Possibly because Franklin Delano Roosevelt, her father-in-law, enjoyed Betsy's company, both Sara and Eleanor gave her a difficult time. Eleanor, her biographers note, was territorial of her place in the family and did not want it usurped by her exquisite daughter-in-law.

Despite the fact that Eleanor was critical of Betsy and perhaps even jealous of her, she did not want her son and his wife to be divorced. When the marriage failed, Eleanor was displeased despite the disfavor in which she held Betsy. It is notable that Eleanor Roosevelt appreciated the public image that her daughter-in-law set forth, yet maintained her negative personal feelings about her.

A CERTAIN IMAGE
* **Often a mother-in-law will not want her son to get divorced, regardless of her feelings toward her daughter-in-law.**
* **The mother-in-law worries that her son, without a wife and mother to his children, will project a negative image upon the family.**
* **A mother-in-law who is concerned about appearances prefers to project an image of wholesomeness and happiness within the family.**

The projection of a flawless family is, however, a heavy burden for all family members to carry, as Dana found out. "I always acted like I was listening to Marcella, my mother-in-law," Dana admits, "when really I wasn't. She is admirable because of her persona, that of a perfect person. She is impeccably dressed and coiffed at all times, but my husband, her son, has zero relationship with her. They are polite but cold to one another. I'd estimate they see each other once every two years. I think about my mother-in-law and I know I would never treat anyone the way she treats me. She has been married several times, but when my former sister-in-law divorced her other son, Marcella never forgave her for casting the family in a bad light. In other words, her divorces are acceptable, but others' are blights on the family record.

"Although I find my mother-in-law to be civil, deep down she does not care for who I am or how I do things. She tells people I am like a daughter to her and no one could please her more, yet I know she feels differently. For example, as far as she is concerned, the fact that her son is flourishing in his career has nothing to do with me or my love and support. I believe she respects me and disparages me at the same time. I doubt she would do any more for her daughter. It is all very superficial. All that matters is that I have the right look and pedigree. What I admire about her is her determination to run the family. That is amazing. The result of her efforts is a family that looks good and behaves when we are with her. We project an image that reflects well on her."

When a mother-in-law truly embraces her daughter-in-law, even placing her ahead of her own daughter as Rhoda did, the resulting relationship can seem very fulfilling. However, such a mother-in-law opens herself up to great pain if her son's marriage fails. "My first daughter-in-law, Louisa, was darling. Then she left my son and broke his heart. Until that time, I was very close to her. We did everything together. We all lived in the same town and her mother did not. I was with her constantly. Because we are a minority in town, it was important to me to hold the family together. However, I have a daughter and I didn't keep her close despite my desire to have a family that appeared tight-knit. You see, Louisa had many qualities that my daughter did not possess. She really pleased me in ways my daughter couldn't. It seemed to work out beautifully because I stopped pressuring my daughter to do things with me and I simply did them with my daughter-in-law.

"Then Louisa left my son and I was devastated, for him and for myself. I could not recover at first. After all those years when I put her ahead of my daughter and she seemed to prefer me to her own mother, I felt betrayed by her sudden departure from my son and my family. Gradually, I came to realize I shouldn't have put her ahead of my own daughter. I have not forgotten this lesson even though my son has remarried. With his new wife, Giselle, I was guarded with my feelings at first. I watched how Giselle reacted to things and I decided I like her, but I will not start a chummy relationship with my daughter-in-law this time. I want her to be there for my son, not for me. I have watched Giselle with her own mother and they are very close. I stay out of the way. I see her as a new beginning for my son, a second chance, and that's all I care about. I respect her for bringing my son happiness. In a few months time, they'll have a baby. I know now that blood is thicker than water. I stay close to my own daughter and my son. I look at this daughter-in-law and how she treats my son and I'm glad for him."

The balance in the relationship between mother-in-law and daughter-in-law is often about who needs what. "Is there equal involvement from each party?" asks Dr. Ronnie Burak. "How much interest does each woman have for the other? Is the balance off or does it work?" In some instances, a mother-in-law will view her daughter-in-law as someone to spend time with and the daughter-in-law responds in kind. However, if this daughter-in-law has a limited amount of time at her disposal, it could be allotted to her mother, sisters or friends. Then the mother-in-law will be disappointed. Conversely, a daughter-in-law whose mother has been absent may now look at her mother-in-law as an available mother figure and her mother-in-law may not have the time or the inclination to become more involved with her.

EXPECTATIONS
* **The mother-in-law believes her daughter-in-law is available and receptive to her as a mother figure.**
* **The daughter-in-law believes her mother-in-law will take her under her wing.**
* **Only if both are looking for the same balance in the relationship will it work.**

A mother-in-law may be too preoccupied with her career to give much time individually to her daughter-in-law. She and her husband might see the son and daughter-in-law on weekends as a couple, but the mother-in-law is not available on a one-on-one basis. A daughter-in-law could have a demanding job and she might travel for work. In this case, she will have little time to devote to her mother-in-law for luncheons and matinees. If the mother-in-law is immersed in her daughters' lives, she may have little time for her daughter-in-law. Many daughters-in-law have been raised to believe their mothers and sisters are the only close female connections they need. These women may be surprised to find themselves desiring a closeness with their mothers-in-law.

OBSTACLES TO A CLOSE RELATIONSHIP
* **The mother-in-law is busy with work and activities.**
* **The daughter-in-law is busy with work and activities.**
* **The mother-in-law is close with her daughters.**
* **The daughter-in-law is close with her mother and sisters.**

If a relationship is not mutually gratifying and works for only one participant, it is not advantageous. Both parties should have their needs met in a relationship, so that it is mutually beneficial. According to Brenda Szulman, there are many times when either a daughter-in-law or a mother-in-law is unsatisfied. "Inevitably, someone will feel let down if a mother-in-law and daughter-in-law do not click. It is, however, a bit unreasonable for the daughter-in-law to assume that because she is marrying into this family that her mother-in-law will become like a second mother. That kind of expectation is doomed to fail. Instead, the relationship should evolve over time."

EARNED DAUGHTER STATUS
* **The daughter-in-law expects her mother-in-law to mother her.**
* **The mother-in-law waits for her daughter-in-law to prove herself.**
* **The two women grow close over the years.**

The distance that Melissa's mother-in-law puts between them baffles her. "I am exhausted from trying to establish a relationship with my mother-in-law," says Melissa. "I have no more energy for this process. I only wish I could be cured of the hope I have of being close to my mother-in-law or of there being some kind change in the situation. I suppose I have been naive about this lack of closeness between us. I keep waiting for my husband to intervene, but he says very little. He listens to me when I say I want to be closer with his mother, but he doesn't do anything. I doubt that he can do anything, because in some ways he is in the same boat as I am. He also craves more closeness with her.

"I have gone to her with some important issues and she has been very aloof. She will listen, but doesn't respond or comment. When I had a miscarriage, she said and did nothing, whereas my mother really helped me through it. My husband has become close with my mother, because she gives him the attention and affection that his mother doesn't. I have a wonderful rapport with my own mother, so I'm not sure why I keep looking to my mother-in-law for attention, but I do."

While Melissa wishes she had a connection to her mother-in-law, Betty, as a mother-in-law, has little regard for her daughter-in-law, Alexis, and remains close to her own two daughters. "My daughter-in-law butters me up. She would never visit with me or invite me anywhere, but she's complimentary and falls over me in other ways. She may do so until the day she dies, but she'll never get what she wants. Since Alexis rarely asks my opinion, when she did recently, I suggested that she ask someone else.

"I believe that my son was thinking with the wrong part of his anatomy when he married her. It's complicated because he actually thought she seemed like me. She's very pretty and sexy and that is very important to him. He wasn't even nice to her in the beginning, but she wanted him badly. Today, she has a firm hold on him. For a long time, he tried to keep her away from me. Then they ended up married. I have been displeased with her from the start. I do not include her with my daughters when we go to lunch. My daughters suggest that I be kinder to Alexis, but I can't. If I have anything to do with it, she is not going to be a part of our clan."

While the antipathy between Betty and Alexis seems extreme, it is not always easy for a new daughter-in-law to find her place in an estab-lished family structure, particularly one in which the mother-in-law has her own daughters. At the start, the new daughter-in-law might be rejected and feel she is not equal to the female members of her husband's family. It is up to the husband to protect his wife if she is not treated well by his mother and/or sisters. "The problems begin," says Brenda Szulman, "if the couple does not have a strong marital relationship. Once the couple is firmly united, nothing can divide or penetrate that bond. A difficult mother-in-law will not be able to wedge herself between them."

Famed psychologist Erik Erikson's theory, Eight Stages of Psychosocial Development, tells us that feminine identity is inwardly defined and that women relate on an interpersonal level. For women, identity and intimacy are more intricately joined than for men. For a mother-in-law and daughter-in-law who, for a variety of reasons, do not bond, there will be disillusionment on one or both sides. Female relationships are valuable to women and when they fail, there is a sense of loss.

"Respect is a big part of the relationship between mothers-in-law and their daughters-in-law," says Alice Michaeli. "When we speak to our mothers-in law, what do we call them? Do we say 'mother' or 'mom'? It is awkward to call a mother-in-law 'mother' if you have a mother. It is also awkward to call your mother-in-law by her first name. This infers that the mother-in-law and daughter-in-law are equals. Yet the relationship should be based on age and position and engender respect for both women."

A respectful attitude toward the other on both the mother-in-law's and the daughter-in-law's part has been beneficial to Sherry, a daughter-in-law. "My husband speaks to his mother, Irene, daily by phone," Sherry tells me. "I soon felt that I should call her every day, too, but over the years, I've learned that his calls to her can be independent of me. She and I don't have to relate in some fantasy of what mothers-in-law and daughters-in-law are like together. On the other hand, I do respect her and I try to be a good daughter-in-law. My mother-in-law objects to some of our family's choices, like when we rent an airplane and take the kids flying. She states her concerns and I listen to her. She will give her view and then I will express with equal firmness my point of view. I have learned from my husband not to become anxious when I talk to her.

"Over the years, we have grown close in a strange way. It happened so gradually it was not something that could be measured or marked. I suppose I wasn't the daughter-in-law she imagined and she wasn't the mother-in-law I imagined. I have learned to do what works best, which I consider a form of respect. I was hesitant at first because I had not found any happiness or joy with any of my own relatives. No one in my immediate family encouraged closeness with our extended family. Now I know that it counts and that it is rewarding. I can even plan my own role as a mother-in-law. I hope to get on famously with my daughter-in-law."

Our culture encourages mothers and daughters to share routines and family life. They bond from one generation to the next by their ability to give birth and raise children. Although we always come back to the "liberated woman," a concept which began earnestly in the 1920's, what women, mothers and daughters alike, seem unable to shake is the gender expectation of home and hearth. Each generation may differ in its goals and dreams, yet the mother/daughter association superimposes itself on changing lifestyles.

If we believe in the solidarity of women, then the mother/daughter relationship ideally can be extended to mothers-in-law and daughters-in-law. Greater longevity means mothering consumes a smaller percentage of our adult lives and not every woman who becomes a daughter-in-law will have children. Of fifty-four million married women, twenty-five million have underage children, according to the United States Census Bureau and twenty-nine million have grown children or no children. Thus, there is room in most women's lives for a mother-in-law/daughter-in-law relationship. Notwithstanding this concept, Dr. Michele Kasson reminds us of the natural competition that exists between mothers-in-law/daughters-in-law. "A mother-in-law still considers her son a part of her household in some way while the daughter-in-law wants her husband completely in her own household. These women may be a threat to each other when both derive self-esteem from their representative homes."

Daughters-in-law and mothers-in-law, in theory, have the chance to share a meeting of the minds, because, for the younger woman, the common adolescent difficulties of a daughter separating from her mother have passed. An emotional and psychological return to the mother figure usually is reestablished by the time a daughter marries. In such a case, a mother-in-law will benefit from her daughter-in-law's emotional maturity and it may supersede a competition between them.

My research has shown, however, that the hope of becoming a mother figure to one's daughter-in-law can be fraught with anxiety and disappointments. Elena, a mother-in-law, also discovered this. "While my son's instincts may be right to have chosen Maddie for his wife, I have been very disappointed with her as a daughter-in-law," Elena tells us. "I don't have the rapport that I wanted or expected. I see mothers with their daughters and I see that kind of devotion. It's the same kind of devotion I have with my mother. I don't have a smidgen of that with my daughter-in-law. She might say she bends over backwards, but I don't see it. There is a wall between us. When her mother died, she said to me that I would become her mother, but the feeling and the action are two separate things. Instead, a feeling of duty persists, not a natural, affectionate feeling. Sometimes, I think the problem is the physical distance between us. Other times I think we have difficulties because of her own issues. For example, over the phone, I sense a cooling of some kind. The worst part is that she has created a distance between my son and me. I've never seen her demand anything of him, but there must be some unwritten rule they have: you do this and I'll do that. It seems to work for them and they cooperate with each other. I was anxious for my son to marry her. I even took him aside and suggested he do so. I was ready to welcome her as a daughter, not just a daughter-in-law."

Similar difficulties and complexities in the relationship exist for the younger woman as well. Heather, a daughter-in-law, experienced this firsthand. She noticed that her mother-in-law resented Heather's closeness with her mother and let it come between a potentially successful mother-in-law/daughter-in-law relationship. "My mother-in-law, Alicia, has three sons. Control is what counts with her. My father-in-law doesn't decide between an apple and a pear for dessert—she decides for him. Alicia is very verbal and can be caustic, even vicious. In the beginning, I saw her once a week, sometimes twice a week, because we lived in the same city. My life consisted of running from my mother to my mother-in-law when I was first married. Then I wised up. I saw that my mother-in-law resented my closeness to my own mother. That was at the heart of the matter.

"My brother-in-law's first marriage broke up over my mother-in-law. Then Alicia became really impressed with his second wife. I watched her in the role of contented mother-in-law and that was a switch. She finally got the daughter figure she had been seeking in me with her other son's new wife. Everyone kowtowed to her; even I was fooled by her in the beginning. I became closer to my mother the more my mother-in-law expected me to be daughterly to her. I found my mother and mother-in-law to be so opposite that it drove me away from my mother-in-law. Although I feel this way, I also know Alicia genuinely hoped for me to be a daughter to her."

Despite Heather's negative feelings for Alicia, a lack of closeness to one's mother-in-law may have nothing to do with dislike. As Dr.

Ronnie Burak explains, "When a mother-in-law and daughter-in-law do not become close and the daughter-in-law and her mother have a strong and exclusive relationship, this may not be about disliking the mother-in-law. The daughter-in-law may simply not be looking for any relationship with his family beyond her husband. Such an attitude can be taken the wrong way and the mother-in-law may easily feel rejected."

Annie's experience demonstrates quite a different example of the mother/daughter/mother-in-law/daughter-in-law relationship possibilities. "My mother-in-law, Lee, loves me very much and is as good as a mother-in-law can be," Annie says. "She's not intrusive and she supports me emotionally. My mother is more judgmental and demanding and she is not as tolerant or patient as Lee. I hold it against my mother that she allowed me to marry so young. She was the one who could have stopped me. My mother-in-law, on the other hand, stepped in and mothered me. Lee treated me as a daughter and I needed that. Our relationship is independent of her son. She will get on a plane and fly to visit me for a day or two. I can't imagine my mother doing the same.

"I can relate to my mother-in-law because she is a basic, hard working woman. Lee is content with her life and extremely giving to me. Everyone loves her. She is a very special person. My mother and Lee are opposites. Being close to my mother-in-law all these years has actually distanced me more from my own mother. Now my mother-in-law is elderly and I worry about her health. When she passes, I'll have a big hole in my life. I count on Lee, because I can discuss certain things with her that I can't speak about with my own mother. Although I have two sisters and my mother-in-law has two daughters, my strongest attachment to a woman is to my mother-in-law."

A daughter-in-law may discover a figure she admires in her mother-in-law. Since mother-in-law/daughter-in-law relationships are relatively new and not fraught with the complexities and harbored resentments that come with family history, they have a unique opportunity to prosper. A daughter-in-law who is not close to her own mother can find solace in the closeness she shares with her mother-in-law, for example. In some cases, these relationships are not mother/daughter oriented, but may exist more as friendships between equals. When expectations are too high, however, the success rate of such relationships may rapidly diminish.

A PROMISING SCENARIO
* **The daughter-in-law relates to her mother-in-law, because there is no strife-ridden mother/ adolescent daughter family history.**

* **The mother-in-law appreciates her daughter-in-law's openness to her.**
* **Stereotypical expectations are pushed aside.**
* **A bond forms between the two women.**

A failed relationship, according to Brenda Szulman, occurs when the unconscious wish of the mother-in-law or daughter-in-law remains unfulfilled. "It is not the mother-in-law or the daughter-in-law's fault when either one wants something from the relationship that is missing in her life. How each woman approaches the other has to do with each one's own personal history, value system and goals."

Accepting the woman one's son has chosen as his wife and accepting the reality of the family situation thus created is of major importance. Lillian, a mother-in-law, recognizes this. "I have always accepted my daughter-in-law unconditionally," says Lillian. "For me, Carla, is the wife of my son and mother of his children. My son had no affection for a long time and he deserves it in his life. He is entitled to some happiness. For years, I had imagined a fantasy daughter-in-law, but in reality, Carla suffices. I have been attached to her since we first began spending time together. I know that my son is not easy to live with and I feel very loyal to her. Carla's own mother does not live in this country, she lives in Puerto Rico. This fact affects my relationship with Carla, because I am not in competition for her attention.

"I think that proximity is one of the reasons why we have grown so close. Carla knows that both of us, her mother and her mother-in-law, are there if she needs us. I think I serve a very different role in my daughter-in-law's life, however, than her mother does."

Another component in a successful or unsuccessful mother-in-law/daughter-in-law bond concerns the type of relationship the husband has with his mother. If the mother-in-law is demanding of her son and the son responds by jumping at her commands, the marriage suffers. A son who puts his mother first or is controlled by her at some level allows his mother to get between him and his wife in their marriage.

Shere Hite, in *The Hite Report on the Family*, describes how often boys are angry with their mothers. Hite asks the question, "Is the anger because the greater love for their mother in the beginning, [was] later betrayed?...Or are we just looking at everyday, plain old prejudice against women?" Hite believes this anger is incorrectly directed toward women because sons think their mothers deserted them instead of the reverse.

"The mother's relationship with the son, which often appears to be a power struggle, can actually be a way of avoiding intimacy in the marriage," says Antoinette Michaels. "In this case, the son might not have ever truly separated from his mother and is afraid of his marriage. This becomes more complicated if the wife is not secure in herself and in the love she receives from her husband. The wife/daughter-in-law will resist spending time with his mother based on principle."

"My husband, Mark, shrugs his mother off while his younger brother sits with her for hours," says Olivia. "My relationship with my mother-in-law is somewhat contained by my husband's lack of relationship with her. It is fortunate for me that my mother-in-law is obsessed with her younger son and his family and she does not treat me with the same affection or interest. I would choose this type of situation any day over the absorbing demands of my mother-in-law. Sometimes I would prefer that she did not favor one of her daughters-in-law over the other, but at least I have a life of my own.

"I think it's been sad for my mother-in-law that she never had a daughter. Neither of her daughters-in-law really make her happy. I am distant to her, because that is how she is to my husband. I purposely don't compete, not when it comes to Mark and not when it comes to her other daughter-in-law. I remember all the stereotypic jokes about mothers-in-law I was told when I first married, but that is not my situation at all. I think my mother-in-law recognizes me as a person separate from my husband, but my relationship with her is still filtered through her interactions with her son."

For different reasons than Olivia's, Phoebe is also not involved with her mother-in-law, Diane. This is unfortunate because her own mother was absent from her life and she is in search of a mother figure. Phoebe's poor relationship with Diane makes her feel cheated. Many of us have a feeling that our mother-in-law or daughter-in-law should behave differently than they do and that we are getting emotionally short-changed.

"It's so sad to me," laments Phoebe. "I really wanted my mother-in-law to love me. I wanted her to be there when I had my babies, someone to shop and go to lunch with. I already know I want to be the kind of mother-in-law who is included and whose family wants to see her. My mother-in-law has these preconceived notions and won't budge. I can't figure out how she could refuse to help us when we've asked for her help. To me, that is the difference between being there and not being there for your loved ones. For our first apartment we needed her help. When my husband, Chris, had business problems early on in our marriage, she compounded the problems by making her own demands. I would never do that to a son and I'll never forget that she did it to her son. My mother-in-law has had her battles with her children. Her position is unchangeable once she has taken it. Unfortunately, the end result is that there is no room in my life for this kind of mother.

"What I see as critical in all of this is the lack of love my husband has for his mother. I want my kids to love me. This is a need I recognize, because I don't love my own mother, who couldn't be bothered to raise me. On the other hand, that very lack of mothering that both Chris and I have experienced has actually held us together as a couple. We feel we are all we have in this world."

Often times, a mother-in-law is perceived as the common enemy between a husband and wife. In a sense, this may serve to unite the couple. The reality is that it is not easy for a daughter-in-law to become like a daughter to her mother-in-law in every instance. It is a happy confluence of events and emotions, a coming together of similar needs, when it does take place.

In many cases, when mothers and sons have less conflicting attachments, it allows the mother and son more space in their relationship. When this occurs, a daughter-in-law may describe her husband's relationship with his mother as detached, negative or nonexistent, but for the son-husband and his mother, this might not be the reality at all. In fact, a little distance may have made it possible for them to salvage a previously unworkable relationship.

MULTIPLE PERCEPTIONS
* **Not every mother-in-law and daughter-in-law are in search of a mother/daughter-like relationship.**
* **The relationship of sons and mothers cannot be compared to that of daughters and mothers in terms of communication and aspirations.**
* **A daughter-in-law might do well to not question the style or depth of her husband's rapport with his mother.**

When Betsy Cushing Roosevelt remarried after her divorce from Eleanor Roosevelt's eldest son, it was to the multimillionaire Jock Whitney. Her new mother-in-law, Helen Hay Whitney, had tremendous control over her son, to the extent that as an adult he lived with his mother. Fortunately, Helen Hay Whitney was in favor of Betsy as a daughter-in-law. This mother-in-law/daughter-in-law relationship was more successful than Betsy's first, because Helen Hay Whitney identified with her daughter-in-law's background. She set out to teach her about the Whitneys and their social group and Betsy was eager and willing to learn.

A mother-in-law might be disappointed if her daughter-in-law does not choose to learn from and emulate her. "Our family is quite upper-class and, frankly, I felt that my son married beneath him," Janet confides. "While I am comfortable with her mothering of my grandchildren, I find Karen, my daughter-in-law, essentially ignorant in all other areas of her life. I am always waiting for that telephone call from my son to say they are getting a divorce, a decision I would support. I have my checkbook ready to help him out, because money is not an issue. Karen's upbringing is much more middle-class than my son's. She is family oriented in a way that I doubt my son understands. His life was more sophisticated and I am surprised that my daughter-in-law did not strive to improve herself, to learn about the arts and to develop more style. I find her helpless in many ways and I always feel theirs is a hierarchical relationship. I cannot fault her, but she is not what I expected in a daughter-in-law. My vision of a daughter-in-law was someone strong-willed and successful. Although my generation is different from Karen's, I would never have objected to her having a career.

"I am disappointed for many reasons. Although I suspect I am seen by her as authoritarian, there might have been a teaching experience or a kind of comradeship between us. I believe she is secretly relieved that there is no closeness between us."

Some experts believe that a mother experiences self-love with her child who, she believes, is an extension of herself. As the years pass and the child is not as perfect as she anticipated, the mother's narcissistic ego is injured, according to Nancy Friday, author of *My Mother My Self*. Furthermore, mothers may attach to their daughters because their own lives are empty. If we take this a step further and apply it to mothers-in-law and daughters-in-law, it is understandable why there is a sense of loss when a potential bond is not cemented.

"I was never looking for any close relationship with my mother-in-law, but I was hoping we could get along," said Sheryl. "As I recall it, my mother's relationship with her own mother-in-law had been terrific. I have had to fight for my rights as a daughter-in-law, because my mother-in-law views me as unworthy, because I'm not her creation. My husband has begun to gravitate toward my family and has broken away from his mother and her values in exchange for my parents and their values. I am aware that my mother-in-law not only contests this, but that she, in fact, is very hurt. I can't handle a close relationship with her, because of what it would entail. I suppose there is no space physically or emotionally for two mother figures. Ironically, my mother-in-law and my mother treat me similarly when it comes to certain things. Both mothers have this urge to give me instructions on how to look and behave. I don't like that treatment but I can handle it when it comes from my own mother."

What works best when there are negative emanations coming from both the mother-in-law and daughter-in-law is that the expectations of each woman are clearly spelled out. If boundaries are not established between the mother-in-law and daughter-in-law, it may feel like an invasion of privacy, emotionally and physically, for the daughter-in-law and perhaps for the mother-in-law, as well. This can cause stress in the marriage as the mother-in-law/daughter-in-law entanglement comes between the husband and wife. The mother-in-law and the daughter-in-law have to understand where their relationship begins and ends. If there has been dysfunction in the families of origin and the wife and her husband have not sorted their problems out before they wed, they bring their unanswered questions about themselves to the marriage.

"When there are no family ties or they are unhealthy ties, a daughter-in-law or mother-in-law will not function in a healthy way," says Antoinette Michaels. "If there is true caring and love coming from these families then there is less misunderstanding. In addition, a daughter-in-law might not recognize her mother-in-law's gestures as positive unless she has had a positive role model in her own mother."

Mothers-in-law with daughters-in-law who have had healthy mother/daughter relationships are fortunate, according to mother-in-law Angelina. "I know that I am a second mother to Sara, my daughter-in-law," Angelina says proudly. "She is very close to her own mother, but I have other talents and we balance each other out. My son and daughter-in-law have a young daughter. I know that sometimes a granddaughter sees more of her maternal grandmother and not her paternal grandmother, but my daughter-in-law made sure when Jenna was small that I saw her as much as possible. Sara is a wonderful wife and mother. My daughter-in-law is so special that my love for her multiplies. My son is an only child and I absolutely got the daughter I never had. In our culture, we welcome daughters-in-law and sons-in-law into our families. My relationship with Sara, however, goes beyond what is usually expected in a mother-in-law/daughter-in-law relationship. I wanted to adopt a daughter after my son was born, but my husband refused. Sara and I even look alike and we treasure each other. When my husband died, she built a room onto their house for me. I felt very welcome, because it was her idea and not my son's. We can discuss anything and we admire each other. Her energy and mine are very similar and, more importantly, we share the same beliefs."

Approximately half of the mothers-in-law interviewed for this chapter envision themselves as second mothers to their daughters-in-law, because of the constancy and heartfelt devotion that exists between them. The other fifty percent were regretful, in varying degrees, that they could not achieve a feeling of closeness to their daughters-in-law.

Fifty percent of the daughters-in-law interviewed expected more from their mothers-in-law than developed over the course of their relationship; over half of this fifty percent do not interact with their own mothers. Thirty percent of the daughters-in-law found satisfaction with the time and energy extended by their mothers-in-law; twenty percent were disappointed in their mother-in-law/daughter-in-law relationships as well as their relationships with their own mothers.

Certainly, a void left by dysfunctional or non-existent mother/daughter relationships can be filled by a mother-in-law or daughter-in-law. And so it seems from those interviewed that many women hope to realize such relationships with each other. Yet there is danger in having such expectations. Often, these women feel disillusioned or cheated by mothers-in-law or daughters-in-law who are unwilling or unable to meet their needs for strong bonds. For those women who do share common needs, who achieve a balance in their hopes and desires for strong and fulfilling relationships, the rewards can be great.

4

Mothers-in-Law
and Their Daughters

"I'm the person best equipped to shrug off my mother-in-law, Danielle, and my sisters-in-law, Kay and Maggie," says Candice, a daughter-in-law for twelve years. My husband's relationship with his mother is equally as distant and strained as mine is, but it didn't start out that way. She and her two daughters became critical of me. At first, they sort of defended my husband, as if I didn't have his best interests in mind. Then they realized how attached Alan and I were and that the marriage was sticking, so they just added him to their list of people they don't think well of. I really expected something else, something better with Alan's family. My sisters-in-law remind me of Cinderella's wicked stepsisters. For his whole life, my husband has been told by the women in his family that he is dashingly handsome. In choosing me, he made a conscious effort to have someone not so obsessed with looks and superficiality.

"The friction in this family is constant and I doubt it will readily improve. My mother-in-law and her daughters have made the decision to consider me as inappropriate for my husband. It is a very painful situation."

Nothing is more excluding to a daughter-in-law than an aloof mother-in-law preoccupied with her daughters. The sisters-in-law may be fundamentally unkind and competitive, particularly if their brother is successful and his wife is living a life of luxury. Other problems surface when the daughter and the daughter-in-law both have children and the mother tends to devote less energy to the daughter-in-law's children.

If a daughter-in-law, who is slighted by her mother-in-law and sisters-in-law has no mother of her own or one that lives halfway across the country, she probably will feel let down and isolated. On the other hand, a sister-in-law or mother-in-law may resent how attentive and giving the daughter-in-law's family is, especially her mother. When and if the mother-in-law and daughter/sister-in-law include the daughter-in-law in their lives, it will be a healthy result for all involved. The children/grandchildren will then be equally a part of the privileged family center and family occasions become pleasurable.

When a mother-in-law and her daughter(s) have a very close relationship, they may not be interested in letting anyone else in. Conversely, if a daughter-in-law is very close with her own mother and sister(s), she will not need that closeness with her mother-in-law and sister(s)-in-law. The ideal scenario would be if a mother-in-law, daughter-in-law and sister-in-law, despite their other bonds, could have a special rapport with each other. "We can look at this in terms of a bell curve," notes Dr. Ronnie Burak. "In the middle, the daughter-in-law would want a relationship with her mother and sister-in-laws or the mother-in-law and daughters would want a relationship with their daughter-in-law/sister-in-law. The extreme is when the mother-in-law has everything she needs in her relationship with her daughter(s) and has no desire to expand beyond this. The other extreme is a mother-in-law who has a poor relationship with her daughter(s) and welcomes her daughter-in-law's attention."

THE BELL CURVE
* **At one end are mothers-in-law who embrace their daughters, excluding their daughters-in-law.**
* **At the other end are the mothers-in-law who have no relationship with their daughters and seek ones with their daughters-in-law.**
* **In the middle are satisfied mothers-in-law and daughters-in-law who are able to engage with each other despite ties to other daughters/mothers.**

"My daughter, Anna, and daughter-in-law, Juliet, get along very well," Natalie tells us. "Although my daughter recently moved away, which upset them both, they are in constant touch. Their relationship is very strong, but my daughter's husband, Brad, is not as successful as my son, Daniel. That is the only problem between the two families, envy. My daughter watches my son and daughter-in-law spend money freely and she resents that. In addition, although I don't think it is true, I suspect that my daughter worries that I take my son's side more often than I take hers. Yet I avoid taking sides; I'm very proud of both my son and my daughter.

"There is no question that my daughter-in-law is more materialistic than my daughter, because she can be—she has the financial resources. There is tension over this and I really see no solution. Sometimes I think to myself that both Anna and Juliet deserve to be on an equal playing field in terms of lifestyle. However, there is nothing I can do. I know that the two women enjoy each other and go out without me. I will baby-sit for Anna's daughter, but I assume that Juliet does not need me for her daughter because she has full time help. Basically, love and good feelings are there for all of us, but there are obstacles. I consider Anna my daughter and Juliet my daughter-in-law. I love them both dearly, but not in the same way."

In a perfect universe where emotional maturity prevails, mothers-in-law, daughters-in-law and daughters would all receive equal treatment. Although the mother-in-law and her daughter may be very close, there could be room for independent relationships between the three women. "What the mother-in-law and her daughter(s) appreciate about the daughter-in-law is the improved quality of life for the son/brother," explains psychotherapist, Brenda Szulman. "While there might be competition between the sister(s)-in-law and the daughter-in-law, in time the daughter-in-law becomes more accepted and her role is better established in the family."

In larger families, of course, things can become complicated. "With three daughters in-law," sighs Golda, "I have to pay attention to how much each daughter-in-law wants to be involved with me. So much depends on the situation, like the arrival of children, which determines how we interact. With two daughters and three sons, however, I find that it is my daughters who are overwhelmed with all the relationships, not the daughters-in-law. Perhaps each daughter-in-law has the advantage of my previous experience with the others. To me, being a mother-in-law is like parenting. Each child requires slightly different parenting and so with each daughter-in-law, I am a somewhat different mother-in-law. Having daughters gives me a broader perspective in terms of the daughter-in-law relationships, certainly a more sympathetic one. I see with my own daughters, one has a successful mother-in-law relationship and the other is very upset by how her mother-in-law treats her. I have to admit, though, my daughters come first with me, ahead of my sons, ahead of everyone.

"My daughters-in-law are not my daughters. I approve of each of them, but I do not embrace them. I try to be fair, as circumstances dictate. It is a full time job as an adult mother of five children, each with children of their own. To my knowledge, I do not interfere with any of their methods or lifestyles. Last week, I did have one of my sons do some work on my house, which meant I took him away from his family. I doubt that my daughter-in-law minded, but I would only ask for help when absolutely necessary and only since my husband died."

While Golda has a caring but basically arms-length approach to her daughters-in-law and keeps her daughters at the center of her life, Samantha constantly compares her mother-in-law to her mother and wants more from her mother-in-law.

"My mother-in-law's background is unique to me. I didn't grow up knowing anyone who went on ski vacations and had piano recitals in their home. I learned about all this from my mother-in-law. My mother-in-law has gone to college, while my mother did not. My husband's family was strong and appealing to me. Although I don't see my sisters-in-law so much, the relationship with my mother-in-law is very important to me. My sisters-in-law do not live close by and my mother-in-law does.

"We go to the theater and to lunch together. She is sort of my dream mother figure and I am very malleable, which she likes. Her daughters are unimpressed with her style and her demands, while I appreciate them. I think this has worked out well because I live nearby and I am such an eager pupil. It is true that my mother might be offended by my affection for my mother-in-law and feel that she is diminished in my eyes, but I can't help gravitating toward my mother-in-law and my husband's family. My sisters-in-law actually complain about her while I really enjoy her company."

The societal expectation of mothers, still today, is to raise their daughters to become wives and mothers. As Marianne Walters tells us in her study, "Caught in the Muddle," published in *The Invisible Web*, the mother/daughter relationship is defined "within the confines and the life space of the familial." Sons, on the other hand, are raised to be participants in public life as "autonomous individuals." Thus, sons can be fathers, but it is not at the center of their lives. Mothers and daughters are placed in opposite positions. As Walters explains, "familial life" is for daughters and "extra-familial life" is for sons. When a mother is estranged from her own daughters or does not see them on a regular basis due to a lack of proximity or other reason, she gets her familial fix from her daughter-in-law. For a daughter-in-law whose own mother is not around or if the two women are not close, her mother-in-law is part of her "familial life." The trick is to have both the mother-in-law and daughter-in-law in the same position, their needs coinciding, looking to the other to be a mother or daughter figure.

If there has been a failed mother/daughter relationship, for example, the daughter and her mother do not share the same values or goals, the mother-in-law and daughter-in-law may provide a second chance for each other. This creates the opportunity for the women to refashion the relationship that has been missing.

ADJUSTMENTS MADE
* **The mother-in-law provides her daughter-in-law with mothering.**
* **The daughter-in-law is agreeable and welcoming of the attention.**
* **The two women benefit from shared goals and values.**

Another component of an impenetrable mother/daughter bond occurs because of geographic proximity. If a daughter-in-law and her husband live nearby as well as the daughter, the daughter-in-law is often the odd person out. When there are several daughters and a daughter-in-law is introduced into the family, she is not always welcome and may be perceived as a stranger. "We see the world as an expansion of our own family," notes psychologist Dr. Ronnie Burak. "When the family style is firmly in place, no one can enter the innermost heart of the clan because they are outsiders. This extends to the son/brother's wife. The question asked is, who is she and why do we need her?"

Of course, this exclusion can work both ways. The daughter-in-law may exclude the women in her husband's family if she views her world, comprising that of her mother and any sisters, as sufficient. Then she, too, wonders what she needs from her husband's mother and his sister(s). For this daughter-in-law, the female experience is already in place and the bond is strong. Thus, it is not always about disliking a daughter-in-law or a mother-in-law, but about already having daughters and mothers who take up all the emotional and physical space available.

Patterns may be altered due to life circumstances. If a mother-in-law becomes ill and only the son and daughter-in-law live nearby or have the flexibility to care for her, for instance, or if a daughter-in-law loses her mother and now looks to her mother-in-law for a role model, then roles and attitudes will shift. "When the responsibility falls on a daughter-in-law to care for her mother-in-law, who is not even her own mother," comments Dr. Burak, "things can change for the better. This is a way of bringing the women together, but the result, to an extent, depends on what the relationship was like beforehand."

"My daughter-in-law, Liza, was a nurse before she had children," says Joanne, a mother-in-law for thirty-three years. "My own daughter is a stockbroker. So when I became sick and had surgery, it was my daughter-in-law who volunteered her services. I would never have expected anything of my son, but I expected more from my daughter than she was able to give. I started to look at Liza in another way. She is so capable and so kind. I suppose this compassion comes with her profession. Now I feel very attached to Liza and I think back to all those years when I wasn't nice enough to her. I suppose I never really knew her, because our interactions were all rather superficial, having to do only with holidays and the grandchildren. I have been convalescing at my son's and daughter-in-law's home and Liza is extraordinary. I think it is a poor reflection on the relationship between mothers-in-law and their daughters-in-law that it takes something like an illness to become close. I admit that I am absolutely guilty as charged. I had always put my own daughter first. Now, I'm learning it can work another way."

Not all mothers-in-law have personal epiphanies when it comes to the value of their daughters-in-law. Many view their loyalty to their daughters as a necessity. This attitude could prevail for many years, perhaps even a lifetime.

"I have been accused," smiles Theresa, "of not treating my one son and my two daughters equally. I know that some mothers-in-law adore their sons and applaud their taste in a wife, but I am not one of them I am not unhappy with my daughter-in-law, Marisa, probably because I was not expecting much. I was raised in a repressed WASP culture where you behave civilly but not particularly warmly. Daughters were emphasized and I gravitate toward my own. I am proud of my son and happy that he has a good marriage, but if Marisa tried to fill the place of one of my daughters, I'd hate her. I have two daughters and I don't need another. I accept Marisa because I do not have any need to be close to her. I would not have chosen her for my son and I would take my own daughters over her any day.

"Marisa is very different from my girls in exposure and upbringing. While I can appreciate her needs, my daughters don't understand her at all. My son has great respect for my daughter-in-law's background and the odds she fought against. What I can't fathom is why she has so little empathy. One would think she would have this trait, this ability, because of her own hardships."

When there are sisters-in-law and a mother-in-law for the daughter-in-law/wife to face, the son-husband has the responsibility to help his wife navigate potentially treacherous shoals with his mother and sister(s). If the mother-in-law and her daughter(s) team up to push the daughter-in-law/sister-in-law away, the husband has to back up his wife and be supportive of her. Psychologist Dr. Michaele Goodman notes that there is often a competition between the sisters-in-law and their brother's wife because they are peers. "When the husband's sisters are close in age to his wife, their sister in-law, this opens up issues of competition. The best advice is to not engage in this, but to distance oneself emotionally."

Sometimes, as in Rita's case, a mother-in-law will defend her daughter-in-law from the rest of the family. "There was one instance where I defended Becky, my daughter-in-law," recalls Rita, who has two sons and two daughters. One son is still a student and remains single. "It made me recognize how tough sisters can be on their sister in law. I had a pretty stone and I gave it to my son, David, when he became engaged. My own daughters do not like jewelry or so they profess. We were all out for dinner and my daughter-in-law showed us the ring that had been made with the stone. Becky and my son thanked me for it as my daughters stared at me. After the dinner, they asked me why Becky was given the stone. I guess they forgot that they hated jewelry, once it was on their sister-in-law's finger. I had to laugh—they never wanted it until she had it. Now I know my daughters would attack her in a minute, over anything and I feel defensive for her.

"My son wanted someone unlike his sisters, he told me that. Despite my preference for my daughters, I find my daughter-in-law acceptable and accomplished. What counts for me is her relationship with my son, since that works in my favor still. My daughter-in-law has taught David to think in a new way and to notice things he would not have noticed before. My son will mature with her and I will have the reward of his maturity. Becky is not a daughter by any stretch, but I respect her and she is good for my son. What more could I ask for?"

In *The Hite Report on the Family*, Shere Hite writes that mothers and daughters are closer today than they were thirty years ago when many daughters were resentful of their mothers for not having careers and for being housebound. Most daughters today appreciate that their mothers work and are able to fulfill their ambitions. These daughters look for role models in mother figures who they perceive as being accomplished and knowledgeable. Mothers currently have more influence with their grown daughters than in the recent past and with this influence comes a certain amount of control. Thus, a mother very often can consciously or subconsciously influence how her new daughter-in-law is treated by her daughters.

"Often, a mother and her daughter(s) form a family unit which views the son-brother as one of their own," says psychologist Dr. Michele Kasson. "When he leaves this unit upon marriage, the mother and sister(s) may feel a sense of loss or abandonment. They have had a long history of being protective of this man and may harbor negative feelings regarding the new wife's ability to protect him." It is only if they see that his wife can do something positive for the son-brother that they will relax in their attitudes toward his wife.

It is wise for a daughter-in-law to take her time when she enters a family with this sort of interpersonal dynamic. If she and her own mother are very connected, then she can identify with her mother-in-law and sister-in-law's closeness. The daughter-in-law should be cautious and size up the situation. If she is very pretty and/or successful, and her sister-in-law is not, it might become more complicated for her to be accepted by these two women. "If the sister-in-law has low self-esteem, no matter what the wife/daughter-in-law does, the sister-in-law and her mother won't like it," says Dr. Kasson. "Hopefully, a mother-in-law will recognize the undercurrents and be fair to both her daughter and daughter-in-law."

UNDERCURRENTS
* **Daughters-in-law should tread carefully when entering the family.**
* **Possessive or envious sisters-in-law can be dangerous.**
* **Mothers-in-law need to be equitable.**

Hurt feelings and damaged relationships are in store when a mother-in-law is blatantly inequitable with her children and their spouses. "Recently, when my sister-in-law's child was christened, none of us were even invited," Kathleen says. "This upset me, especially because my mother-in-law did not intervene. I've always wondered why she refuses to make waves. When this daughter got married three years ago, my youngest child was not invited to the wedding, while my older three were in the wedding party. I was furious at the time and so was my husband. He fluctuated between making a fuss and saying nothing. Finally, he asked if we could bring our son and we were told no, we could not. My mother-in-law was aware of the entire thing, but she never got involved. It still irritates me to this day.

"What bothers me is how my mother-in-law will never see her daughter as doing anything wrong. There is no conversation we could have that would improve the situation. She doesn't have an interest in our feelings, and if my children are slighted, even if her son is slighted in the process, that's okay with her. Our families are not alike, which is why these things keep happening. I do not feel comfortable with my mother-in-law or sister-in-law and still, the charade goes on. We do holidays together and a weekend each season. My mother-in-law will stay with us and I will do everything I can to please her. All the while she is here with me, she tells me how she can't wait to visit Darcy, her daughter."

Sociologist Alice Michaeli notes that in modern life, the disadvantage is that all too frequently no one from an extended family is really there for each other. "A daughter-in-law may not be able to admit to her mother-in-law that she needs help. This may pertain to helping her with her children or visiting and caring for the grandchildren while the daughter-in-law is away from home. In the reverse, the mother-in-law cannot admit to her daughter-in-law that she needs her help. Perhaps she is widowed or has to have a medical procedure and needs someone to go with her." Because of this lack of expectation and communication, this intense desire not to impose on others, both the mother-in-law and daughter-in-law lose out. However, when there is a daughter for the mother/mother-in-law or a mother or sister for the daughter-in-law, that person can be counted on and trusted in these instances.

"In my dreams," says Virginia, "my son would have married someone like me when I was younger. I always had lots of energy and I had a creative streak. My daughter-in-law, Delilah, is also creative, but in other ways we are so different. She prefers to do things with her mother anyway, although I've made some gestures toward her. I wanted to paint with her, but Delilah would rather take any free time she has and devote it to her mother. Since I have no daughter, I am always watching my daughter-in-law and her mother with envy. When my son married her, I thought we would share some kind of closeness. Instead, I tend to hear about her adventures with her friends and her visits to her mother. This has been going on for years. I admit, at the beginning, I was disappointed with her. But I tried to make her feel like part of the family because that is what we do, and of course, now that she is having a baby, I have new hope. Of course, now I worry she'll take the baby to her mother and not to me.

"In our culture, we embrace our extended family. My daughter-in-law was raised this way, too, and my friends say her behavior is odd. There should be room for me and for her mother. I know what my daughter-in-law thinks to herself, that daughters and daughters-in-law are not the same. I want her in our family, though. It would please me."

While Virginia has an openness about her daughter-in-law and looks for a better relationship, Beth, as a daughter-in-law, has felt her mother-in-law's iciness.

"From the minute I met my husband's mother and sisters, I knew I was in trouble. They watched every move I made and judged me. If I landed a new job or if I bought a new suit, they talked about it. I told my mother, who couldn't quite believe that they would act that way. Then I observed my mother with my brother's wife and, ironically, I noticed she wasn't very open or friendly. She made a few futile efforts to spend time with her or have some kind of relationship and then it slipped into holidays and obligatory family dinners. So my mother and I are very close, but she is not close with my sister-in-law, who is very close with her own mother and sisters. Then I have my own mother-in-law, Lydia, who does everything for her two daughters and wouldn't do a thing for me. She is distant and at the same time she seems to be watching me. If she engages me in any way, say she calls and is very friendly and chatty, there is an ulterior motive, like she wants my husband to come for some family event and she knows I have the power to make that decision. I always acquiesce to her wishes or family demands for my husband's sake. Since I have no sister, I cling to my mother, who is devoted to me. In this extended family, none of these other relationships work—everyone goes to their own mothers or sisters."

If a mother-in-law has several daughters or daughters-in-law already and her son marries late, she may not be particularly interested in forging a closeness with his wife. Perhaps there are enough females in the immediate family and she feels there simply isn't room for anyone new. The son is pivotal in his approach to such a situation when his wife is shut out because of a surfeit of daughters and/or daughters-in-law. While the son should not be put in the middle, he also has to make it clear to his mother, sisters and other female relatives that his wife should be welcome into the family. "Of course," Dr. Ronnie Burak remarks, "if the son is put in the middle, it becomes a tough situation. He really does not want to have to choose between his wife, his mother or his sister(s), which is why everyone should try harder to get along. If the husband/son's wife is nagging him about how his mother acts and how his sisters act, he'll resent it. And if his mother and/or sisters do the same, he'll resent that too."

In her essay on midlife interpersonal relationships, "A Longitudinal Analysis of Midlife Interpersonal Relationships and Well-being," Elizabeth L. Paul points out that at this point in life, parent-adult child relationships can become particularly strong and vital, especially for women. If this occurs, the mother's and her daughters' relationships with extended family also improve. The reasons for this are partly due to a death or loss in the family (often the husband-father) and partly due to what Paul describes as "the fluidity of relationships over time." If we apply this theory to mothers and their daughters, it becomes clear that as both women age, the ties become more important and necessary. Paul observes that in midlife and later adulthood women's well-being depends to a large degree on extended family relations as well as friendships. If this is the case, the mother-in-law could still develop a successful rapport with her daughter-in-law later in the marriage. Because of the mother-in-law's need to expand connections, this new closeness can take place even if she is close to her daughters. The same theory applies to the daughters/sisters as later in life, they too may relax and invite their sister-in-law into the fold.

A SIMPLE SOLUTION
* At midlife, both the mother-in-law and her daughters, regardless of their attachment, make an effort to include the daughter-in-law.
* This improves the mother's and daughters' relationship with the extended family.

With care and effort, a comfortable, amiable relationship can be achieved between mothers-in-law, their daughters and their daughters-in-law, as the following story shows. "In this family, we are very careful in what we say and how we do things," says Athena, a mother-in-law for fourteen years. "My daughters were trained to be kind and civil and to invite both daughters-in-law whenever there is an occasion. I imagine that the two daughters-in-law, who are close and have young sons only a few months apart, must sometimes resent me and my daughters. I respect both my daughters-in-law, but I do not treat them as I do my daughters. I view both women as helpmates for my sons, who each seem happily married. Neither of these women has ever denied me access to my sons. Everyone behaves well and, although there is no deep closeness, there are no altercations either.

"I try not to judge my sons' wives and their marriages. I see no reason why we can't all get along. Nor do I see any reason why we should have constant contact. My sons are dissimilar and have married very dissimilar women. My first son is loud and aggressive and can be provocative with people. He may be too much for my other son's wife, who is married to the quiet son. I cannot say I prefer one daughter-in-law to the other and I respect both. Everyone lives nearby so there are no favorites in terms of time or travel. As I get older, I tend to spend more time with my daughters and I find it rewarding. Lately, though, I have wondered if I should have encouraged everyone to be closer, not just united by the occasional holiday or family event."

Although it is less common than fifty years ago, when women raised their children as a full time occupation, there are mothers today who may work and still be entrenched in their children's lives to an unhealthy degree. Once the children grow to adulthood, the stakes are raised in terms of expectations and separation becomes more difficult. A mother who does not let go of her adult son or daughter is attempting to fill some emptiness in her own life. She may have no resources of her own and her identity is invested in her children. "Here then is a form narcissism," comments Dr. Ronnie Burak. "The self-esteem of the mother is wrapped up in what her children accomplish and how much her children love her. She then shows them love for what they have achieved. In such cases, when this woman becomes a mother-in-law, she has difficulty handing her son over to her daughter-in-law. The mother is proprietary out of fear of losing her son to his wife and along with that, losing his love, attention and the pride she gets from his accomplishments."

PROPRIETARY MOTHERS
* **Mothers put their entire lives into raising their sons and daughters then suffer when the children grow into adults.**
* **If the mothers have not developed other skills and interests, separation is especially difficult.**

An example of a controlling mother-in-law is illustrated by Brianna's story. "My mother-in-law is controlling because she always got away with it," says Brianna. "She does it with her daughters and with her sons. When my first child was born and my in-laws were abroad, I was very hurt because my mother-in-law spoke with my husband about the birth and then she called her daughters with the news. She never even spoke with me or asked how I was doing. Her concerns are with the immediate family members and, I guess, that doesn't include me. They are a highly overachieving family. It wouldn't matter, however, what the members of the family accomplished or didn't accomplish, they each would still be more important than anyone else in my mother-in-laws' eyes. I won't forget that she ignored me when our baby was born, but on the other hand, I'm not sure I want to be an insider in this family.

"Twenty years later, things aren't much different, although I care much less. My mother-in-law's mother, who has always been wonderful to me, is leaving all of her jewelry to her granddaughters and nothing to her grandson, my husband. I don't say a word and I don't want the jewelry, but I want to feel like I count. What I wish is that my mother-in-law would not be so into my husband's life and into her daughters' lives and still ignore me. Of course, her son counts, but his children, with me as the lowly oven who baked them, do not count as much as her daughters' children. My husband is very content with the attention his mother gives him and my children will have to survive without feeling particularly special in their grandmother's eyes. It's such a slight to me, really. But I can't compete, so I don't even try."

Contrary to Brianna's feelings of insignificance, Martha is comfortable with her mother-in-law and sister-in-law. "My mother-in-law, Edie, lives three thousand miles away from us, but her eldest daughter lives ten blocks away from our home. This works well for our relationship, because my sister-in-law and I do so many things together. I come from a close family and so does my husband. His sisters and I are very similar in looks and in our taste. I have always wanted to have sisters-in-law, because I never had a sister. At first, it was a little tricky to be accepted because my sisters-in-law are very close, but they include me anyway. The second sister lives about two hours away. When my mother-in-law comes into town, we all get together. My mother, who also lives a distance, is happy to hear it. There isn't any competition between the two mothers, although my husband retains some sibling rivalry with his sisters, but I don't get involved. We are each married with young children and everyone is busy. Any time we make for each other is appreciated.

"I know that my mother-in-law is not like my mother, but I find that a plus. Both women have strengths and weaknesses. I take the best from each and try to learn from them. I would call my mother-in-law about something I would not call my mother about. I know she is flattered and pleased. People say they've never seen an in-law relationship as solid as ours. As I get older, I need less lessons, but the mothering part seems to last. I want them both to treat me like a daughter and I want to be accepted by my sisters-in-law for the sister relationship I never had."

As evidenced in the previous chapter on mothers-in-law who seek out their daughters-in-law and daughters-in-law who seek out their mothers-in-law, this mutual need can come about because of missing pieces in the women's lives. The benefit of a mother-in-law and her daughters having a connection with the daughter-in-law/sister-in-law is undeniable. The role relationships enhance the extended family and are in everyone's best interest. "We marry the entire family, for better or for worse. It is most successful for everyone when we explore and reinvent to be accommodating," Alice Michaeli emphasizes. "This brings about stability and peace."

Problems often arise when, somewhat unusually, a mother-in-law shows her preference for her daughter-in-law over her own daughter, as in Jeanne's case. "My mother-in-law, Anya, is critical of her own daughter, but not of me," says Jeanne. "She thinks of me as the perfect daughter-in-law while she finds fault with Isabelle, her daughter. Of course, I also aim to please her and Isabelle does not. I have watched closely and I also see that my mother-in-law is critical of Isabelle's kids and not mine. I always go along with Anya's wishes and I do not disagree with her. If anyone disagrees with her, there is trouble. My mother-in-law has done more for me than she has for her own daughter."

Jeanne confides, "Although my mother-in-law is so good to me, it makes me uneasy that all the family members do not get along and it makes me feel guilty that she favors me over her own daughter. I have a daughter and son of my own now and I would not want to favor my future daughter-in-law over my own daughter one day. I suppose it is impossible to know how you will react ahead of time in a given situation, but one has to keep in mind the basic premise of a healthy relationship. There has to be give and take and the relationship has to withstand strain and stress. In the case of my mother-in-law, I find it difficult to enjoy my relationship with her, because her daughter does not get along with her. I feel guilty about it every time we do something together.

"Sometimes I think it is only a matter of time before my mother-in-law becomes critical of me, too. My husband has warned me to be careful and not to get too close to Anya. She's his mother, so he knows what he's talking about. I have seen her ugly side and I do want to keep my distance. However, at the same time, I do not want to offend her by saying no to her overtures."

When a daughter-in-law begins to recognize her mother-in-law's style of interaction, she finally has some insight that can help her navigate the relationship. If a mother-in-law finds fault with both her daughter-in-law and her daughter, then the daughter-in-law will begin to understand that this is how her mother-in-law relates to everyone. The daughter-in-law realizes she should not take it personally. "It is always best," says Dr. Michele Kasson, "to learn about each other and to observe each other over time. People's behaviors follow patterns across a range of situations. This works in the other direction as well. For example, if the daughter-in-law is quirky at a family dinner, the mother-in-law needs to understand that this is probably how she relates to people in general, not just with family members."

PERSONAL STYLE
* **When the mother-in-law displays idiosyncratic behavior toward her daughter-in-law, chances are she is that way with other people, too.**
* **Once the daughter-in-law realizes this, she learns not to view her mother-in-law's odd or unpleasant style of communication as an attack on her.**
* **When a daughter-in-law possesses an unusual, even quirky, personality, her mother-in-law may find her behavior unexpected and unwelcome.**
* **It will be beneficial if the mother-in-law can accept that this is simply how she operates in life and how she interacts with others.**

Finding a balance between what a mother-in-law and daughter-in-law want from their relationship can often be precarious, as Sandra learned. "There was no particular expectation on my part, as a mother-in-law," Sandra reports, "because my son's courtship was so short. I had no idea what my daughter-in-law, Gabrielle, would be like. I knew she didn't need a mother substitute, because she is so close with her own, as I am very close with my daughter. However, I wanted some kind of give and take, some kind of relationship with her. Unfortunately, I think I offended Gabrielle by making her feel replaceable—I once told her there was no such thing as one woman for one man. In retrospect, because my son is so special to me, I think that I might have intimidated her.

"I speak to Gabrielle when I want some information, because my son is so uncommunicative, but I speak to my own daughter on a daily basis. She lives nearby while my son and Gabrielle live half way across the country. My daughter-in-law is totally attached to her mother and her sister who live close to her. Both my daughter and my daughter-in-law have children. I admit that I am more interested in my daughter's children and more involved with them. The two sets of children have been raised in opposite ways, in keeping with the different lifestyles that the two couples lead. I think that since I am not as close to my son and daughter-in-law, I have less curiosity about their children."

Even in the best of mother/son relationships, there is a delicate balance to be found. According to Olga Silverstein, in her essay, "Mothers and Sons," while a mother is loving and nurturing, she must never smother her son. "And she must always be aware of the right moment to pull out and turn her son over to his father and the world of men." It is a quandary, however, because the "good mother," Silverstein tells us, "is expected to facilitate a pattern of emotional development in her son that stands in direct opposition to her own."

While the goal is to have a successful mother/son bond, there are those sons and mothers who are not close. When the relationship between the son and his mother is not healthy, it may filter into the marriage and the daughter-in-law will be affected as well. Only if the mother-in-law realizes, in time, that his wife is a positive factor on her son, can the situation improve for the two women. Whatever problems might exist between the mother and son, the mother wants her son to be content and cared for. "If the daughter-in-law enhances the son's life, the mother-in-law usually becomes more gracious," says Brenda Szulman. "The mother-in-law then recognizes the value of the marriage, which is that her son is taken care of in a certain way. Her daughter-in-law now sustains her son and she likes that. This gives her son credibility and maturity."

Sometimes all it takes to achieve harmony is a genuine effort, as Charlotte learned. "It has taken a long time for me to become close to my sister-in-law and my mother-in-law," Charlotte confides. "At first I was intimidated because they were so brainy and I was not. I have been a model and an actress, but my mother-in-law, Lois, is a scientist and her daughter is a professor. I was definitely not what they had in mind for their son. They imagined someone who also had several graduate degrees and had some intellectual pursuit. We have become close, however, because all three of us have made an effort. I tell them about my life and they tell me about theirs.

"My sister-in-law, who is bookish and rather plain-looking, recently became engaged and that took the pressure off, too. While she was single, it was a bit rocky, especially after our first child was born. Now that she is getting married next month, though, and wants to begin a family, I feel less self-conscious and as if we are on a level playing field. My husband has been sensitive to some of these issues from the start. I now realize that he did not want someone who was a cookie cutter of his mother and sister."

Again, when a daughter-in-law is very pretty and the sister-in-law is not, there can be competition between them and the mother-in-law may feel protective of her own daughter. A similar situation may occur if a daughter-in-law is successful in her career and the daughter does not have that kind of success. On the other hand, if the sister and her mother are very glamorous and the son marries someone very plain, the son's wife may feel inferior. At the same time, the mother-in-law and sister-in-law may have trouble understanding why the son/brother made the choice he did. Often in such cases, he chose as he did because he values a type of woman who is different from the women in his family. Though such a choice may make waves in the family, when the son is made happy by his wife, his mother and sisters will usually be more accepting of his wife.

DIFFERENT WOMEN
* **The mother-in-law and sister-in-law are similar in type.**
* **The daughter-in-law is the opposite.**
* **The son purposely chose a wife who is different from the females in his family.**

Fifty percent of the mothers-in-law interviewed for this chapter revealed that they put their relationships with their daughters ahead of their relationships with their daughters-in-law. Thirty-five percent of the mothers-in-law have made strong efforts to become close to their daughters-in-law, although they consider themselves closer to their own daughters. Fifteen percent are estranged from their daughters and find comfort in their closeness with their daughters-in-law.

Of the daughters-in-law interviewed, thirty-five percent are close to their mothers and sisters and do not seek strong bonds with their mothers-in-law and sisters-in-law. Twenty-five percent actually wanted a relationship with their mothers-in-law initially, but found it too difficult and daunting to pursue. Forty percent of the daughters-in-law are very happy with their relationships with their mothers-in-law and share their closeness with the daughters/sisters-in-law.

Whatever kind of woman a man marries, it is with the expectation that his mother and sister(s) will, at best, embrace her and, at the least, accept her. Mutual respect is a basic requirement above all, along with the hope that the extended family profits and grows. Repeatedly, we see mothers-in-law who find themselves "off the hook" in terms of creating relationships with their daughters-in-law, because their daughters-in-law have solid relationships with their own mothers and sisters. Other times, we see mothers-in-law who feel competitive about their daughters-in-law's relationships with their mothers and who are envious of such loving relationships.

A daughter-in-law who feels her mother-in-law and her sister-in-law are a locked unit and cannot be infiltrated, is often disheartened and embittered. The daughter-in-law who sizes up the situation between her mother-in-law and sister-in-law early on in her marriage is at an advantage. If she accepts the situation as it is and does her best to work within its framework, her husband will be grateful and there will be less tension in both the extended family and in their marriage.

5

Religion, Race and Ethnicity

"My kids go to my church, which really bothers my mother-in-law," Megan tells us. "When my husband comes with us, she is very unhappy, but I don't care. My feeling is my kids are getting religious training. What religion we are is not as important as what that religion provides. My husband has always been completely supportive of this. He has explained how he feels to his mother and she finds it objectionable. She does not complain about it though and I think that is a compliment to me. She knows better than to get in the way, but it bothers her that her grandchildren are not Muslim but Catholic; this is what she always dreaded, from the moment my husband brought me to her house.

"I look at all our cultural differences and how much my husband and I have had to learn from each other. No matter what my mother-in-law thinks, religion is only a small part of our marriage. My mother-in-law is very polite to me and never lets on if she cares about my not being the same religion as her son. She masks everything and I have to watch for clues and signals. She once made a noise in her throat to indicate she was not happy with our Easter egg hunt. Her approach is so alien to me."

Preconceived notions of race and religion may be changing as intermarriage increases in America. Yet for some families, it will always be a serious matter. For centuries, mothers have disapproved of their sons marrying someone of a different race, religion or ethnicity. While a mother-in-law of the past might have summarily dismissed her new daughter-in-law, whether she converted to the husband's religion or not, there are mothers-in-law today who appear to be more broad-minded. Today, the number of interfaith marriages and interracial marriages is at an all time high. Fifty percent of current brides and grooms are marrying outside of their respective religions. It is estimated that eighteen million Roman Catholics in the United States marry outside their faith, as do forty percent in Canada and seventy-five percent in England, according to Fennella Temmerman in her "Letters to Columbia." While interfaith marriages between Protestants and Catholics were once disapproved of by both religions, eighty percent of the population accepts them today.

One reason we tend to marry into our own culture or religion is because it simplifies aspects of how to raise our children in the complex world we live in today. The establishment of kinship, as Juanita Williams notes in her essay, "The Importance of Marriage," was, historically, to transmit property and power from one generation to the next within one's class and social strata. In today's world, a mother-in-law may justifiably worry that her son will marry a woman from a completely different culture or religion and she will then lose him. If the mother-in-law believes that a marriage takes priority over everything else, this is a very real threat to her. In addition, a mother may worry about cultural differences creating confusion or miscommunication between her son's new wife and the rest of the family. A lack of common beliefs or shared language of gestures and behavior can make daily interactions difficult and create tension for both the couple and their respective families.

How much importance we place in these differences depends on our own sensibilities. In Ida's case, the differences between her son and daughter-in-law loom large. "My daughter-in-law, Pamela, and my son are not the same religion," Ida says. "Although they had both clergymen at their wedding, I do worry for my grandchildren today. She is a non-practicing Catholic and we are ardent Methodists, who take it seriously. This is my son's second wife. His first wife had chosen a non-denominational church. I try not to let it bother me that my grandchild has never seen the inside of my church. This really irks me, but it would have to be monumental for me to interfere. I can't let religion get between us. I see this as a successful marriage from the outside looking in. They are totally absorbed with their child and the fact that my family's religion is absent from their lives is beyond my control."

Contrary to Ida's experience with her daughter-in-law, Jessica and her daughter-in-law, Connie, are the same religion. "Just because someone is the same religion does not mean you would choose her for your son. I admit it makes it easier on one level, but it isn't everything. I did want my son to be married and I thought it was time for him to make a commitment. The fact that my daughter-in-law is the same religion is a plus. I find her sensible and pleasant enough, but I can't say that our common religion binds us. I am very involved with my son. I actually preferred the woman my son did not marry. She was Greek Orthodox and we are Roman Catholic, but it didn't even bother me—I was absolutely crazy about her. What I have learned here is that sharing a religion does not make someone right for you, but it is a myth that we are taught all the same. I changed my religion for my husband and I would not expect someone to do it for my son. It is really not the answer."

Antoinette Michaels, an interfaith minister and relationship counselor, views having the same religion as part of a joint value system. Michaels recommends that couples consider this before they marry and warns that if one partner's belief system is foreign and different to the other's, it causes more hurdles in the marriage. "Do they see themselves going to church or temple together with their in-laws and extended family?" Michaels asks. "If one partner cannot do this and is not interested, then there is antagonism because the two people do not have the same sensibility." When there are similar religious and spiritual beliefs, this builds a foundation for the more trying times and challenges of marriage.

According to B.A. Robinson, in his essay entitled "Facts About Inter-faith Marriages," the definition of such a union is one "in which two spouses follow different religious traditions." The forms vary so that one partner might practice a specific religion while the other believes in a non-theistic ethical system. An example of this is would be if one partner followed Judaism and the other, Humanism. Another form of inter-faith marriage is when one person follows a Western faith and the other an Eastern faith. The example Robinson gives is Christianity and Taoism. Christianity and Islam are both Abramic religions, indicating they share in some beliefs. In this case, the two religions view Abraham as a patriarch.

A frequent type of mixed-faith marriage is one in which the two people are both Christian, but one is Roman Catholic and the other is Protestant. This type of union is categorized as an intra-faith marriage. A further differentiation is when both partners are Protestant, but one is Evangelical and the other is main-line Christian. What narrows this further is when the spouses come from separate traditions of the same religion. Robinson's example is when one partner follows Assemblies of God and the other worships as a Baptist.

For the daughter-in-law who expects to raise her children in her religion and feels pressure from her mother-in-law to raise the children in the mother-in-law's family's religion, this can cause ongoing disputes in the marriage. For many of us, religious affiliation and indoctrination is an intimate part of our psyches. With a mother-in-law and daughter-in-law of different religions, such conflicts may be viewed merely as a battle of wills, but they are also about issues that are intrinsic and highly personal.

ONGOING CONFLICT
* **For those mothers-in-law and daughters-in-law of different but strong faiths, there usually will not be much yielding.**
* **This creates ongoing, deep-seated struggles.**

"Religion raises the question," according to psychologist Dr. Michaele Goodman, "of how many differences are tolerated in the family. Frequently, whatever image the mother-in-law had of her daughter-in-law, the right religion was a part of it. Now, a daughter-in-law materializes and she is not the same religion as the family. In this situation, the daughter-in-law has to look to her husband for support."

"My mother would have reacted strongly if I had converted to James' religion," Allegra tells us. "But James converted to my religion instead and this pleased my mother to no end. Of course, my mother-in-law is not happy about it. It infuriates her that he is now Episcopalian, because he was born Jewish. My family is this proper Bostonian family and I think my husband found it appealing. My husband and I had spent many years together before he made the decision to convert. While his mother never thought we belonged together, we have a history that made it important for him to convert. My mother-in-law is cool towards me every time she sees me. I've given up any hope of mutual support between us. I worry that one day I'll have to nurse my mother-in-law despite her treatment of me. I think religion was such a big deal to her that any other criticism she has of me is negligible. At this point, I just concentrate on my husband and we gravitate toward my family, especially at holiday time."

In America, the Judeo-Christian religious tradition prevails. Although there are different religions within its parameters, each is monotheistic and shares similar values, ethics and moral sensibilities. Yet we each hold on to our own particular religious identity. "Often when a mother-in-law holds it against her daughter-in-law because she is of another religion, it is the daughter-in-law's behavior in specific situations and daily conduct that seems so unlike the mother-in-law's," observes sociologist Alice Michaeli. "Someone so 'different' is clearly not the mother-in-law's choice of wife for her son."

For Dara, a mother-in-law of ten years, her son's decision to marry a woman of another faith was devastating. "I only have one child, a son, and my gut instinct was that his choice of a wife was wrong for him. I said nothing, because he was old enough to make his own decision. My husband felt the same way and we kept quiet. She was from another religion and she was Asian. We are Baptist and American. I can't think of how they could be more different. My daughter-in-law was raised too differently for them to find a common ground. She was really on foreign territory, literally sent here for graduate school when they met.

"My opinion is that my son found her when he was lonely and she was also. That was their common bond. I suppose, too, her being foreign was very curious to him; he had never met anyone like her. She has a lot of good qualities and she is kind and witty and very presentable. She and my son are the same age and her family is solid. So what is really odd is that from day one they did not get along. Ironically, I grew fond of her, not as the right wife for my son, but as a person. I liked her, but I knew it was a mismatch. There was such a huge culture gap. There was no way they could fit as a couple nor were they successful at family life together. After eight years, they split up and their two children have suffered. The differences in their religion and race that bothered me at first are hardly my main concern now. With the divorce, I have more to worry about than what religion my grand-children are raised in."

The author, Thomas Moore, in his book, *Soul Mates,* writes about how valuable the concept of family is to the soul. Moore does not discuss the family unit per se, but rather "a family of human kind" where the family is looked at "with a poetic mind that is tuned to the deepest emotional needs and yet able to imagine the nature of the family broadly." So often, Moore notes, people live in a family structure, but it is not satisfying to the soul.

While the answer might not be a traditional, cookie cutter family, a family of any kind and of any religion has great influence over its members. Moore observes that rituals and customs preserve a family and keep it intact. When a husband and wife are from different religions and cultures, they may not be able to reconcile their unique approaches to creating a successful family and marriage. The "fantasy daughter-in-law" or "fantasy mother-in-law" which each woman imagines, perhaps for years before the actual meeting, often includes a common religion on the wish list. The reality is that with interfaith marriages at an all time high, this wish may not materialize.

For many mothers-in-law and daughters-in-law, it is a major disturbance when family backgrounds are not alike. This manifests in separate rituals and causes opposition in some marriages. For example, as a

Jehovah's Witness, one does not celebrate holidays or birthdays. "If a Christian marries a Jehovah's Witness," counselor Antoinette Michaels observes, "there will always be one person in the marriage who celebrates holidays and birthdays and one person who does not. For the one who does, and who celebrates alone, there is the sense that she or he is being cheated."

According to the 1995 National Jewish Population Survey, over fifty percent of those members of the Jewish religion marry outside their faith. Yet Dr. Bruce A. Phillips, a professor of Jewish Communal Service, points out that the grown children of intermarriage "will become an ever larger shadow Jewish population with weak ties to the Jewish Community." Phillips writes, "…formal Jewish education had less impact on intermarriage than did informal experiences such as Jewish camp or trips to Israel." In 1997, the *Jewish Post of New York* reported that over one third of the Jewish population today are intermarried and one in ten children in an intermarried family will marry a Jew. There are more children under the age of four in half-Jewish mixed marriage households than in all Jewish homes. The 1998 edition of the *American Jewish Year Book* reports that one third of Jewish parents whose children decide to marry outside their religion contest their children's choices and two thirds do not.

INTERMARRIAGE FOR THE JEWISH FAITH
* One in ten children of interfaith marriages with a Jewish parent will marry a Jewish partner.
* Two thirds of Jewish parents do not actively oppose their children's decisions to marry outside the faith.
* The influence of a Jewish education has less impact on discouraging intermarriage than informal experiences comprised of all Jewish participants.

As I discovered in my interviews, the issue of different religions can be a serious, knotty problem. "Patricia, my daughter-in-law of twelve years, is not Jewish, but she converted," Annette explains. "I told my son at the time that it was a ploy to ensnare him and that she would not raise their future children as Jews. I just knew it to be so. He was so taken with her, however, that he failed to hear me. And now, all these years later, my grandchildren are not Jewish, despite her conversion. Patricia will observe the Jewish holidays and then she will celebrate Christmas and Easter with her sisters. So the children are learning two religions, which, to me, is the same as an 'interfaith marriage.'"

Annette goes on, "This has been going on for five years, since my first granddaughter was born. My son says nothing, even though my husband is a Holocaust survivor and this is very important to him. We cannot look the other way. The issue of not having a Jewish daughter-in-law and Jewish grandchildren is extremely serious for us. The irony is that our daughter-in-law pretends she is Jewish and that their daughters are being raised in the faith. It isn't so. To me, my daughter-in-law's example is one that condones and encourages intermarriage and nothing more."

James Davidson, a sociologist at Purdue University, notes that interfaith marriage today is "at least twice what it was in the pre-Vatican II era." This is due to a large segment of society which does not emphasize religious education and has less attachment to the concept of religion. With a twenty-three percent decline in church sanctioned weddings between 1975 and 1995, according to Davidson's article published in *Commonweal Magazine* in September 1999, civil ceremonies have become increasingly popular and accepted. Among Catholics today, many parents accept interfaith marriages rather than lose their children to her/his spouse's religion or to no religion at all.

Some daughters-in-law who convert to their husbands' religion, hope for their in-laws' approval and an invitation into the family fold. For these women, the hope is that their commitments to convert will be repaid by being welcome as part of the family. Many mothers-in-law, however, often find conversions suspect and afterward still do not feel their daughters-in-law are of their heritage.

When Melanie converted fourteen years ago to Judaism from Catholicism, she believed that she was pleasing her husband and his family. "I expected my mother-in-law, Sylvia, to appreciate me for having gone through the conversion rites. Instead, I think she was very disappointed in her son's choice of a wife and saw me only as a woman who was born Catholic. Her hopes were crushed, but so were mine. I am from the South and I have no family nearby. I really made a sacrifice in marrying Joel, living on the east coast and in becoming Jewish. I was hoping, in return, that I would have a relationship with my mother-in-law and that we would even plan to celebrate some of the holidays together.

"At the same time," Melanie explains, "I do see Sylvia's point of view, especially with what Jewish people have been through. What I wanted, I suppose, was my mother-in-law's respect for converting and recognition of how much I love her son. My husband has not defended me. He says it is a miracle that his parents even talk to me, they are so clannish. He views it as a tribute to my personality that they are civil to me in a sort of superficial way. His take on it is: *I married you, isn't that enough proof for you?* When I tell him that his mother isn't friendly and our relationship is only fair, he shrugs and accepts it. I keep waiting for them to remember I am now Jewish and that our boys are being raised in that faith."

Alice Michaeli remarks that in some cultures and in certain religions, the mother of a son is pivotal in granting permission for his marriage. She is in search of a mate for her son who not only shares his instincts, values and knowledge, but is of the same religion and culture. The goal is to perpetuate the religion and culture and to carry on the family traditions. If a prospective wife comes from another religion or race, she simply doesn't fit in.

THE MOTHER-IN-LAW'S SEARCH
* The mother- in-law seeks a daughter-in-law of the same faith and culture.
* She is looking for someone who shares her family's value system.
* The grandchildren are to be raised in this shared faith.

Race and ethnicity are other contentious issues in how mothers-in-law and daughters-in-law react to one another. When the *New York Times* did a series of articles in spring of 2000 entitled "Talking About Race," and then devoted an entire Sunday magazine to the topic on July 16th 2000, many opinions on the topic of "How Race is Lived in America" were expressed. In this special issue, an article written by Ruben Martinez of the Institute for the Arts and Civic Dialogue at Harvard, explains that those of different races, ethnicities and nationalities, "are being thrown together and torn apart by the churning forces of first the post-industrial and now the information economy." Noting that "When we say race, we mean 'nationality' or 'ethnicity' or even 'religion' or 'culture,'" he advises that, "We cannot speak of one race in isolation from the others or apart from the other forces that divide and unite us, like our religion and our work."

Susan Fales-Hill's article, "My Life in Black and White," in the June 2000 issue of *Vogue*, discusses her childhood as "living proof of a happy mixed marriage." Growing up biracial in the early 1960s was "an extraordinary adventure," according to Fales-Hill. Her parents had met in 1958, her mother a daughter of Haitian political exiles and her father a scion of a powerful and wealthy family. Fales-Hill describes evenings with her maternal Haitian grandfather in his Brooklyn brownstone and

Sunday lunches with her paternal grandmother in her townhouse on the Upper East Side of Manhattan. As for the mother-in-law/daughter-in-law rapport between Fales-Hill's black mother and her Colonial Dame of America grandmother, she writes that her mother was accepted "fully" and became a favorite daughter-in-law.

Despite Fales-Hill's impressive family, most mothers-in-law do not happily conjure up images of a daughter-in-law from another race. Almost always, the prevailing desire for mothers of sons is that their family's culture and heritage will be passed on through their children and grandchildren. "It is a subconscious wish that one's culture will not die and will not disappear," remarks psychologist Dr. Ronnie Burak. "Another component of wanting one's son to marry within the family's race is feeling comfortable with people who are like us. What makes us feel alike is being from the same place culturally and ethnically."

According to the United States Census Bureau for Statistics, interracial married couples totaled 5,078,000 as of 1998. Mirta Ojito, a journalist for *The New York Times*, has written on how race is lived in America and has commented that people from different races still come from different worlds. "It's differences in socioeconomic status more than anything else," writes Ojito. And yet, when people from different worlds are united in marriage, mothers-in-law and daughters-in-law have to deal with the issues which arise.

INCREASE OF INTERRACIAL MARRIAGES
* **According to United States Census Bureau Statistics, interracial marriages have more than doubled in the past two decades.**
* **The number of interracial marriages reported in 1980 was 2,341,000. In 1998, there were 5,078,000 such unions.**

"While I see now that in some ways my mother-in-law tolerates me because my husband and I have children, I will always remain the outsider, someone who not only stole her son, but kept him from his true destiny," Lee says. "My mother-in-law, Gertrude, is prejudiced and I'm Asian. I consider her very narrow-minded and ignorant. She is proud of her son, but not proud of his law practice. She sees him as an ambulance chaser, although a successful one. We live in a suburb with a lovely home and a pool, but it is not what my mother-in-law had in mind. She wants her son at home in Pennsylvania, where she can control him, his friends, even who he has chosen for a wife.

"I am thankful that we live at a distance and see my mother-in-law only once a year. My husband is such a special person that he unconditionally loves his mother despite her feelings. He won't compromise our family and my dignity, but he also genuinely has deep feelings for his mother. During our visits, there have been bad incidents. When we were last visiting, there was a family wedding. My husband seemed to find this wedding important and insisted that we go to Pennsylvania for it. When we arrived at the church, his mother made a big scene insisting that we interrupt the ceremony to sit up front with the family. My husband had to appease her as usual so even though we were humiliated, we walked up to the front while everyone in the church looked on."

A mother-in-law may be unforgiving of her daughter-in-law belonging to another culture, rather than blaming her son for marrying outside of his ethnicity. Often, she is still looking for a daughter-in-law with whom she can share time and common interests and a comfort level that stems from these similarities. If a daughter-in-law is the same religion or ethnic background, much of the interaction between the two women is based on this mutual association. When this isn't the case, it becomes stressful and there can be animosity for the daughter-in-law and mother-in-law because their cultures are different. Because the daughter-in-law does not mirror her mother-in-law's race or ethnicity, the mother-in-law might feel wounded by this or betrayed. This may be very disappointing to a daughter-in-law who believes that her mother-in-law will accept her immediately, because she loves the older woman's son and has made a commitment to him.

AN UNDERSTANDING
* **When the mother-in-law and daughter-in-law are from the same culture, they share the same rituals and customs.**
* **Even if they have their differences, their similar backgrounds provide common ground.**

When the mother-in-law and daughter-in-law are from separate cultures, the mother-in-law may be hurt and disappointed in her son's choice of wife. The daughter-in-law is made unhappy by the mother-in-law's reaction to her and fails to see why she is not accepted. This is the scenario that has played out in Rorie's marriage. "I remind myself that my mother-in-law is attached to her grandchildren who are half-Indian, half-American," Rorie confesses, "because she is attached to Samuel, her son, not because of anything else. My children and I exist in a fictionalized version of the people her daughter-in-law and grandchildren should be. She wants a daughter-in-law whom she can control in her own way, someone of the same culture. Sometimes I find myself feeding into her antagonism. I encourage observances of certain Indian holidays just to aggravate her. It's wrong, but I can't help it; I have to fight back. Because my husband and I have a clear understanding of the situation, it doesn't come between us. He's very tolerant and his loyalty to me and the children is strong. Our family unit comes first. Early on in our marriage he had insisted that it would all be fine with his mother, despite the odds of that happening."

Rorie sighs. "I put up with his mother for his sake. I don't want him to suffer. I've been married long enough to know how it is with her, what to expect and how to keep it smooth for my husband's sake. My mother-in-law simply cannot forgive me for being Indian. I just wonder if he had chosen someone who was also Episcopalian, whether she would have been a different sort of mother-in-law, a more kindly mother-in-law. I also think my mother-in-law is prejudiced, on top of being angry that her son did not marry one of their kind, so her rejection of me is based on personal preference, but begins with racial bias to a degree."

In some cases, the mother-in-law has very high expectations for her son and this includes a daughter-in-law who is from the same ethnicity. Dr. Ronnie Burak, clinical psychologist, cautions us that the cause of prejudice is fear of the unknown. "Race is unlike religion in that it is usually visible. A mother-in-law may fear her child will be ostracized because of the high level of prejudice in our world. This prejudice can extend to her grandchildren who are racially mixed and this concerns the mother-in-law as well."

Rosanna is a mother-in-law who has had difficulty adjusting to a daughter-in-law of another culture. "My daughter-in-law, Maria, is unacceptable to me," Rosanna admits. "Food is such a priority in our family and she is not Italian. It makes little sense to me that she is Catholic if she is not Italian. In our family, you have to be both to fit in. I see her trying to prepare my recipes and I laugh. We only get together on holidays and then we are distracted because of the children. I always tell my husband to spend Easter with her family, because I can't stand my daughter-in-law at Easter time. She doesn't know how to observe the holiday in a manner that's in keeping with my family's traditions. We go to their house for Mother's Day and Thanksgiving, because those holidays don't matter to me and it makes my son happy. But I don't like her way of cooking and I don't like her cold manner.

"I suppose I am complaining, because Maria is Hispanic and not Italian. The religion issue, which I always thought was so important, isn't. I can't believe that with all the nice Italian girls in our neighborhood, he had to choose her."

According to Gloria Yamato, in her essay, "Something About the Subject Makes it Hard to Name," the definition of racism is "the systematic, institutionalized mistreatment of one group of people by another based on racial heritage." Yamato talks about people being "stratified into various classes." Evelyn Nakano Glenn, in her essay, "From Servitude to Service Work: Historical Continuities in the Racial Division of Paid Reproductive Labor," reveals the complex interaction of race and gender oppression in the lives of minority women. Glenn points out that gender and race have been studied as separate systems of hierarchy. Yet we cannot deny that there is prejudice against all women, not on the basis of race but gender. The question becomes, why is there so little solidarity between women as mothers-in-law and daughters-in-law, in terms of race? "Race is an overt issue," Dr. Michaele Goodman tells us, "more than religion, which can be put on the shelf."

While some ethnic or cultural differences may seem minor, to family members they may loom large, as in Kathleen's first marriage. "I am from a different ethnic background than my former mother-in-law, Mireille," says Kathleen. "I am Irish Catholic and she is French Canadian. She seemed okay with it until my husband and I had a child. Then she seemed to become really angry about our ethnic difference. I would say that Mireille looked down on me and my background to the point where I doubt she would have crossed the street to say hello if not for her grandchild.

"I only asked for respect and that I be treated like a human being. It became a big problem in my marriage, because my husband was so affected by what his mother said and how she behaved towards me. I suppose it's odd, but I kept trying to help my mother-in-law. As long as she was on her good behavior around me, I tried to help. But it was no good; she always hated me for being Irish. She never believed I belonged with her son and, finally, we got divorced because of it."

In her book, *Composing A Life*, Mary Catherine Bateson points out that marriage is a less than optimal method of learning cultural differences. This is because, "The contrast between cultures can easily become confused with the contrast between male and female, and any two-way comparison can be interpreted as better and worse, high and low."

What Bateson describes correlates with Lorraine's situation. "I am black and my husband is white. We went to graduate school together, which is where we met. Back when we were dating, I thought there would be a problem. My mother-in-law makes me feel like an outsider and my husband sees it. There will be family discussions while there are guests in her home—which was once her son's home, too. When I walk into the room where they are gathered, they will become silent. My in-laws have no regard for what is mine and my husband's, as if our value system is so radically different from theirs.

"Although my husband puts me first now, he suffers from his filial duty. What pacifies me is my closeness with my own family. Clearly, I belong to my family and he belongs to his. I know the situation will never improve, and in fact, it might deteriorate. I can't imagine what it will be like when we have children. I remember what my mother told me about life being tough enough even if you marry one of your own. I know in my culture, a mother-in-law exists long after the marriage. She will still take care of her grandchildren, even if her son is no longer with his wife. Sadly, I can't rely on such loyalty from my mother-in-law."

"What happens," explains Alice Michaeli, "is that in a divorce situation in specific cultures, the extended family prevails. However, the significance of the extended family is not the same in the United States as in other countries." A continuing connection between the mother-in-law and the daughter-in-law, who is now a single parent, is frequently the case in some cultures or in struggling or disadvantaged families, Michaeli points out, because the daughter-in-law needs her mother-in-law. "The choices made between mothers-in-law and daughters-in-law vary according to race and culture."

In sociological theory, there is the principle of homogamy, which translates into "like marries like" in terms of social characteristics. This means that the story of Cinderella or the message of many popular films, such as *Pretty Woman* (poor, but beautiful woman from the wrong side of the tracks meets and begins a romance with a wealthy, sophisticated man and they live happily ever after), cannot often be found in the real world. The United States Census statistics on marriage and family reveal that ninety-seven percent of Americans marry within their own social classes. "The most salient feature in marriage is social class," says Alice Michaeli. "Most people choose to marry within their social class and race, ethnicity and religion are all examples of social characteristics."

The second principle is the theory of complimentary, which simply means that opposites attract. An example of this is when a very shy person marries a gregarious partner. Alice Michaeli reminds us that the principle of homogamy, in which the partners are similar, causes less discord. In terms of the health and success of the marriage, less friction and more equanimity over a length of time are meaningful components.

LIKE MARRIES LIKE
* The husband and wife come from the same area of the country.
* They are of the same socioeconomic background.
* Both partners are equally educated.

OPPOSITES ATTRACT
* The husband and wife were raised in very different environments.
* One partner is an extrovert and the other an introvert.
* They may be of different races or religions.

Social status and educational achievement are issues that may be as divisive as religion and ethnicity in some families, such as Sonya's. "I see that mothering-in-law is like walking a tight rope," sighs Sonya. "It's been difficult for Patsy, my daughter-in-law, to blend into my family, despite the fact that I'm careful to be inclusive. I think it's her background. Here she is in a sophisticated, educated family, which is culturally dissimilar to hers. She has integrated somewhat, but it took a while. At first, she seemed to resent our lifestyle instead of wanting to learn about it. I would say Patsy has improved a bit, but the bottom line is she just doesn't comprehend how we live, nor does she care to.

"My daughter-in-law is certainly not who I imagined my son would bring home. I imagined someone of quality and intellect with a sense of responsibility. I think Patsy is a good mother to her children despite the fact she is not stimulating and she is limited in her abilities. She allows the children to watch far too much television, although she has cut down a bit recently. To her credit, she views her daughters as her greatest achievement and that is something on which she and I can both agree."

An important issue for some mothers-in-law is social status. Just as women have a certain expectation of the sort of man they will marry and what their lifestyle will be, some mothers-in-law anticipate a particular type of daughter-in-law. If a daughter-in-law is from another culture, but has achieved something of note in her field, it may assuage the disappointment of a mother-in-law who expected her son's wife to be similar to her family. The prestige brought about by this daughter-in-law's achievements or status may cause her mother-in-law to be more enthusiastic about her. For instance, if a daughter-in-law is from another country and heritage, but her family is highly regarded there, this may be enough of a trade-off for a mother-in-law. A mother-in-law may be satisfied if her daughter-in-law is prestigious in terms of her career or her lineage. In turn, a daughter-in-law may love her husband, but be disappointed by his parents' lack of social status or intellectual pursuits. The daughter-in-law in this example represents for her husband something his parents never had but aspires to and admires in others. The son-husband appreciates not only his own ability to rise socially, but appreciates the fact that his wife has already experienced a level he hopes to achieve.

On July 16, 2000, the *New York Times* published an article by Richard Stengel entitled "Let us Now Praise Social Climbing" about the attributes of social climbing. Stengel points out that social climbing has taken on a new face and attitude, one in which people are encouraged to unabashedly social climb and use others for their personal benefit. What is striking about the article is that today, celebrities and film stars are pursued by social climbers, rather than the *grande dames* of society as it was in times past. Neither race nor religion seem a part of one's aspirations. "Social climbing these days revolves around celebrity," Stengel writes. This has so much value that even average citizens who are not celebrities still seek partners who display attributes associated with the rich and famous. For example, people are often congratulated for marrying "up" when paired with men who have some status money or status or with women who possess beauty and youth.

ROPE BURNS
* **A man comes from money.**
* **A woman offers youth and beauty.**
* **They marry and "trade goods."**
* **Together they climb the social ladder.**

"From the start, I thought that Abigail, my mother-in-law, was terrific, elegant, bright and had a good sense of humor. She was very friendly without being overly solicitous, but she definitely brought me under her wing in the beginning," acknowledges Natasha. "I look back at how it began with my mother-in-law. Although my husband and I are similar in how we were raised, I came from a broken home and I think I was hungrier for acceptance than my husband or his mother. Abigail once called me a lunatic and that really bothered me. I think she believes that her son pampered me. I was the only woman of the same religion and background that her son had ever brought home and she was grateful. My mother-in-law also recognized my ambitions—that I wanted to be recognized as the leader of our social crowd. At first, Abigail encouraged me, because she had been that in her day. Eventually, she saw me as too flashy and somehow she no longer approved of my ambitions and my social agenda. I believe that her initial encouragement compelled me to try harder socially and yet this very effort came between us later."

The converse situation occurs when a daughter-in-law persuades her husband to become a part of her culture and family history. Judy's influence over her husband was palpable. "My connection to my mother and sisters was so intricate that there was no way that my husband could convince me to put his family first," Judy remarks. "Originally, it mattered to my husband and to me that we married people from the same culture and religion and then it didn't happen for either of us. I see our marriage as one in which our differences make it more interesting and we are constantly teaching each other. My mother-in-law seems to create an undercurrent of hostility and criticism towards me and so we gravitate to my family, because my husband is so welcome there along with me.

"My mother-in-law never expected that I would become her daughter-in-law. She kept writing to her son about me after we were a couple as if he and I were just friends. She sees our marriage as a hostile act, possibly against her family, and can't fathom that it's just about our love. I don't think it's my religion that bothers her, but my ethnicity. I am Korean and my husband is American. I have agreed to raise our future children in his faith, which is Protestant, but it is very important to me that I influence them in terms of ethnicity and culture. My mother treats my husband so well that a positive relationship has developed between them despite ethnic boundaries. Of course, my husband and I chose each other, although we are dissimilar, and somehow we have begun to blend. I see that his deep feelings toward me have extended to my mother."

Mothers-in-law may deal with daughters-in-law of another ethnicity as if they are outsiders. As they observe their sons immersing themselves in a life devoted to a woman who seems a stranger, they feel threatened. The mother-in-law has an idealized perception of the family and has been performing its rituals her way for many years. When her daughter-in-law is from another culture, it seems to the mother-in-law that the younger woman is taking something away from her family. The mother-in-law fears she will lose her son and that her influence will wane. The daughter-in-law, in return, considers her mother-in-law's attitude and behavior to be an imposition upon the new marriage.

"In a family of the same culture," psychologist Dr. Ronnie Burak points out, "mothers-in-law and daughters-in-law speak the same language and share the same values. If instead, a daughter-in-law comes along that does things in another way and speaks a foreign language, it becomes a false reality. The mother has a sense that there is a young woman out there like her, but she is not this daughter-in-law."

Part of the rationale for the mother-in-law not wanting an "outsider" in the family is that it will cause disharmony in raising her grandchildren. Another concern is that the goal of holding the family culture together and perpetuating it through the children is defeated. The mother-in-law wants her son to be a keeper of the faith, to contribute to upholding it and not allowing it to become extinct.

STRANGERS AMONG US
* **The mother-in-law does not want her son to lose his religion, culture and heritage.**
* **For this reason, she behaves coldly to her daughter-in-law, whom she perceives as an outsider.**
* **The daughter-in-law may be devoted to her husband, but is disappointed in the unenthusiastic welcome from her mother-in-law.**

Even when there are no cultural differences, class and economic disparities can come into play. This can cause dissension between mothers-in-law and daughters-in-law, as Susanna has experienced. "They have their lives planned out," Susanna says of her daughter-in-law, Marta, and son. "I find them inflexible and goal-oriented in a way my husband and I never were. Marta is Slavic, which is our culture, and we all come from the same part of the world. I couldn't imagine that there would be so many differences between us. Still, I know their lives will be a departure from the way my husband and I lived ours. I find myself questioning their values more than anything else. However, if they choose to live differently from my husband and me, what can I say? I have to accept it. At least, she and my son have many similarities in style and tempo.

"One contentious issue for Marta's family is that they have always been wealthy and very formal while we have been less privileged. She and my son met in high school and my son was determined to marry her someday. Her parents treat us with some distance although we are from the same cultural background. I suspect that at one time they tried to break up the relationship, but my son and daughter-in-law were in love. Although they don't share my husband's and my values, I believe that each generation has its own path to follow. I am proud to have a daughter-in-law like Marta, because of her origins."

Approximately sixty-five percent of the mothers-in-law interviewed regarding cultural and religious differences were disturbed by their sons' marriages to women not of their ethnicity, race or religion. Of the daughters-in-law interviewed—all of whom are of a different race, religion or culture from their husbands—most reported having problems, some major, some relatively minor, in dealing with their mothers-in-law because of their differences.

INFINITE POSSIBILITIES
* **The possibility of marrying someone from another religion and/or race will increase in the twenty-first century.**
* **The challenge for family members on both sides is to practice tolerance and acceptance.**

In the new century, the chances of partnering with someone from another religion or race increase. Yet what men and women learn about culture begins with both subjective and objective influences of their families of origin. The media has also been influential in exposing cultural norms and beliefs, making it apparent that there is an expansion in social and cultural development in America today. For a daughter-in-law of another religion or culture than her husband, there is no road map for how to relate to her mother-in-law. If this husband is a special son or the only son, the emotional and psychological "loss" for the mother-in-law might be felt more profoundly than if she has several sons and other daughters-in-law of the same or similar culture. Although daughters-in-law may miss the mother-in-law bond, in some instances, the lack of attention may be a relief. This is especially true when there exists seemingly unbridgeable differences in the two families' cultures and/or religions.

6

Desperate Situations

"I had always wanted a mother-in-law who did not have her own daughter," says Regina. "I had boyfriends who were only children or who came from families where there were only sons. I saw that those mothers were very supportive of me. I was just the type they wanted for a daughter-in-law. I suppose my desire to have a loving relationship with my mother-in-law, Mary-Rose, came about because my mother and I have a very poor relationship; in fact, we can't stand each other. Unfortunately, that has remained with me and spills over into my experiences with my mother-in-law.

"I do not fight with Mary-Rose directly, because I am a believer in not confronting one's mother-in-law. She irritates me and at times she behaves poorly towards me or my husband. But I believe that either Steven or I should be an intermediary and try to solve the problems with my mother-in-law. Sometimes I deal with a set of problems and other times he deals with them. I find this approach much more comfortable, but still, sometimes there are these huge confrontations anyway. I take all her nonsense, because I know that Steven is behind me. I am confident that my husband stands up for me. If I thought he didn't support me, I would be more confrontational with her."

Brenda Szulman, psychotherapist, notes that each spouse should attend to his or her own parents' behaviors and expectations. "The husband has to resolve the issues with his mother and father and the daughter-in-law shoulders the same responsibility for her parents. When there are ongoing problems, the couple has to address them together. This is the work of the marriage, to create a new family from two individuals. Unfortunately, some mothers-in-law are unwitting saboteurs of their sons' marriages, because they have difficulty letting go of their sons."

"My daughter-in-law, Catherine, is a big disappointment," Henrietta confides. "Her attitude is that life is difficult being married to my son. She is unforgiving and behaves poorly towards me. I would do anything to fix this marriage for him. In the beginning, for the first year of their marriage, I expected that everything would work out. My daughter-in-law looked to me to be another version of her mother and I anticipated that my daughter-in-law would be giving and kind.

"We had a big fight over celebrating my son's birthday while Catherine was pregnant. Her mother was planning the party and my husband and I were invited at the last minute. When we arrived, all we brought was a birthday gift. Then Catherine claimed that I promised to bring the cake. I was shocked and angry and I accused her of inviting us as an afterthought. She said I should have planned the party, as it was for my son and I said I couldn't compete with her and her mother. Catherine and I have barely spoken since that day. We are equally angry with each other."

In her book, *The Dance of Anger*, author Harriet Lerner points out the confusion surrounding the question of "who is responsible for what." Lerner tells us this family turmoil is a "source of non-productive self-blaming and other blaming." In Henrietta's case, both she and Catherine seem to engage in this destructive behavior. Both women wish the other was different. Although it is never wise to attempt to change someone, some family members, including mothers-in-law and daughters-in-law, make this attempt again and again.

In certain instances, mothers-in-law and daughters-in-law loathe one another and harbor anger with little hope for reconciliation. It appears that there is nothing to assuage their discontent or to compensate for their bad feelings. Locked in long-standing battles of wills, their negative relationships are ongoing, sometimes without recourse or compromise.

BATTLE OF WILLS
* **The mother-in-law has an intense dislike for her daughter-in-law.**
* **The daughter-in-law feels similarly.**
* **Both women are disappointed.**
* **They remain embroiled in negative feelings.**

Martine found herself locked a protracted battle of wills with her mother-in-law. "My husband agrees there cannot be two more opposite people than my mother-in-law, Lily, and myself. That's enough reassurance for me and sometimes keeps me from fighting with her," Martine remarks. "I try not to contest every issue between us, because I don't want to put my husband in the middle of our disputes. On the other hand, there are so many contentious issues that it's inevitable that we fight. I see Lily as a woman who wants to be in charge at every chance and she does hurtful things on purpose. One time, she invited everyone in the extended family as well as close friends to a Sunday afternoon at her house except for me and my husband. She claimed she couldn't reach us and that our answering machine was broken. I happened to run into a family friend who remarked that we were not there. That was how I found out about the get-together.

"My husband tries to pretend none of it matters. Sometimes he'll distance himself, a kind of survival technique. He has hinted that I might want to do the same thing, but I can't look the other way. My mother-in-law will always judge me and always be in my face. I know that when she comes to my house, she watches how I serve food and entertain. Lily knows that I work and yet she will insist on coming on a week night. She will tell my husband that she hopes we are not having take-out again. Then she'll complain that my cooking is mediocre. I can't win."

From Martine's and other daughters-in-law's points of view, their mothers-in-law are intrusive and unwelcome. These daughters-in-law may feel that their mothers-in-law are unable to let go of their sons and to refrain from trying to influence the marriages. The wives are waiting for their husbands to put the marriages first and to put their families of origin, especially their mothers, second. For those mothers-in-law who hope that their sons will continue to put them first, rather than their marriages, such expectations are unhealthy and unrealistic. It would be helpful for these mothers-in-law to recall their own positions as daughters-in-law, when they, too, needed their husbands to place the marriages and themselves as couples ahead of all else.

The son's ability to separate from his mother and achieve maturity is necessary to make his marriage a success. As Stephen A. Shapiro describes in his book, *Manhood: A New Definition*, the plight of man is that when men are divided in their hearts from wives and friends, the family unravels. It is the depersonalization in a man's life that causes such problems. Shapiro also points out that if a man hasn't a healthy attitude and is skeptical and critical of women, then he will withdraw from them. Unless men are reconciled with their own feelings about needing women and their mother/son conflicts are resolved, men will be ambivalent in their relationships with their wives. Many men who have not reached this level of emotional maturity are those husbands who say and do nothing when their mothers and wives are battling each other.

Agnes, a mother-in-law, realizes that she and Elise, her daughter-in-law, are opposites. "I believe my son, John, chose Elise because she was the antithesis of me in every way. My daughter-in-law is tall and large boned, not very bright and not very friendly. Her entire approach to life is so unlike mine that I feel he purposely made his choice based on this. There have been altercations between us from the start. We have never agreed about anything. Now that they have children, it is worse.

"In the beginning, I really made an effort. I overlooked Elise's behavior and I kept hoping she would warm up to our family. After eight years, I know this is not possible. My daughter-in-law has made it quite clear to me that she has no interest in an amicable relationship. There are fights over every holiday and in between there are arguments about ridiculous things. Something as simple as brunch together becomes an issue. I once overheard her on the telephone, when John was at our house and he called her at their home. He had Elise on speakerphone in the den. John suggested that she and the kids drive over for dinner in an hour. Elise began to curse, saying she had no intentions of having dinner with her in-laws and that he had no right to invite her. She said, 'What the hell am I supposed to do with that wretched mother of yours?' That was when I knew there would be little chance of a relationship between my daughter-in-law and myself. At the end of the day, my son will take his wife's side over mine. So while he comes to the house by himself and he calls me from the office, he needs peace at home. He wants his marriage to succeed."

While Agnes's story illustrates a mother-in-law who sees no hope for improvement, Stacey, as a daughter-in-law, is locked in a standoff with her mother-in-law. "My husband's view of his mother, Nettie, is that she will disappear if he ignores her," says Stacey. "She tries to control him and she can't. Gil has a thing about being told what to do and that comes from his upbringing. It was a red hot button because his mother told him to do things all the time. He never did anything she told him to do. She went about raising him the wrong way. I understand the positions of both my mother-in-law and my husband. I can definitely get Gil to do things, but I can't get my mother-in-law to do anything I suggest. Nettie tries to be aggressive with me, but it never works. My mother-in-law and my sister-in-law get into major arguments. I avoid such confrontations, but that doesn't mean I'm not constantly fighting her."

Stacey continues, "When Nettie comes to my house and tells me how to do everything, I ignore her. I nod my head, but I don't mean it. If she says to do something one way, I do it the other way and so would my husband. My mother-in-law and my husband are in a constant battle for power and both of them are bossy. I don't get involved like that. I simply think my mother-in-law is wrong and I don't like how she tells people what to do. What my husband and I share is the idea that somehow, whether we fight or let the issue go, his mother will leave us alone. Although my husband resists her, I see that Gil also has guilt. Nettie raised him like that and it hurts our marriage. On top of my mother-in-law being difficult and not someone I want to spend time with, my husband's unresolved conflicts and unfinished business with his mother are problems in our marriage."

Brenda Szulman would discourage a daughter-in-law who engages in a combative relationship with her mother-in-law. "The daughter-in-law is making an error and is placing herself in a no-win situation. If she tries to change her mother-in-law or if there are arguments, the mother-in-law and her daughter-in-law are off to a poor start. There is no way that a mother-in-law will allow herself to be changed and the daughter-in-law has to face this. What the daughter-in-law is really looking for is acceptance and respect." Above all, the daughter-in-law wants the marital unit and herself to be recognized and treated with the utmost respect.

DESTRUCTIVE BEHAVIORS
* **The daughter-in-law contests her mother-in-law's wishes.**
* **The mother-in-law will not change.**
* **The son retreats from any confrontation between the two women.**

POSITIVE PERSPECTIVE
* **The mother-in-law acknowledges the sovereignty of the marriage.**
* **The husband-son defends his wife when necessary, even if he and his mother are close.**
* **The marriage comes first.**

For a son who has not left home emotionally, but nevertheless is married, his mother's expectations will probably take precedence over those of his wife's. Also, the son may begin to experience feelings of guilt, because he is no longer as available to his mother now that he has a wife. In such situations, the mother-in-law may become resentful of the daughter-in-law's demands of her son. The style the mother-in-law has used to govern her family may be challenged by the arrival of a new daughter-in-law, indicating that the old rules no longer apply. The mother-in-law may become anxious about her status with her son and angry with her daughter-in-law, who she views as an intruder. At the same time, the daughter-in-law is resentful of her mother-in-law's expectations. The daughter-in-law insists that her husband's attention is to be focused on her and on the marriage. Both women believe they are being cheated out of the appropriate amount of time and attention from the son-husband. If the two women never liked each other or didn't connect in some way to begin with, the trouble escalates and a dangerous triangle, consisting of mother-in-law/daughter-in-law/son-husband, is formed.

TRIANGLES EVERYWHERE
* **The mother-in-law cannot accept her son's new obligations to his wife.**
* **The daughter-in-law will not tolerate any interference from the mother-in-law.**
* **The son is caught between them.**

Moira's husband is entangled in his wife's and mother's battles. Moira, who at thirty-nine has been married for fourteen years, has never gotten along with her mother-in-law. "We always hated each other. We are polite in each other's company, but it is a hopeless relationship. I see my mother-in-law as a very selfish woman who wants to wreak havoc. When I was pregnant with my second child and bedridden, Vivian rarely visited or helped with my older child. One day, my mother was unavailable so Vivian picked up my older child. They were late returning and naturally I became frantic. When they arrived they were eating frozen yogurt. My mother-in-law said nothing about being late, she just apologized for not bringing any frozen yogurt for me. I could have cared less about getting frozen yogurt. I wanted my child brought home at the agreed upon time, or she could have at least called to say they were running late. I saw her behavior as an effort to undermine me as a mother.

"In every instance, my husband acknowledges that I have a terrific family and that he doesn't. He accepts who his parents are more readily than I do. I can't excuse people when they behave as my mother-in-law does. My children are her only grandchildren and she doesn't even celebrate the holidays with them. I keep remembering that my husband said he had an unhappy childhood. He is devoted to our children, which, I believe, is a reaction to having had a mother who was never around for him."

Difficult mother-in-law/daughter-in-law relationships are found at all levels of society, from the most disadvantaged to the most prestigious levels. Over the years, we have been witnesses as Queen Elizabeth II wrangled with her former daughters-in-law, the late Princess Diana and Sarah Ferguson, before both women were divorced from Prince Charles and Prince Andrew respectively. Although the Queen found Sarah Ferguson, "Fergie," to be "headstrong and giddy" at first and hoped time would serve to calm her down, Elizabeth II had her doubts about the vivacious redhead from the start. The queen's message to her daughter-in-law, when Sarah requested a divorce, was that Fergie should not have married her son unless she intended to stand by him. In this way, she let Sarah Ferguson know that she did not consider her worthy of the House of Windsor.

After Sarah Ferguson's divorce from Prince Andrew, Queen Elizabeth was fearful that Princess Diana would follow suit and end her unhappy marriage. Diana did indeed follow Fergie's footsteps and in 1996 she, too, became divorced from her husband. Diana's tragic death in 1997 left the world wondering whether she would be alive today if she had only remained married to Charles and a part of the Royal Family. With Princess Diana, who possessed her own element of power as the mother of the future king, Prince William, Queen Elizabeth, in her role as mother-in-law, needed to be flexible from the start. The queen's goal was always to portray the royal family as the embodiment of stability. Once the Queen's confidence level in the marriage of Charles and Diana waned, her concern was to placate Diana and prevent a public relations nightmare and scandal for the royals. It was this intriguing position that allowed Diana to leverage her divorce.

Whether a mother-in-law and her daughter-in-law are royalty or not, the intention of the mother-in-law should be to ensure her son's happiness. The essential question she might ask about her daughter-in-law is: Is this woman enhancing my son's life? In a healthy situation, the mother-in-law views her role as the only woman in her son's life as ending and the daughter-in-law's role as the new woman in his life as just beginning. Negative situations develop, however, when the mother-in-law does not let go of her son emotionally. Problems occur if she worries more about competing with her daughter-in-law for her son's affections than whether or not her son's marriage is a successful and happy one. A daughter-in-law needs to be secure enough in her role as wife/daughter-in-law to take the initiative in moving the relationship between her mother-in-law and herself to a better place. Both women, in a best case scenario, need to make the mature decision that the marriage has merit and value in spite of the fact that the two women are not naturally compatible.

Unfortunately, Jane has not been able to implement such advice and considers herself and her daughter-in-law in a "cold war." "I have chosen to distance myself from my daughter-in-law," says Jane. "We are not from the same social class and our values are not the same. My daughter-in-law, Lara, is spoiled and educated, while I am working class. My son's achievement, that of becoming a surgeon, is a tremendous accomplishment to me, but seems to mean nothing to my daughter-in-law. I see how she removes herself from my company and my son has done it to a degree, too. But there are children and an ex-wife in the picture from Tim's first marriage and it gets complicated. Lara is the opposite of my first daughter-in-law. On top of everything else, I find that I am constantly comparing the two women.

"If I really believed that my son was happy in this marriage, I would think more highly of my daughter-in-law. But I see how hard she pushes him and how he has to live in a certain way to please her. I think she pressures him terribly. Lara rarely invites us to visit. Tim is always asking her if they can stop by my house, and she refuses. She doesn't want anything to do with me. Lara keeps her distance from me as a way of feuding. It is an ongoing cold war."

The "cold war" that Jane describes is, unfortunately, not an unusual situation between a mother-in-law and daughter-in-law and can easily be instigated by one or the other of the women. All too often, the woman who perpetuates it causes great damage. The son-husband is forced to choose between two women who are battling it out. Whatever the causes, pain is inflicted on both sides and the marriage suffers. The negative energy and ill-will generated by this has long-lasting, unhappy repercussions.

COLD WAR TACTICS

DAUGHTER-IN-LAW AS PERPETRATOR
* **The daughter-in-law decides she dislikes her mother-in-law and wants nothing to do with her.**
* **She becomes manipulative, holding herself apart from her mother-in-law.**

* **In this passive resistance stance, she forces her husband to choose between his wife and his mother.**

MOTHER-IN-LAW AS PERPETRATOR
* **The mother-in-law distances herself from the marriage, because she dislikes her daughter-in-law.**
* **The son-husband is distressed, but his mother refuses to be cooperative.**
* **The son-husband feels disloyal to both women.**

"My mother-in-law, Helen, is the most difficult woman on earth," begins Susan, ten years into her marriage. "In the beginning of my relationship with my husband, I was very young and I tried to be accepting of her. I expected her to be my friend, but I should have known better, because as soon as I became engaged to her son, she was manipulative and not nice. When Roy asked me to get married, the only thing that she said to him was that she hoped I didn't expect a ring. Then she suggested to her husband that he buy Roy a new set of golf clubs. Since we all live in the same town this treatment is ongoing. Roy has learned how to avoid his mother's manipulations and knows her moves by heart. He doesn't seem to be bothered by them, because he is immune by now. Paul, his brother, who lives nearby, has also finessed these skills. But his brother's wife, my sister-in-law, Taylor, has terrible problems with Helen. Helen treats Taylor as she treats me, but I've been married longer so I'm somewhat accustomed to it. I don't feel any differently about my mother-in-law than I did when I first became engaged, I just know what to expect.

"Taylor and I talk about Helen because Taylor is consumed by their bad relationship. There are no daughters in my husband's family, which my mother-in-law bemoans constantly. She always tells her 'cute story' of how when her third healthy son was born, she wept because he wasn't a girl. When she describes me as a daughter to her, I don't buy it for a second. No one would treat her daughter as she treats me. She mouths this sentiment all the time, but she argues with me constantly and calls Roy to tell him what I have done wrong. The only real solution is to keep my distance, which isn't easy when we all live in such close proximity."

In her book, *The Dance of Anger*, Harriet Lerner discusses how adult children decide to be distant emotionally and/or geographically from their parents to avoid their anger or frustration. Lerner discourages emotional distancing from ones family of origin, because it keeps one from resolving past issues and entering into any new relationship in a healthy way. Once a daughter-in-law becomes a part of her husband's family, she may inherit her husband's history with his mother. The mother-in-law might shift her focus so that whatever transpired between her and her son, she now assigns to her daughter-in-law. In addition to causing confusion for the daughter-in-law, who is caught unaware, the issues do not disappear, but remain unresolved.

Dr. Ronnie Burak reminds us that a daughter-in-law who is secure in her relationship with her own family may not be as emotionally invested in her husband's family, whatever kind of mother-in-law she has. "For the daughter-in-law who expects something from her mother-in-law or who is very insecure, disappointment may be overwhelming if the relationship isn't working out." This works the other way as well. If a mother-in-law is not secure or happy, she could look to her daughter-in-law to enrich her life. The daughter-in-law might not be interested, and whatever her husband's family patterns are, she will be reluctant to participate. Not every daughter-in-law wants to marry the entire family and not every mother-in-law is looking for a daughter. When the two women cannot share a mutual respect and flexibility, contention occurs.

"My daughter-in-law, Willa, has always disliked me," admits Sophia. "Even after fourteen years, her feelings have never changed. We see each other every six months and during those visits, I get to talk with her children, my grandchildren, for ten minutes before she whisks them away. I think her children are too thin and I have said so to my son. This caused a big stir.

"When I am invited to their home, which is once a year, Willa expects me to help in the kitchen. I do not appreciate it, but I do it. I always try to compliment her and say she looks well. The truth is that she is quite unwilling to make it easy for my son, Ben. If I suggest anything to Ben, she tells him I am too dominating. She says that I am interfering and deliberately excludes me from family events to get back at me. Willa is determined to make me aware that my opinions do not count and she has been that way since the first day of her marriage to Ben. Had he known she would be like this, I wonder if he still would have married her. He knows exactly how I feel because I have been openly critical when necessary. I am sure this infuriates her, but I don't always approve of her behavior."

While Sophia cannot see why her critical attitude offends her daughter-in-law, Allie explains how she suffers with a tyrannical mother-in-law. "Nothing has improved in fifteen years. If my husband did not have this contorted relationship with his mother, Carol, he wouldn't survive. But for me, it's not like that because I am not guilt ridden as he and his sister are. They take pity on their mother since she has had a difficult life, although she has never been a martyr for her children. Guilt, however, they have bought into one hundred percent. I think it's even worse than that, actually; I think they are also fearful of her. I resent how authoritative my mother-in-law is. I resent that she comes between me and my husband, which poisons the marriage. How can I get along with Carol when she is obtrusive and unkind at the same time?"

Allie shakes her head sadly. "When each of my children was born, my mother-in-law somehow became involved with what we planned to name the baby. She had such a fit over my first child's name that my husband agreed to change her name despite the fact that we had chosen this name together before her birth. My mother-in-law put a rift between my husband and me at one of the happiest moments in the marriage. After that, at our daughter's christening, she came with a stranger, a man she had dated briefly, without telling anyone she was bringing a guest. Then she fought with him, making a scene, so that people noticed. Again, it was a great day of happiness in our lives and Carol had to spoil it. That is one of the reasons that I simply cannot have any good feelings about her."

Antoinette Michaels, relationship counselor, has been helping a mother-in-law who is coping with her daughter-in-law's wrath. "What happened was that the mother-in-law was oblivious to her daughter-in-law's anger," explains Michaels. "The daughter-in-law announced that they could not work out their differences because she saw her mother-in-law as passive aggressive and negative. Through therapy it became apparent that both the mother-in-law and daughter-in-law were actually quite similar and had blind spots when it came to seeing their situation clearly. Both women are controlling, but in this case, the mother-in-law genuinely wants to make amends. Her concern is for the greater good, that of the family."

Sometimes, as in Peg's case, it takes a while to reach the point of conciliation. "I keep waiting," sighs Peg, "for my daughter-in-law, Fran, to be someone who I can respect. I keep waiting for her to do the right thing. Fran, it seems, keeps waiting for me to disappear. As the years pass, I say to myself that I have to try harder and I have to stop making suggestions, but then I think that she also has to try harder and she has to be more responsive to my needs. Fran simply breezes in and out of my life. There are times when she will call and take me to lunch, but it is awkward and I can only imagine what she tells her friends later. I know what I confide to my friends: Fran is a superficial, unfocused girl who wanted my son because he is so solid and such a fine person.

"One day I told her that she was thirty years old and that she ought to know better than to act as she does. That was when my son called me from his office and told me to stop making life so difficult. Then, a week later, we all had to go to my other son's house together for Palm Sunday. My husband tried very hard to be charming, but I was seething. I am still waiting for the relationship to become better, because I know that she and I both dread occasions when we have to be together."

Peg frowns. "Fran and my son have just announced that she is pregnant, which worries me. I am afraid she will not let me see the baby or have any input with this child. This is a terrible position to be in, especially since my time is flexible and I will be available to help her out with the baby. If we both have such trepidation, isn't there some way to fix it? I admit I am changing and I want to end this war we're in. I am looking for some solution."

The approaching birth of a grandchild seems to have inspired Peg to work more diligently to repair the situation with her daughter-in-law. Thomas Moore, in his book, *Soul Mates*, writes of the culture of a family as not only influential in how we live our lives, but as a place of direction, meaning and style. "Our families," Moore observes, "even though they rarely seem to be perfect models for us, offer plenty of raw material that we can shape into a life in our own creative fashion. When we become parents and create our own families, we may want to be conscious of the importance of family traditions and other aspects of our family heritage."

Despite their best intentions to create a loving, healthy family, when misunderstandings begin to grow between a mother-in-law and her daughter-in-law, they frequently experience common reactions. The mother-in-law feels that she has been ignored by her daughter-in-law and the daughter-in-law feels that her mother-in-law is trying to manipulate her. The two women relentlessly blame each other for the bad feelings between them. Over time, it seems that neither the mother-in-law nor the daughter-in-law is confronting her own issues that have contributed to the stress of the relationship. The downward spiral of a failed mother-in-law/daughter-in-law affiliation can contribute to a poor marriage. If there is hatred between the two women, this takes its toll on the marriage. What can help, Brenda Szulman advises, is a meddling mother-in-law who stops meddling or a daughter-in-law who gives up on her unfulfilled expectations of her mother-in-law. A husband who communicates effectively with his mother and wife, in an attempt to show each woman the other's attributes, is making a positive effort.

SORTING IT OUT
* **Mothers-in-law should stop meddling.**
* **Daughters-in-law should give up their hope of a perfect mother-in-law.**
* **Husbands-sons should intervene on both women's behalf.**

There are many reasons why a marriage ends in divorce. Sometimes this happens when the daughter-in-law/wife cannot handle the attitudes and actions of her husband's family and receives no emotional support from her husband. According to Brondi Borer, divorce mediator, in-laws are a definite factor in divorce. "When people file a complaint, one of the things they often cite as a problem about is the way that a spouse treated their family or how they were treated by the spouse's family. What we have to remember is that when things fall apart in a marriage, a fairly common refrain is unhappiness with in-laws. If there has been some kind of friction and a marriage breaks up, there is no doubt that those chronic problems between in-laws and spouses added a layer of strife to an already fragile relationship." If daughters-in-law and mothers-in-law could learn to cope better with each other, this extra strain on the marriage could be avoided.

LAST RESORT/DIVORCE
* **If a marriage is already fragile, the added stress of animosity between the mother-in-law and daughter-in-law may cause its failure.**
* **In extreme cases, mother-in-law/daughter-in-law feuds may be responsible for the marriage ending in divorce.**

From personal experience, Rayanne understands the danger of extra stress on the marriage caused by dissension between a daughter-in-law and her mother-in-law. "The one person I did not miss for a minute when I got divorced was my first mother-in-law, Stella," says Rayanne. "She and I were oil and water and she really did make things impossible for me. I would be reduced to tears and my husband would alternate between defending me and berating me for upsetting his mother. For years, she would make comments about how we had no children. Then, when we had two children, she made comments about how spoiled and uninteresting they were compared to her other grandchildren, so I kept my distance. Then she complained that I avoided her as much as possible. Well, why would I want to be around someone so meanspirited and manipulative? My father told me she had to do something right to have produced such a lovely son. But I saw her as nasty, vitriolic and undermining. I couldn't see anything positive in her.

"Stella talked about money constantly. She was always telling us how her friend's children lived and comparing them to us. She would try to make me feel small and insignificant. Whatever I did at work, she always knew someone who was much more accomplished. Although my marriage was unhappy even without my mother-in-law's influence, she did not help. My husband's strange behavior toward her baffled me at first and angered me later. He would ask me to invite his parents over and then he would schedule a racquetball game. I was left to entertain them and I realized he just didn't want to deal with them. Who could blame him? I was the one, however, that Stella really laid into. My last time spent with her was when I cooked a meal and invited some relatives over. Stella spent the entire night telling my sister how mediocre everything was. I look back and wish I could have separated myself from it all and risen above it instead of defending myself so fiercely."

Unlike Rayanne's experience, Hallie's mother-in-law, who seemed not to be supportive for years, came to her defense when she separated from her husband. "I never trusted my mother-in-law, Mildred. In our culture, there is a real need for an extended family and I wanted her to help me with the kids. I had four children by the time I was twenty-three. My mother worked and so I thought my mother-in-law would help and she did, but only once in a while. Still, any amount of help was appreciated and needed. Then Mildred decided that she also needed to work and she found a job. I couldn't depend upon her anymore to help with my children when I was at my job. Since Mildred had always been standoffish with me, when she canceled our babysitting arrangement, I was very angry.

"My husband and I fought from the start. I think it was partly because we had all these little children and we were not much more than children ourselves. Eight years later, I look back on it and I realize our marriage didn't have much of a chance. There was too much pressure on us. Then my mother became ill and had to not only give up her job, but couldn't take care of the kids at all. My mother-in-law would help sporadically then, but I still couldn't count on her.

"Mildred always came up in the conversation when my husband and I argued. I accused her of being lazy and not helping enough and my husband would say she didn't approve of me and that I was too demanding of her. He defended her, because they were close. Finally, I told him I wanted a divorce. I had all these youngsters and a husband who was away from home a lot, a sick mother and sisters who had their own troubles. Eventually, when I found a better job and the two older kids were in school all day, I separated from my husband. When he left our home and went to his mother, she called me. She told me she turned him down. She said she didn't want to help him or let him live with her after the way he'd treated me all these years. That was when I became sorry I'd never tried harder to have a relationship with her. I decided that even if I wasn't married to her son anymore, I would keep up with her, for the children's sake."

What often happens as daughters-in-law mature is that they recognize that they have little choice but to get along with their mothers-in-law. The reality is that the two women have to share in the lives of the children and must participate in family events, whether they like one another or not. If a daughter-in-law or a mother-in-law refuses to accept such conditions, the distance between them grows larger and larger. "Unless the two women work to make it better," comments psychologist Dr. Michele Kasson, "they are holding onto a fantasy. The mother-in-law holds onto the relationship with her son that she had before the daughter-in-law entered the picture and the daughter-in-law nurtures the fantasy that her husband will be less attached to his mother now that he is married."

IRREFUTABLE CONNECTION
* The fantasy mother-in-law does not exist.
* The fantasy daughter-in-law does not exist.
* The two women will share a connection for many years.

Edna has reached the point where she realizes that she must cope with the daughter-in-law she has, not an idealized figure. "Christine, my daughter-in-law, is a major disappointment to me," Edna says, shaking her head sadly. "When my son first brought her home to meet us, I thought everything would be fine. She was the same religion and background as we were and we sighed with relief. That is why it is so incredible to me that she is not a worthy wife. Christine is a poor wife and yet my son is very tied to her all the same. She is harsh and unfair to him.

She is demanding and critical. When I compare her to who I thought she was, my image of her, I want to weep. I don't contest anything, because I don't want to make things hard for my son.

"There have been many stresses and strains in the marriage, in all fairness. Christine wanted to be pregnant and is not. She is not doing as well as she expected with her career and my son works long hours, so she is lonely. I see all this and I tell myself that it would be best if I could make some kind of gesture toward her. The problem is that I do not see her as supportive of my son and that is my main worry. Whether she is kind to me or not is of little importance, but if she is not kind to my son, that is a big problem for me. I think about her often and I almost wish they lived far away so that it wasn't so obvious to me what goes on. Lately, I have wanted to talk with her, to patch things up between us. I would do this for my sons' sake, because, after all, it appears that we will remain connected for many years to come."

In Edna's story, we see how she has evolved over time in her attitude toward her daughter-in-law. Although she is not enamored of Christine, she recognizes the value in forging some kind of bond. Tanya, a daughter-in-law of six years, also seeks a truce in her relationship with her mother-in-law.

"On every count, my husband has stood beside me, one hundred percent," Tanya tells us, "and that has helped me to finally accept where my mother-in-law, Nina, is coming from. Several years ago, when I first met her, I kept expecting something more from her and when it wasn't forthcoming, there would be all this tension. I saw her as a selfish woman, one who had little to offer and who kept herself much too insular. Today, I realize that Nina has difficulty coping with everyday life. This explains her moods and the way she has behaved in the past. Initially, I believed she should be reaching out to people and doing charity work, such as reading to the blind or some other community service since she has so much time on her hands. Over time, I have learned that it isn't going to happen like that, she just isn't the type.

"I have come to the conclusion that just because I wanted Nina to do something positive with her life and to be stronger and more giving doesn't mean she will. She isn't a bad person, because she won't do it my way. I am acutely aware that my mother-in-law viewed me as too aggressive and too outspoken when we first met. It has taken her a while to understand and accept that this is how I am. I also have no further expectations of her and I won't let anything she does or doesn't do annoy me anymore. I've stopped pressuring her to relate to me as I want her to and I've come to the conclusion that we can work through this together. We are both getting to a place where we are able to yield to the other. I am proud of our growth. I think we will both benefit in the long run."

Of the mothers-in-law interviewed, over sixty percent reported serious difficulties with their daughters-in-law, although half of that number desire better dynamics and hope to improve their relationships.

Unfortunately, almost eighty percent of the daughters-in-law interviewed see no hope for progress in their connections with their mothers-in-law. The remainder expressed their desires to mend the breaches between themselves and their mothers-in-law.

"It is only when a mother-in-law or daughter-in-law feels threatened by their differences that the altercations begin," Antoinette Michaels reflects. "If the two women want to grow psychologically and spiritually, they must stop insisting the other one is wrong."

There are, however, practical solutions for those mothers-in-law and daughters-in-law who remain antagonistic toward each other. A daughter-in-law who sees that her husband is close to his mother has to concede and put more effort into her relationship with her mother-in-law. A daughter-in-law who has a mother-in-law who is not overly involved with her son can follow his lead and keep a friendly distance. The motivation, either way, is to avoid conflict with one's mother-in-law. A mother-in-law who has a high regard for her son and his marriage, even though her daughter-in-law might not be her dream daughter-in-law, will not make herself the cause of conflict in the relationship. Rather, she must determine how much effort on her part is required to be a positive influence on the marriage. Over the entire lifetime of the marriage, this can be as little or as much as seems necessary to keep the peace.

TRUCE
* If her husband is close to his mother, a wife needs to try harder to maintain good relations with her.
* If her husband is not close to his mother, a wife only has to meet his level of involvement with her mother-in-law.
* A mother-in-law has to give up her idealized vision of a daughter-in-law.
* A mother-in-law should be guided by her son and daughter-in-law's wishes as to how much of her presence is wanted in the marriage.

A daughter-in-law and mother-in-law who know they do not have to love one another are at a great advantage. What is essential is that both women love the husband-son. Out of this love comes the ability to respect each other's differences.

7

Shifting Patterns: Grandchildren, Careers, Mothering

"Recently, my son and daughter-in-law had a baby and I kept hoping that my relationship with my daughter-in-law would improve as a result," says Marguerite. "I offered to stay with the baby on a weekly basis. She said no in the beginning, but now she has asked me to come on Monday afternoons so that she can get out and do some errands. I am flattered that she's asked and of course I do it. I love to be with my granddaughter who is only three months old. But I am always in fear that my daughter-in-law will ask her grandmother or her mother or her sister to help instead of me.

"We had one unhappy incident in the beginning. It was the first day I stayed with the baby. My daughter-in-law came home as I was playing with my granddaughter. She flew to the telephone and called my son at work to complain that I was taking away her child. Then he asked to speak to me and he asked me what I was doing to his wife. I was very upset, but I tried to think about the future, about the baby who will grow up to be a beautiful girl, my granddaughter."

Once a child is born, the mother-in-law/daughter-in-law relationship may be ameliorated or it may disintegrate further. If the mother-in-law offers to watch the baby, the daughter-in-law may be grateful or she may resent the mother-in-law's intrusion and want only her own mother to be involved with the child. Usually, however, when children become the focus, the hostility between the mother-in-law and daughter-in-law will lessen.

As our society evolves, opportunities for women change. Motherhood is no longer held up as the only role for adult women, nor is it viewed as a vocation. Some women today not only wait to have babies and establish themselves in the workplace first, but they frequently choose not to depend upon family or extended family to watch their children while they remain in the work force. For the mother-in-law who is traditional in her outlook, this may be a confusing time. She wonders if her daughter-in-law will ask her to help with the baby or if she will be passed over, replaced by day care or her daughter-in-law's mother or her other family members. As society changes, mothers-in-law and daughters-in-law do not necessarily respond in the same ways as they have in the past.

Husbands are also changing. As described in Gail Sheehy's book, *Understanding Men's Passages: Discovering the New Map of Men's Lives*, the "post-patriarchal man" performs some of the responsibilities of a mother or grandmother for his child. In doing so, he is also altering the historical expectations of middle class family life. Although these modern men work and have careers, they are willing to care for their children and they may have flexible schedules that allow their wives more autonomy.

This undoubtedly causes some mothers-in-law concern as they worry if their sons, while making themselves available, really are capable of caring for their children. The focus may then shift from doubts about the sons as caregivers to dissatisfaction with their daughters-in-law to apprehension for the well-being of their grandchildren.

Alice S. Rossi notes in her essay "The Bio-social Side of Parenthood" that new mothers today are more insular than in the past, because the extended family frequently is not geographically close and/or has less influence. This observation works both ways since the new mother has more choice than before in the form of friends she can depend upon, playgroups and preschool. What is striking is how often the young mothers whom I interviewed sought baby-sitters and outside sources rather than utilizing the help of their mothers-in-law. What we have to remember is how much the mother-in-law has also revolutionized her life and discarded the traditional role of grandmother. Longer, healthier lives and more disposable income allow her to work, travel or engage in hobbies and activities that leave little time to take responsibility for her grandchild. She may also avoid this responsibility due to strong memories of what it was like to be alone with small children all day.

Nancy Chodorow asserts in her essay entitled "Family Structure and Feminine Personality," that the middle-class mother's daily life is isolated and "she is likely to invest a lot of anxious energy and guilt in her concern for her children and to look to them for her own self-affirmation." By the time a daughter-in-law asks her mother-in-law to help care for her children, it may only be because she is feeling desperate.

Fanny, one daughter-in-law with whom I spoke, regrets that her mother-in-law does not want the responsibility of helping to care for Fanny's and her husband's children. "Whenever we visit my mother-in-law, Etta, she says things to the kids like, 'Don't make noise, don't ruin this meal.' She gets on my nerves, because she is so disinterested in who they are and she only worries about her furniture and tablecloth. I should have known from the beginning that our relationship would be a one way street and that my husband and I would be catering to my in-laws after we had children. Why should it be any different just because my children were born? Why did I imagine my mother-in-law would be generous with them and make time for them?"

"While I think the relationship between Etta and me is okay because we don't argue," Fanny continues, "I also resent that my mother-in-law is relieved that her obligations as a mother are completed. This extends to grandparenting. She feels she has raised her kids and it's over for her now. At the same time my mother-in-law is judgmental, so she has this detachment combined with criticism. My husband feels very obligated to his mother. I dread the day when she needs money and it goes to her instead of paying for quality childcare while I am at work. I suppose that is one of my fears."

"When a daughter-in-law asks her mother-in-law to baby-sit," psychotherapist Brenda Szulman advises, "it can make the relationship more difficult. Of course, some mothers-in-law will be delighted. But others may resist because they don't want the obligation or they may accept, because they don't know how to say no and then are miserable in their newly appointed role. This causes more tension between mothers-in-law and daughters-in-law."

MISCOMMUNICATION
* **The daughter-in-law expects her mother-in-law to baby-sit.**
* **The mother-in-law agrees grudgingly.**
* **Both women have false expectations of the other.**

With the addition of children to the family, there are other problems besides whether a mother-in-law wants baby-sitting duty, as Yolanda explains. "I do not bother to call my son and daughter-in-law at home anymore," Yolanda remarks. "If I have something to say I will call my son at work and tell him what I am feeling. I hope he will iron the problems out without getting me involved. Mostly, my problems have to do with the kids. I can't understand why he won't come and bring the kids to see me a little more often without his wife.

"At Easter time, I bought my grandchildren special clothes and Evelyn, my daughter-in-law, said she didn't want them and that they didn't fit. She has returned every gift I have ever given the children with one exception, the gold crosses I bought them. I find her behavior very harmful and what's worse is my son is weak and won't stand up to her. I admit that my daughter-in-law keeps a nice clean house and is a good mother to those kids. She doesn't work anymore and takes great care of them. They have just built a house and my son needs to do well. In all fairness, my daughter-in-law is the type of person who will easily return to work if it is necessary. Whatever is required in the marriage she will do. I only wish she would share my son and my grandchildren with me. I am ready to baby-sit whenever she asks."

The arrival of children not only alters the marriage, but the mother-in-law's expectations of her daughter-in-law may increase. For the daughter-in-law, her husband's parents who previously had no particular rights, are now directly related because of the child. "There is a deeper connection for the mother-in-law once the grandchildren arrive," Dr. Ronnie Burak remarks. "There is a blood link through this child who is biologically related to her. For the grandparents, it is like having another child, their child's child. It now becomes a more intimate relationship between the mother-in-law and daughter-in-law." While some may resist this new bond, almost always the expectation of the mother-in-law is that she gets to see and interact with her grandchildren.

Grace has been disappointed to differing degrees by all three of her daughters-in-law. She is estranged from her second daughter-in-law, Kelly, the mother of Grace's grandchildren. "I love my grandchildren, but I rarely see them. My daughter-in-law has been deliberately keeping them away from me for years. It has been a long, unsettling process with Kelly. From the time she would not speak to me at her wedding to my son, until she had these children, I have been miserable.

"My grandchildren do not really know me. I have made many attempts to see them, to take them places. I feel I am being cut off from my own flesh and blood. My son has done little to work our problem out, to help me with my grandchildren. But no matter what, I can't give up hope. I continue to call and try to make plans. I invite them over and she refuses. I call every Sunday and they are quite unfriendly to me. It has been a year since I have seen my son, his wife or their children."

Linda, by contrast, is a mother-in-law who has not had the difficulties Grace has endured. However, she believes that she has a relationship with her daughter-in-law, Betsy, only because of her grandchildren. "I would not seek out my daughter-in-law except for my grandchildren," explains Linda. "Our mutual adoration of these children, two girls and one boy, helps us. I make myself as available as much as I can, for myself and for the children. So while I'm baby-sitting for my daughter-in-law, it's really for me.

"I look the other way when it comes to Betsy's parenting, her materialism and how she treats my son. I ignore the big issues I have with her for my grandchildren's sake. I do not allow myself to think about Betsy. Rather, I look at the children, who are truly lovely children and I know that they are worth everything. One of my best friends is now watching her son go through a terrible divorce. The children are in the middle of the mess and I remind myself that this is not what I would want for my son and for his family. That is why I try to be so accommodating."

Although in previous chapters I have discussed divorce and the consequences for grandparents, it is notable that some mothers-in-law become quite focused on the matter once they have grandchildren. They may look with trepidation upon daughters-in-law they have never liked, because the power has shifted in the daughters-in-law's favors through the birth of their children. Grandparents fear losing their relationships with their grandchildren. As divorce mediator Brondi Borer points out, often a grandparent who has been involved with her grandchild before the divorce will lack accessibility to her grandchild during and after the divorce. "A grandmother will be separated from her grandchild although her input might have been invaluable," notes Borer. "If the grandmother has been a parental figure in the grandchild's life, the courts do not always recognize this. A biological or legal parent will trump a grandparent's rights."

"I was like a mother to my grandson," Hilda says, "and my daughter-in-law, Janine, counted on me. She would say she couldn't do it without me. Janine and my son were so young when they married. They really needed me for their baby—they couldn't take care of him on their own. While they were at work, I watched Andy all day long. Then my son and his wife began to fight. They stopped getting along after four years of marriage. By then, Andy had been with me everyday since he was three months old. I was more of a mother to him than Janine ever was.

"The courts didn't see it this way. We went to family court, because neither of us could afford a private attorney. It was decided that Andy belonged with his mother and his father could have visitation. My role was finished, just like that. I can't even telephone Janine and speak to Andy. All of my love and hard work devoted to that child and now I never see him."

To prevent such a loss on the part of grandparents, Amy Reisen, divorce attorney, suggests that the father of the child allot some of his custody time to his parents. "Since there are so many divisions in a divorce, we have to look at what can be done for the children. One thing which works is when the husband, during his time with the children, takes them to his parents to visit. This way the continuity between grandparent and child is not broken. The good news is the pressure is lessened between the two women, the former mother-in-law and former daughter-in-law, because they are not forced to interact with each other. Now it is about the kids still seeing their grandparents."

VISITATION
* **The divorced son takes his children to see his parents.**
* **The mother-in-law and daughter-in-law need not interact.**
* **The children benefit from their grandparents' input.**

Sometimes, mothers of sons, like Olga, can see trouble ahead, but are unable to affect the outcome. "My son had many problems even before he married Lori," Olga says sadly. "I tried to warn her so she knew what she was getting into. Today, they are divorced and she has remarried, but I still have contact with my grandson. Lori has been very generous to me in that respect. It took me years to accept who my daughter-in-law is and, more importantly, who my son is. My son is someone who has geared his entire adult life in such a way that he doesn't have to deal with any pressure. He lives with a woman now, but will not remarry. She is not demanding or threatening on any level, but I have no contact with her, because there are no children."

"I have remained in touch with my first daughter-in-law, Lori, because of my grandson who is now seven. I give her credit for how well she has raised him. I believe that she never fit into our family, because, frankly, my son doesn't fit in either. Until she had a child, my entire reaction to her was that she was chosen by my son as a slap in the face to me. I acknowledge, finally, that it wasn't her fault. It is my son who is so difficult. I secretly sided with her during their divorce."

Olga's case notwithstanding, the mother-in-law who sides with her daughter-in-law in the face of divorce is rare. Usually the grandparents are too concerned with their rights as grandparents once the divorce ensues to think about much else.

"A mother-in-law," Amy Reisen notes, in response to Olga's situation, "has to respect her son's wishes in a divorce although she knows sometimes that her son is not right. Usually, regardless of what the son has done, his mother defends him and waits out the custody schedule, hoping she'll see her grandchildren often. There is the unusual divorce case where I see a mother-in-law who supports her daughter-in-law. This woman appreciates how her daughter-in-law has cared for the grandchild. Her feelings for her daughter-in-law are not tainted by the breakup of the marriage."

Even in families that are not fractured by divorce, issues often arise between the parents and the grandparents of the children. A common occurrence is when a competition arises between the mother-in-law and her daughter-in-law's mother over a grandchild. The mother-in-law's point of view is that her daughter-in-law is ungrateful whenever she offers to baby-sit and her offer is not accepted. The mother-in-law may also feel she is being excluded in favor of her daughter-in-law's mother who is equally willing to take care of the child or children. In some cases, from the daughter-in-law's point of view, her mother-in-law's gestures are intrusive since the daughter-in-law wants only for her own mother to be involved with the baby. When this happens and the daughter-in-law overtly prefers the children to be with her mother instead of her mother-in-law, hurt feelings and negative repercussions in the mother-in-law/daughter-in-law relationship are bound to ensue.

WINNERS AND LOSERS
* The daughter-in-law chooses her mother to be the primary grandmother.
* Her mother-in-law is insulted and disappointed.
* A rivalry over the grandchildren may ensue.

A side effect of such preferential treatment is the rivalry that may spring up between the two grandmothers. Betty, a mother-in-law of nine years, holds both her son and his wife responsible for how distant her connection is to her two grandsons. "I blame my son as much as his wife, Johanna, for the restricted time I have with my grandchildren. I look at my son and I remember how close he was to me as a youngster.

It's amazing how that has changed. The boy I was once so mad about is a man who does not impress me. I know I have to let go and I've given up long ago. He can't be who I want him to be anymore. As far as my daughter-in-law goes, one day her sons will be married and have children. Then she will regret what she has done to me, how alienating she has been. Not for one moment do I think she's done the right thing. Her mother is the one who sees the boys, not me. One would think there would be room in the picture for both grandmothers.

"When I consider what has happened over the past seven years, since my first grandson was born, I see that my respect for my son has dwindled as a result of his marriage and lessened further once he had children. I know what a richness it would have been to have had a daughter-in-law I could relate to, someone who would allow me a real relationship with the boys. It seems I have to fight for their attention. I'm a good grandmother and I have always been available to them."

Roxanne's history with her mother-in-law, Eileen, is the opposite of Betty's with her daughter-in-law. Roxanne would welcome any energy her mother-in-law would give toward her children and regrets that Eileen is not ready or willing to help with the children. "How I wish my mother-in-law would spend time with my three children," says Roxanne. "While my parents have little money, but are willing to spend it on the children, to say nothing of giving their time, my mother-in-law is wealthy, yet unwilling and ungiving. She is completely self-centered, both time-wise and in terms of material things. She knows I need some help and that I still work part time. She disregards my predicament completely. Instead, she gives advice about everything, none of it solicited. Her advice is worthless to me, when what I really need is an extra set of hands, something she would never provide.

"After our third child was born, I had the flu. The other kids were so small they were both in diapers. I called to ask my mother-in-law to come and help since my mother also had the flu. My mother-in-law suggested I call an agency and hire someone, because she was too busy. I called my husband at work and told him to come home immediately and that if he didn't, I'd leave him. He knew his mother had refused to help me and I was at my breaking point. I don't usually do things like that, but I was sick and furious."

When a daughter-in-law has a poor relationship with her mother-in-law, like Roxanne, she might not be able to ask for her help or she may be refused help with the children. Instead, she must depend on her own resources. According to Brenda Szulman, many times grandchildren are used in these instances to fuel the rage between mother-in-law and daughter-in-law. Whatever occurred to inflame relations between the two women before the children were born is now extended to the children and how they are being raised. As the children grow older, a mother-in-law who is critical of her daughter-in-law may watch closely and be overtly judgmental. The daughter-in-law feels violated. "The boundaries blur," remarks Szulman, "when a mother-in-law tries to mold her grandchild in a way she could not do with her own child. As a result, the relationship with her daughter-in-law may become untenable."

Heather finds herself in such a situation. "My mother-in-law, Raquel, told me that I put her in a position of being a grandmother before she was ready—that I got pregnant too young for her," says Heather. "Then, after her ego recovered, she favored my daughter, Missy, over my sons. Missy has been totally aware of this favoritism and is spoiled all the time by my mother-in-law, not just on her birthday and during the holidays. I suspect my mother-in-law is trying to be close to Missy because she recognizes that she made many mistakes with her own daughter. Missy looks just like my sister-in-law and my mother-in-law compares them all the time. I am opposed to this unequal treatment of one grandchild over the other. Although my sons are not suffering, they are aware of her preferential treatment of Missy. I'm afraid it will become worse as they grow older."

"Sean, my husband, is reliving his past. His mother chose his sister over him and made him miserable his entire childhood. I see how he suffers and how little he thinks of his mother in some ways. I try to tell him that even if his mother preferred his sister, she still made mistakes with her or she wouldn't be seeking another chance with Missy. The irony here is that my sister-in-law, Jackie, whose problems started this whole thing, just watches my mother-in-law and laughs. Jackie says she'll never get it right and that Raquel's a poor mother. My mother-in-law isn't even interested in being a grandmother. This is just about my daughter giving her an opportunity to address her past mistakes."

Unfortunately, motherhood does not automatically confer perfection. Yet our society has conditioned us to expect this ideal standard of mothers. Carol Tavris writes in her book, *The Mismeasure of Woman*, "Mothers are held responsible for almost any disorder that their offspring might develop," and this idea is "a widespread assumption in clinical psychology and family therapy." Although Tavris views mother blaming as "truly insidious," she also concedes that some mothers "deserve blame and responsibility for the awful things they do."

THE SECOND TIME AROUND

* **The mother-in-law wants another chance to mother, through her grandchildren.**
* **The daughter-in-law does not want her mother-in-law to use her children to right the older woman's past wrongs.**
* **The mother-in-law/daughter-in-law relationship is harmed.**

"I am very disappointed by my mother-in-law," says Nancy, a mother of three with a full time job. "I had always assumed that mothers wanted to do *for* their kids and *with* their kids. That was how I was raised. Not until I was engaged to my husband did I realize that someone could be like my mother-in-law, Elsie, for whom none of that applies. My mother-in-law has no interest in what goes on in her son's head or in his life. She has never been able to see him for who he really is.

"Her attitude is the same with my children. When the first child was born, Elsie wanted to be called 'Supermom' and I refused. My husband said, why not let her, but I didn't like the presumption of it. I thought she should be called 'Grandma' and act like one. This became a real source of trouble between us and my children never knew what to call her. Mostly they call her nothing, because I call her 'Grandma' when I refer to her and she calls herself 'Supermom.'

"Elsie treats my kids as if they are still babies, although they are adolescents and they resent it. She is not generous with them in terms of her time and energy. Mostly she spends her time at the hairdresser or with her friends and she is not available for the kids. She once told my son he could not go to his school play because she had a hairdresser's appointment—it was her third that week. No one expects much from her anymore; it would be useless."

In certain situations, it becomes apparent that a mother-in-law does not desire the conventional, historical role of mother-in-law, let alone grandmother. She would prefer to follow her own interests or lifestyle without the burden of assigned familial roles. There are those daughters-in-law who also do not seek out traditional mothers-in-law or those who will be hands-on, active grandmothers. What is unfortunate is when the two women do not share the same ideology on this issue. In Nancy's case, if she had anticipated that her mother-in-law wanted no time commitment to the children, she might have been less surprised and better prepared to expect less.

A MEETING OF THE MINDS
NONTRADITIONAL VIEWS
* The daughter-in-law is not invested in her mother-in-law's role as grandmother.
* The mother-in-law is not interested in fulfilling the role of grandmother.

TRADITIONAL VIEWS
* The daughter-in-law appreciates her mother-in-law's active participation with her children.
* The mother-in-law relishes the opportunity to be instrumental in her grandchildren's lives.

When a mother-in-law's narcissism becomes a part of the quotient in her function as grandmother, she may look to her grandchild to fill her needs. In this instance, she will hope that her granddaughter looks like her or has some family traits and features. A mother-in-law/grandmother might plan for her and try to guide her granddaughter's future, one that will achieve the older woman's own incomplete hopes and dreams. More problems with this kind of identification as a grandmother may occur when a grandchild is adopted. "There is no biological link with an adopted child and no transference," sociologist Alice Michaeli remarks. "This may disturb a grandmother who is looking for signs of herself in her grandchild. She will not find this in an adopted child."

Because of her own needs a mother-in-law might question her daughter-in-law's decision to adopt and perhaps draw incorrect or unfair conclusions. She might believe that with the advancement of technology today, her daughter-in-law has other options, such as in vitro fertilization. When a child is adopted, this may raise subtle issues as to how the grandmother will bond with her grandchild. Of course, if her own child has been adopted, the mother-in-law will be much more open to her daughter-in-law's and son's decision.

Paula experienced a disappointed mother-in-law when she and her husband adopted a child. "We adopted a baby after years of infertility," relates Paula. "It wasn't our first choice, but in the end, we are very happy. My mother-in-law, Jean, was not very kind about the whole thing. She actually told me that we could have a happy marriage without children and that we didn't need to take such a risk. I had the feeling that she would be telling her friends about the adoption and feel embarrassed. But Jack and I wanted a child very much and this was what we decided.

"I was so turned off by my mother-in-law's manner that I didn't even want her near our baby at first. Eventually, however, she came through, which surprised us. Jean saw us with our daughter and she understood what parenthood means to us. For once she thought of us and not of herself. That's the biggest, happiest surprise of all."

Tabitha, another mother-in-law, had positive feelings about her daughter-in-law and son adopting a child. Unlike Paula's mother-in-law, she was open to the concept and supportive from the start.

"I saw my daughter-in-law, Janice, go through hell to get pregnant. She and my son were spending money hand over fist at the infertility clinic. It became such a preoccupation that it was destroying their marriage. All of their friends were having babies and they couldn't. I was the one who suggested they look into adoption. I think my opinion mattered to them and this freed them to explore the process.

"My sister has an adopted daughter who is now in her mid-twenties and she is delightful and a treasure to us all. While I am aware of the risks with adoption, I also know that there is tremendous joy in raising a child. My daughter-in-law was unable to get a baby of our culture, but she has a lovely Asian daughter and the three of them make a beautiful family. She and I take the baby everywhere together."

ADOPTION AND GRANDMOTHERS
* **Some grandmothers may not welcome adopted grandchildren.**
* **They should try to overcome this feeling, because their support, in many cases, will be warmly received.**

As in adoption situations, supportive, non-judgmental mothers-in-law/grandmothers are usually highly prized by working mothers. A notable, fairly recent shift in motherhood involves the working mother, who in the past thirty years has made her mark on society. According to the 1998 United States Census Report, thirty percent of working mothers with young children enroll them in organized day care programs and forty-one percent leave their children in the care of family members. The young mother who makes the decision to place her child in day care is seeking an independent, efficient method of conducting her life and her mothering. A mother-in-law may be offended by this and critical of the system, even if she is not willing to take on the daunting task of watching her grandchild from nine to five on a daily basis. In such instances, the mother-in-law might be comparing her experience in mothering to her daughter-in-law's although, in fact, the two are not comparable.

Thirty years ago, Germaine Greer wrote in her revolutionary book, *The Female Eunuch*, "the professional women who struggle to continue in their vocation after marriage are a tiny minority." Since then, women have evolved as their opportunities broadened and they do not necessarily close the door on a career in order to open a door to marriage and motherhood. Women's choices have expanded, although their struggles to combine family and career continue. Working mothers often complain bitterly about the burden of responsibilities like running the household after work hours. Nonetheless, compared to thirty or forty years ago, there now are other options. Greer describes motherhood of the sixties as a bleak and narrow existence: "The family of the sixties is small, self contained, self centered and short lived....Children live their lives most fully at school, fathers at work. Mother is the dead heart of the family....The wife is only significant when she is bearing and raising the small children."

FIFTIES AND SIXTIES STYLE MOTHERHOOD
* **Mothers were relegated to their roles as housewives.**
* **Women were not encouraged to work once they were married and raising families.**
* **Some women confessed to their isolation, others were true believers.**

Greer, like Chodorow and Rossi, writes about the isolation of the young mother coinciding with societal expectations of impeccable mothering. What Greer attests to is how much more difficult and ill equipped the "working girl" of the sixties was for the isolation of the family home when she became a mother. Once the children were ready to attend school, the mother was left to her home, her "province" where she was so very alone. Some women were able to express their dissatisfaction and sense that life was passing them by. Yet for others, including many of the mothers-in-law interviewed for this study who have lived the life described by Greer, there is a sense of defensiveness and an insistence that their way is the only way. Other women, once their children seemed officially grown or entrenched in their adolescence, decided to go back to work. Many seeking fields where they did not need to acquire new skills or finish a degree. Thus, they became real estate brokers, travel agents or part-time teachers. Of the population of mothers-in-law who did not join the work force at any time, there seems to be a residual, negative judgment of their daughters-in-law's choices to do so and they continue to question the impact upon their grandchildren.

Today, mothers-in-law and daughters-in-law can have very different philosophies in terms of children and careers. "Ellen, my mother-in-law," Nell begins, "cannot handle the fact that I have gone back to work and put my two children in day care. She doesn't understand that the children are happier there than stuck with her all day and that there is little reason for her to be involved with their day to day scheduling. My son, who is the older child, will be entering kindergarten in the fall and that seems to be a great relief for her because she can justify his day better. Somehow, I have less patience for her now that I have children and work. Ellen remains very concerned about her relationship with the children and attempts to control them.

"I would be happier if she wanted less time with the children and if she stopped trying so hard to be a part of our life. I keep waiting for her to move to Florida or to some retirement village, where she can play cards with other widows and be preoccupied with her own life. Then I think of how much she loves my boys and I try to invite her over once a week just to make her happy."

Unlike Nell's mother-in-law, Sally's mother-in-law, June, wants no responsibility for her grandchildren and Sally would appreciate more input. "I swear my mother-in-law moved away once my daughter was born, because she suspected I would be looking to her for help with my child. I work in an emergency room at a hospital and my schedule changes constantly. I was really hoping that she could watch Elizabeth on occasion, say twice a week. This never happened and it has caused a strain in our relationship. My mother-in-law's mantra as a grandmother is: *I get to see my grandchild as little or as much as I want without obligation.*

"June's attitude is that she has raised her children and that role is over for her now. This is her point of view. This is the choice she has made. Before Elizabeth was born, I really expected our relationship to be better. I thought my mother-in-law would be a hands-on grandmother. Another factor for me is the cost of baby-sitting and I think that my mother-in-law is aware that money is a consideration for us."

While June is not alone in eschewing a caregiver grandmother role, her attitude does reflect a departure from tradition for the modern day mother-in-law/grandmother. Unlike grandmothers of the past, once faced with the prospect of constant care for her grandchild, a grandmother today may run for the hills. Unfortunately, a daughter-in-law who is looking to her mother-in-law for involvement in her children's lives may find herself with a hands-off mother-in-law, just as often as the daughter-in-law who is delighted not to have the input.

HANDS OFF GRANDMOTHERING
* **The daughter-in-law needs a scheduled baby-sitter.**
* **The mother-in-law is not interested.**
* **The daughter-in-law resents it.**

A good example of a healthy balance between a mother-in-law's and a daughter-in-law's expectations is that of Felicia, a mother-in-law, and Colleen, her daughter-in-law. "I see my grandchildren," Felicia says, "on my daughter-in-law's terms, which happen to coincide with my terms. It is a bit unusual for our family's style, but it is successful for the two of us. What is also unusual is that I have a full-time job. So while Colleen works, which many women do today, in our family a working mother-in-law and daughter-in-law is not common. I am unlike my own mother-in-law, who lived a block away from our family and grew old happily, assuming the traditional roles of wife, mother, mother-in-law and grandmother. She did exactly what was expected of her and probably liked each stage of mothering. I look back at her life and I realize that she was defined as a mother from the time she was a young bride, destined to have children and grandchildren. She was a wonderful mother-in-law to me, always there to help me with the kids. I think she saw my career as absurd, because no one else in our neighborhood had a daughter-in-law who worked, but she never said a negative word. My children benefited from her love and care.

"I understand that my daughter-in-law takes the little one to day care and the older ones are in school. When Colleen needs back-up help, she calls her mother, who lives about half an hour away. I might be around on a weekend, but usually I am doing what every working woman does on weekends, which is playing catch-up with household chores. My daughter-in-law and I are both running around doing errands and neither of us has much leisure time, but we like it this way. Colleen and I speak the same language and operate in the same universe. As for her children, I think they are terrific. I love them and they get quality time not quantity time from both their mother and from their grandmother."

At times, day care gives off a singular, rather negative message to a mother-in-law/grandmother. If a grandmother offers her time and her daughter-in-law opts for day care in lieu of her mother-in-law's help, this may be perceived as a slap in the face. The older woman feels that she was passed over. The message she receives is that her input is not as valuable as what her grandchild will experience at the day care center. This can be devastating to the mother-in-law/daughter-in-law relationship.

Alice Michaeli notes that a daughter-in-law may have a preference for her own family of origin or for a benign entity like a day care center, over her husband's family's influence. "When a daughter-in-law chooses day care over her mother-in-law's assistance, the implicit message to the mother-in-law," explains Michaeli, "is that I'd rather not have my child socialized into my husband's family's values. To attain her ends, the daughter-in-law will even pay for day care rather than relinquish her child to her mother-in-law." When the grandmother lives near to her grandchild and is available for child care, but is turned down on her offer, her relationship with her daughter-in-law may be irreparably damaged.

Grandparenting roles seem not as clearly defined as in the past, in large part due to women in the workplace. As the roles of young women change, they impact the roles of women as grandmothers. While I have mentioned longevity as it affects the length of mother-in-law/daughter-in law relationships, a longer life span also affects the decisions and life styles of both women. If a grandmother is still working, she is less accessible to her grandchildren. However, the children do have a role model in their grandmother and if she makes time as best she can, this works positively for the relationship. The two women understand one another by virtue of being working mothers. Both of them identify with the sense that their vigor comes from more than the label of motherhood. They may, as a result of their schedules, have a similar style in how they "mother" and "grandmother."

A traditional work ethic has been ingrained in many of us. The implicit message is that work is good and it doesn't matter what one does, as long as one is working. While putting work as a first priority sometimes causes conflict and pressure on families, the idea still remains that the breadwinner puts her/his work ahead of everything else. In most parents' cases, particularly mothers, this choice includes how one deals with the children. A working mother faces the dilemma of her child's schedule conflicting with her work schedule, holidays and unexpected illnesses on many occasions. Despite all the difficulties, a mother-in-law and her daughter-in-law might want the chance to be a part of the vital work world, avoiding long days with small children. Possibly, the mother-in-law has learned her preferences the hard way, after raising her own children. Perhaps the daughter-in-law has always planned on working and has confided in her mother-in-law that although she adores her children, she wants to be in the world as well. Joan Borysenko, in her book, *A Woman's Book of Life*, documents the modern woman's desire in midlife to be "potentially wise, still vigorous and in possession of a kind of fierce power." These qualities enable women to carve out meaningful, multifaceted lives for themselves, long into grandmotherhood.

WORKING WOMEN UNITE
* **When the mother and the grandmother both work outside the home, they often share experiences and speak the same language.**
* **Mutual respect usually results between the two women.**
* **The children profit from these strong, female figures**

The relationship between Kristin and her mother-in-law, Gretchen, has, in some ways, benefited from this kind of shared sensibility, but still has its difficulties. "There is nothing I can do that would encourage my mother-in-law to take my side on the small issues of my mothering," explains Kristin. "I don't worry, though, because she is there for the big problems. We never talk about the fact that I leave the kids to go to work. We never talk about the fact that she works, too. Those are givens. But we argue over how the children are being raised. She thinks I spoil them and I think I'm doing what everyone else does. I'm just trying to give my children opportunities like other families do. My nine-year-old daughter wants ballet lessons and it so happens that my husband, who works a night shift, can get her there. That is why she got her way, because it fit into our schedules.

"What I find is that my mother-in-law watches me closely and questions every move I make. I try to tell her that children today are not like her son was as a child. I tell her that I want my son and daughter to have every opportunity they can and that is why I'm working so hard. Why won't she agree this is a good idea? My husband says she is always comparing how she brought up her children with how I am bringing up ours."

Although it is ideal that a mother-in-law and daughter-in-law bond when there are children, Dr. Michaele Goodman reminds us that children are not raised today as they were in the past. "Over the past twenty years, a shift in how children are brought up has begun. There is a generational difference and a movement toward permissiveness. A mother-in-law could think that her grandchild was indulged, emotionally and materially, when really this grandchild's existence is like all of her friends' and classmates' lives." When a mother-in-law does not approve of how her daughter-in-law is raising the children and she is not accepting of her daughter-in-law's decision to pursue a career, tension builds between the two women.

"My mother-in-law, Emily, thinks that too many women are career oriented today," says Jeannette. "She will be much more accepting of a mother who has a financial need to work, but her point of view is that if a mother of young children has no economic need, but only the desire to work, she's somehow wrong to work outside the home. Her view of me is that I can do anything: knit, sew, make a birdhouse. From her point of view, these activities should be enough for me. She will see the children often and encourage them to be creative, but it all seems like a very 1950s sensibility to me.

"The reality is that her first daughter-in-law, Kailyn, who is divorced from my brother-in-law, was a successful entrepreneur. My mother-in-law's take on that marriage was that Kailyn was aggressive and too involved with her career. Kailyn left my brother-in-law and tossed the kids in his direction. No wonder my mother-in-law encourages me to be a homebody. Meanwhile, I have my own plan. I plan to return to the workforce within two years, when my youngest child goes off to kindergarten. My dream is to resume my career and work hard at combining it with a solid family life."

In her essay, "Dreams vs Drift in Women's Careers," author Pamela Daniels discusses the fact that having women in the labor force is not a new phenomenon, but the way that women seek a career and work with pride is "intrinsic to psychological and moral well-being." Daniels encourages a transcendence of the traditional in order for women to reach their goals.

Some modern mothers-in-law fee; their daughters-in-law should work. "I am somewhat perturbed by my daughter-in-law's lack of career drive since she had children," comments May. "I was ahead of my time when it came to career and children and I find it surprising that my daughter-in-law, Winnie, does not have the same aspirations. I do not mean that she has to be like me, because I am not attempting to be her role model, but I would think that a woman of her generation would want to be working, with or without children. She will do an occasional freelance job, but before the children she had a full-time position in a big corporation.

"I believe I have carefully processed how the relationship works between a daughter-in-law and mother-in-law. At work, I am brisk and forceful. It is not the role I have wanted to play as mother-in-law. Subconsciously, I see my daughter-in-law as a conduit to my son and to my grandchildren. So while my personal belief is that my daughter-in-law is actually limiting her children's outlook by not working, I say nothing. She has two daughters and I would admire her if she devoted herself to her children and to a career. Maybe my son didn't like the fact that I worked while raising him and this was a factor in his choice of wife. He and the children are well tended to, I will say that. I always made time for the children and for work. It wasn't easy and it was exhausting. But I expected something better from my daughter-in-law—a current version of what I had done thirty years ago."

The son-husband and/or his wife may opt to work from home, which enables one or both parents to have a hands-on position in raising their children. A mother-in-law might find this curious and foreign, but she cannot fault the arrangement. Not only does such a situation relieve her of grandmotherly responsibilities, but she has a clear conscience, because her son and daughter-in-law are there for the children.

"Dave, my husband, gave up his job at a big firm to be a consultant after our son was born," says Samantha. "At first, I was worried about medical benefits and the kind of income he would be capable of pulling in away from the buzz of those big offices. I have always worked at home on a freelance basis, so I was also worried that there would be too much togetherness, the baby, Dave and me. As for my mother-in-law, Dottie, she was in shock. My working at home pleased her once the baby was born and, of course, absolved her of any responsibility as a baby-sitter. Dave's decision negated all that she had taught him to be. In her stereotypic view of the world, men do their work outside the domestic sphere, eat and sleep at home and women run the home. If a woman works part-time from home, as Dottie knows I do, that is acceptable to her. For Dave to be home working, however, is unthinkable to her and for us all to be together at home makes us look like we are goofing off and have no work ethic in her eyes.

"After two years of regarding our life and work style in this unforgiving way, my mother-in-law concedes that it has been a rich experience all around. Dave has built up his consulting business, I am doing more work than ever before and our daughter is thriving."

Traveling and a busy social schedule were easier for Nadia once she saw that her daughter-in-law, Maggie, would be setting up a home office. She did not struggle with the idea of it, as Samantha's mother-in-law had, but saw working at home as a perfect solution. Nadia relates, "My daughter-in-law, who is now the mother of two toddlers, never asked me to baby-sit, because she set up a home office and conducted her work from there. There have been days when the children were so sick that she couldn't get anything done and she lost business. Certainly, she must discipline herself to create an aura of professionalism while she's really at home with babies, but she manages to do it. I had mixed feelings about this in the beginning, but she has proven herself. And my son, who is very involved with the kids, seems so happy with the arrangement. Of course, when I watch Maggie juggling her busy life, I don't envy her.

"My contact with the children is as much or as little as I want. I believe this kind of loose and easy approach is part and parcel of who my daughter-in-law is. I listen to my friends complaining about how they see their grandchildren too little and I listen to those who are obligated to baby-sit their grandkids, because both the daughter-in-law and son work. I have none of this to deal with, so I feel really blessed."

Another variable for grandparenting is that most grandparents no longer live around the corner from their grandchildren. The undeniable factor of geographic distance looms in the grandmother/grandchild relationship. The contacts between mother-in-law and daughter-in-law, grandchildren and grandparents are diminished when a mother-in-law/grandmother lives halfway across the country. The extended family is divided physically by thousands of miles and their time together frequently is relegated to yearly or semi-yearly visits back and forth. While this definitely lessens the competition between a mother-in-law and the mother of the daughter-in-law in terms of time spent with the grandchildren, it also establishes the grandmother who lives closest as the primary grandmother.

With the large numbers of men and women over retirement age migrating to parts of the country where the weather is mild, for example Florida or Arizona, the day-to-day contact between extended family members has lessened. Long distance telephone calls and E-mail replace neighborhoods. The roles of mother-in-law and daughter-in-law as well as grandmother and grandchild exist in a vacuum. Any strong feelings, negative or positive, between a mother-in-law and her daughter-in-law are diluted by the lack of frequent interaction. As for the son-husband, his relationship with his parents exists in its own sphere. His closeness, built on years of family history, hopefully supersedes physical distance.

HALFWAY ACROSS THE COUNTRY
* **The reasons for arguments between a mother-in-law and daughter-in-law are lessened by the geographic distance that separates them.**
* **Neither mother-in-law nor daughter-in-law are able to overstep their bounds.**
* **Whatever initial sentiments the mother-in-law or daughter-in-law have toward one another continue to exist.**

Alice Michaeli warns that a lack of physical proximity to the extended family can limit the relationships. "No one in the family can really know the other members," Michaeli says, "when they seldom see each other. Relationships form over time and with ongoing contact between in-laws. If contact is missing from the equation, the relationships will be stunted."

One mother-in-law with whom I spoke, Corinne, was distraught when her son and his family moved away. "After seven years of marriage to my son," Corinne says with a smile, "my daughter-in-law had a baby. I couldn't wait to baby-sit and I knew she would be a terrific mother because she has been so kind to my daughter's children. I told her right away that I would take their child on weekends and that I would help her out any time at all. She seemed so happy and we felt very close. My girl-friends warned me that I would be controlling and have strong opinions about how my son and daughter-in-law reared their child, but I was determined to do better than that.

"It seemed that everything was working out and I did baby-sit after the baby was born. This lasted for six months and then my son was relocated abroad by his company. I was devastated. I think my daughter-in-law was, too, because she had grown accustomed to having me around. My grief was so great that I couldn't even think of not being with my grandson. It was as though we were being torn apart."

"Geography is a strong component in how the grandparent relationship plays out," says Dr. Ronnie Burak. "When the mother-in-law and daughter-in-law live far apart, it is difficult to share the same intensity of feeling. A mother-in-law who, in terms of her grandchild, felt she was shut out when she lived a mile away and now lives five hundred miles away, is going to have less of a problem coping with infrequent contact. The distance can help."

Conversely, when a couple settles down in an area of the country for career or economic reasons and finds themselves growing more and more aloof from their extended families, a daughter-in-law with young children may feel adrift. The reverse holds true when a grandmother chooses to live far away from her children in order to pursue her own lifestyle and perhaps to avoid the responsibilities of parenting, this time in the role of grandmother. Her attitude is that she already raised her children, so she shouldn't have to go back to that stage of her life. Here, then, is a departure from the traditional stereotype of a grandmother, a woman who impatiently waits for her grandchildren to be born once her children have grown up and married.

Rebecca, a daughter-in-law I interviewed, sees both the advantages and disadvantages in having a long-distance mother-in-law. "My husband and I have never lived in the same town as my in-laws, which helps," admits Rebecca, a daughter-in-law of sixteen years. "My mother-in-law, Amelia, lives thousands of miles from us in a warmer climate and is very close to her daughters. While she might surprise us with material gifts that come by mail, it isn't the same to me as a real support system. In the beginning of my marriage, my mother lived nearby and it was very meaningful to me. Amelia found it a relief not to be around for several reasons, mostly because my mother was there and my husband gets along so well with her. Also, my mother-in-law seemed uninterested in being the stereotypical, attentive grandmother. I know that her one regret is that all the grandchildren in the extended family do not live close enough to play together.

"But my mother-in-law set the tone by moving away to a retirement community that is a kind of camp for adults. I remind myself that my mother-in-law has a 'no boundaries' view of family life even from afar, so I can only imagine how difficult our relationship would be if she lived nearby."

In our culture, it has been traditional that women are valued for childbearing and lose status once this stage of their lives is over. As this perception of value changes, so do women's roles. Gail Sheehy writes in her book, *New Passages: Mapping Your Way Across Time*, of a "revolution in the life cycle" and indicates that the norms have shifted in the past twenty-five years. Sheehy views "true adulthood" as not beginning until the age of thirty and middle age not occurring until people are into their fifties. With this theory, she has labeled forty-five to sixty-five the "age of mastery" and sixty-five to eighty-five the "age of integrity." It is the "age of integrity" that becomes an exploration for grandmothers, one in which they are not beholden to their children, their in-laws or their grandchildren.

"Grandparents today are trying to discover themselves outside of their familial roles," notes Alice Michaeli. "Once their children are grown, they do not always want to return to a world of schedules, after school pick-ups and grandchildren who have croup. In the past, when people died at younger ages, the family was more closely bound to its designated role. Today, there is freedom for women as they grow older and begin to ask themselves questions never considered before. Such women have the opportunity to decide what lifestyle is best for them and who they really are, or want to be, at that stage."

LIBERATED GRANDMOTHERS

* Mothers-in-law/grandmothers rediscover themselves once their children are grown.
* They avoid or resent being relegated to staying home with their grandchildren
* They live in or move to a community that offers them opportunities to indulge their interests.

"I did not encourage my mother-in-law, Dolly, to see my children when they were small," admits Gloria, "because she poisons their minds. She is very possessive of them, probably because I have given birth to the only daughters in the family in eighty years. She said to me once, 'Why were you the one to have a daughter?' The underlying message was, *How dare you outshine me.* She was very close to her sons, including my husband, and the boys were very obedient and did not cross her. No matter what I said, my husband didn't see his mother negatively like I saw her.

"My mother-in-law was socially connected, very active in the community and organized. She was the queen bee wherever she went and everyone tried to please her. I always felt Dolly tried to buy my girls' affection, but it didn't work because of me. Then she became older and two things happened. One was that she wanted another kind of life with her friends, in a resort community. When Dolly moved away, she was no longer around to lavish attention and control over my girls. The other outcome was that after the early years, when I tried to avoid her and to exert my own power through the children, I realized that it wasn't fair. Whatever I felt about Dolly, they were her grandchildren and my children deserved a relationship with her as much as she did with them. The girls are older now and they love to be with her and she keeps up her relationship with them on a schedule, which also provides her with a life independent of being a grandmother."

With a similar reasoning, we see that Peggy, a grandmother of teenage boys, has also made a separate peace with her daughter-in-law, Jessie. "At first, I wasn't completely satisfied with my daughter-in-law, but my feelings changed once she had the children," Peggy reports. "The years have gone by, the boys are bigger and everyone is busier. Our schedules are heavier and more demanding and my daughter-in-law cannot meet me in the city as much as she did before. I miss Jessie and the children terribly. I have actually grown closer to my daughter-in-law, in some respects, than to my son. It must be due to the children, because I was closer to my son before he and Jessie had the boys.

"I speak with my daughter-in-law all the time and she tells me about the kids. My son hasn't any time for this. Jessie and I developed this closeness because of the children. We have better conversations about the boys than about anything else. I have become her willingly captive audience. Besides, you can't win a war with a daughter-in-law, it's foolish to even try."

"It is very common for a daughter-in-law to say she doesn't like her mother-in-law, but then doesn't deny her children access to this woman because she is the children's grandmother," comments psychologist Dr. Michaele Goodman. "Despite any negative feelings toward her mother-in-law, a daughter-in-law does this because she wants her children to enjoy the benefits of having a caring grandmother. The daughter-in-law's behavior and attitude are all about what is best for the children."

As time passes and she matures, a daughter-in-law frequently will move beyond her initial, averse reaction to her mother-in-law. There is the distinct possibility that the mother-in-law is an excellent grandmother although her daughter-in-law may consider her deficient as a mother or mother-in-law. The shared goal of daughter-in-law and mother-in-law alike is to provide the children with the richness and advantages which a relationship with grandparents provides.

THE BIGGER PICTURE
* **The daughter-in-law does not deny her mother-in-law access to her children.**
* **Regardless of her personal feelings about her mother-in-law, the daughter-in-law wants her children to have grandparents.**
* **The mother-in-law's schedule does not intrude on the family.**

"Alexia, my daughter, is so close to her grandmother that I can't complain about my mother-in-law anymore," says Wendy, who for years fought with her husband over his mother. "My mother-in-law, Roberta, takes my daughter everywhere and at a time in Alexia's adolescence when she is very negative about most things, she is always willing and happy to see my mother-in-law. I think they trade secrets and have a wonderful trust in each other. They get manicures together and go to early Sunday evening movies. There is a mutual respect between them and a chance to learn from each other. I advocate this totally, for both their sakes.

"Whatever I felt at first about Roberta is not relevant now. I am, finally, not threatened by my mother-in-law. I see there is enough love to go around. She definitely gives Alexia something special."

In time, the grandchildren grow up and the relationship between a grandmother and a grandchild must stand on its own. As Elizabeth Paul comments in her essay, "A Longitudinal Analysis of Midlife Interpersonal Relationships and Well-being," women are affected in midlife by a positive relationship with their grandchildren. Grandchildren return the affection, particularly when they are young. As they approach early adolescence, they may pull away from their parents and parental figures. However, in late adolescence, Alice Michaeli explains, they often rediscover their grandparents. It is the historical perspective that has great value for the grandchildren. When they are willing and ready to learn from their grandparents, grandchild and grandmother alike will almost always find their lives enhanced by the interaction.

ADOLESCENT GRANDCHILDREN
* **In later adolescence, grandchildren seek out their grandparents.**
* **The grandmother and her grandchildren spend time together.**
* **The mother/daughter-in-law is in favor of this because she views it as an enriching experience.**

Forty percent of the mothers-in-law interviewed wanted a better relationship with their grandchildren and felt their daughters-in-law discouraged this. Thirty percent of the mothers-in-law found their daughters-in-law to be acceptable mothers and agreeable to their interactions with their grandchildren. In terms of making opportunities for interaction with the grandchildren or assistance in scheduling time with their grandchildren, approximately thirty percent felt their sons were deficient in any aid or intervention.

Almost half of the daughters-in-law interviewed welcomed relationships between their children and their mothers-in-law. The remainder of the daughters-in-law felt there were problems and issues with their mothers-in-law regarding the children. Fifteen percent of these women expressed relief that their in-laws lived far away.

The husband has a great deal to do with the way in which his wife and his mother interact. It is important for a daughter-in-law to remember this in response to her mother-in-law's role as her children's grandmother. Undeniably, a daughter-in-law is inclined to spend more time with her own mother than her mother-in-law once her baby is born. It is only natural since her mother was the one who nurtured her. Yet there is room to include the mother-in-law, as she so desires, in the grandchild's life and for the grandchild to reap the love of two grandmothers, not one.

Thomas Moore encourages readers in his book, *Soul Mates*, to bear in mind that the basic structure in life is family and the shelter it offers children. Moore writes, "Other members—grandparents, cousins, uncles, aunts, nephews and nieces—are connected through the family to others, no matter where they live and how they behave." It is "guidance, education, physical and emotional security and love" Moore emphasizes, as well as the profound influences children receive from their families which enables them to achieve adulthood.

8

Endless Competition

"I often wonder if I could have stopped them from marrying," says Phyllis, a mother-in-law of twenty-eight years. "However, it may not have made a difference what I said, even then. They were married in Europe and once they lived in the United States, I always made it my business to defend Ursula, my daughter-in-law, to others. I saw how alone she was in this country. She could be the most wonderful daughter-in-law anyone could have prayed for and then she would go off the deep end. Several times the marriage broke off and she went home to Europe. I was the one who sent money for her to return, because I still thought she and my son cared for each other. I sent the money selfishly, for my peace of mind in terms of my son and grandchildren. All the while, Ursula looked to me as a mother and I looked to her as a daughter. The problem was, in the role of mother and daughter, we couldn't get along for one moment. There were fights and disagreements at every turn and we competed for both my son and for their children's affection. To this day, we are still competing and still disagreeing."

We often hear it said that if we are able to look at the relationship a son has with his mother, we might be able to predict what kind of relationship he will have with his wife. In her essay 'Woman's Place in a Man's Life Cycle," Carol Gilligan writes, "Boys are likely to have been pushed out of the pre-oedipal relationship [now] and to have to curtail their primary love and sense of tie with their mothers in order for them to develop in terms of masculinity. However, men have difficulty in relationships with women if they have had difficulty separating from their mothers." While this definitely impacts what goes on between a husband and wife in a marriage, another factor for a son-husband, regardless of his history with his mother, is the issue of competition between his mother and his wife. Despite conventional thoughts on unresolved issues between mothers and sons, it is difficult to predict the duration or level of disharmony caused by competition between his mother and his wife or from where it stems.

This competition involves lifestyle, parenting and who yields more influence over the son-husband. There are instances where the condition between a mother-in-law and her daughter-in-law does not change, despite the passing years and the many phases in both women's lives. If there has been competition between the women since day one, it will probably persist over the long term with the stakes rising incrementally. It seems as if there is no personal evolution taking place on either the part of the mother-in-law or her daughter-in-law which could ameliorate the situation.

Sometimes, as in Emma's situation, other family members are brought into the competition. "It sickens me how Diana, my mother-in-law, and my sister-in-law play out the competition between us," Emma confides. "Diana set this up from the start of my marriage and it has been going on for years. She is dedicated to her daughter, Angela, whom she constantly praises to me and to Angela's children. She has little time or energy for my children. Diana has explained to me that because Angela needs her and I am so self-sufficient, it is necessary for her to be this way. So she makes herself available to Angela and then tells me about it. If my husband so much as buys me a coat, she buys herself a coat or she buys Angela a coat.

"When I turned thirty, my husband chose a beautiful watch for me as a birthday gift. He asked his sister if she would go to the jeweler and approve the gift, which was a surprise. Not only did she approve, but she had to have the same watch. This has happened over and over again. Angela decided to have a second child after we had twins, although she had always claimed she only wanted one child. I think that she couldn't bear the idea that we had more children than she. Although all this goes on with my sister-in-law and we are only two years apart in age, it is really fostered by my mother-in-law. Diana's form of competition, since it can't be about having babies, is about who went where and when. If my husband and I go away for a few days, she then has to go to a similar or the same spot. Since nothing is sacred and just for us, nothing feels special."

A daughter-in-law who has a very controlling or competitive mother-in-law has to learn how not to engage the older woman in antagonistic competitions, advises Dr. Ronnie Burak. "A daughter-in-law can become very resentful of a competition which is devised by her mother-in-law. On occasion, I have seen the daughter-in-law who puts her husband in the middle of the war between the two women, hoping this will help. It may or may not work. Other times, the daughter-in-law will attempt to work things out, forcing herself to be compromising and determined to find levels of tolerance." It is always best if a mother-in-law and daughter-in-law can set limits.

SETTING BOUNDARIES
* **The goal is to avoid a lifetime of competitions and repeat problems with mothers-in-law and their daughters-in-law.**
* **If the mothers-in-law cannot disengage, the daughters-in-law must.**

Jane has begun to learn how to disengage from her mother-in-law's interference. "My marriage is in continual jeopardy because of my mother-in-law," Jane begins. "She started this game from the beginning of my marriage and she and I are always vying for my husband's attention. I have tried very hard to respect the relationship my husband has with his mother, but it is easier to accept in theory than in fact. Only last week he left me at a cocktail party on a Saturday night to take his mother to dinner. I was not invited, ostensibly because she had some financial matters to discuss with him. Why it had to be dinner on a Saturday night when we had plans beats me. When I said something to my husband, he agreed, but implied it was better to meet her than to fight with her about it.

"The larger problem with my mother-in-law though is not that she acts like my husband is at her disposal, but that she is abusive to me. She will be verbally cruel and pushy at the same time. During the week, she calls at night, knowing my husband is working at the store until nine or ten. She will ask me why he isn't home yet and how he would never be late for her. I am so mad about it that I am trying a different tactic—instead of complaining about her, I am looking to be important to my husband in my own right."

Much of how a daughter-in-law responds to her mother-in-law has to do with her family of origin and her upbringing. Antoinette Michaels, relationship counselor, tells us, "If there has been no consistency and security for a daughter-in-law when she was growing up, she may not have formed a healthy self-image. As a daughter-in-law, she may feel threatened by her mother-in-law, because she has issues of abandonment or perhaps she grew up feeling insignificant and unworthy." On the other hand, a mother-in-law could be very unhappy with her husband or in her own life and this may spoil her contribution to the mother-in-law/daughter-in-law relationship. "If a mother-in-law is not healthy in her approach to her daughter-in-law, the relationship suffers," Michaels adds, "and as it declines, the negativity seeps into the marriage."

UNHEALTHY WOMEN
* Either the mother-in-law or daughter-in-law have unresolved emotional issues.
* The mother is unhappy in her life.
* The daughter is unhealthy emotionally.
* The mother-in-law/daughter-in-law relationship is bound to suffer.

Often times, a daughter-in-law harbors anger toward her mother-in-law over how they interact. She believes that her mother-in-law is the instigator of conflicts and that she cannot escape. This feeling of help-lessness is what causes her to feel anger. As Dr. Harriet Lerner describes in her book, *The Dance of Anger*, the daughter-in-law becomes the "nice lady" who remains silent during these episodes. Instead of exhibiting anger, the daughter-in-law is hurt and tearful. Dr. Lerner recommends that women plan to do something different with their angry feelings in a rela-tionship and to break the pattern of swallowing that anger. As discussed in previous chapters, mother-in-law and daughter-in-law relationships are fraught with expectations and differences, but in situations like these the daughter-in-law feels particularly vulnerable.

Of course, there are those mothers-in-law who feel just as vulner-able and put-upon by their daughters-in-law. In Marla's case, she and her daughter-in-law have achieved an "armed truce." Marla explains, "There have been jealousies and competitions for years between me and my daughter-in-law. I don't believe I started them, but it's been so long, I can't even remember. I'm beginning to think that we are both jealous people. There is no trust on my part and I feel that her word is unreliable. What I see is that she doesn't like me, but goes through the motions. And then she gets back at me by telling me what she did with her family or with my son and the children, without ever inviting me. She and my son are a team and recently they have formed a line against me. I get their vibes and they get mine. So we all play the game, knowing it's a game. It's sort of like an armed truce. We do this instead of expressing our anger.

"I suppose I am getting back at my son for choosing a woman I thought was wrong for him. From day one, I felt his wife didn't fit in with our family. He and I were so close before the wedding, but not now. I have no more influence over him and my approval no longer matters. At first he attempted to please both me and her and I couldn't stand it. I saw him in this go-between role and I knew that was bad for his marriage and for our relationship. I advised him to take a side, and to be responsible for himself. I know that I'm a hard act to follow. That is why she is jealous of me and, because he wanted her, I am jealous of her."

Dr. Michaele Goodman advises her clients to be aware of the more common eruptions in extended families, usually over time, money, visits and holidays. "These blowups and issues cannot be avoided, but what can be done is for all parties to make an effort to minimize the damage between the husband and wife. It is better for the couple, or for the mother-in-law and for her daughter-in-law to accept the severity of these situations. If there is competition between a mother-in-law and her daughter-in-law when they come into contact, it is wise to lessen that level of contact."

MINIMIZING THE DAMAGE
* **Admit there are problems.**
* **Face the fact that issues are chronic.**
* **Lessen the level of contact between mother-in-law and daughter-in-law.**

Matilda, a mother-in-law, has had a stormy relationship with her daughter-in-law, Aimee, for the entire eleven years she has been married to her son. "I postponed their engagement party and she was blazing mad about it. Although it was rescheduled, she never forgave me. It never worked out from day one. Once or twice, she attempted to visit or to spend time with me, but she really didn't care about our relationship. I knew it was an effort made solely on my son's behalf.

"Their marriage is volatile and angry and it is best if I keep my distance and she keeps hers. What I object to is how my daughter-in-law has turned my son against me. Aimee resents me and anything I have ever said to my son. I don't know why. She wants total control over him and there is very little I can do. Recently, my son left the family business, because she wanted him to. This caused great pain in the family. First, she antagonized him about working there and then she talked him into leaving.

"To me, their marriage is about infatuation and not about love and commitment." Matilda sighs. "She never had children because she wanted to be in shape, to preserve her body, an attitude which I found to be selfish. I think about this whenever I see her and I wonder what kind of person she truly is. Unfortunately, I have no expectations that my feelings will change and I do miss my son, who I devoted myself to raising."

As Shere Hite reveals in *The Hite Report on the Family*, most boys "leave" their mothers emotionally and switch their allegiances to men and the system their fathers represent. Hite defines this dynamic as "the lynch-pin of the social system of patriarchy." Her research concludes that despite the social pressure for sons to "disassociate themselves from their mothers and show contempt for all things female, men have positive views of their mothers." This bodes well for the marriages of the sons who respect their mothers and thus, one assumes, respect women in general. Such men will transfer that respect to their wives.

When the two women in his life, his mother and his wife, are feuding or are competitive and antagonistic toward each other, it forces the son-husband to choose sides. Although he has a good relationship with his mother and he views his wife positively, there are occasions when he will have to side with one or the other. Dr. Ronnie Burak describes clients in her practice who have been unable to abide their mothers-in-law under any circumstance. "I have seen women," says Dr. Burak, "who have had husbands hospitalized after car accidents or who are gravely ill and still these daughters-in-law cannot contain their feelings toward their mothers-in-law. There was one daughter-in-law who could not cope with her mother-in-law while her husband was recovering from a terrible accident. The husband resented that his wife couldn't rise above her negative feelings. He sided with his mother, his attitude being that while his mother was neurotic, he had grown up with her and he was accustomed to her ways. He wondered why his wife couldn't just deal with it and be magnanimous. Once he recovered, his wife's behavior toward his mother during this stressful time had a devastating effect on their marriage."

THE BIG PICTURE
* **When battles persist, especially in times of stress or illness, the mother-in-law and daughter-in-law owe it to themselves and to the marriage to find a way to get along.**
* **For the son, especially if he is ill or has a problem, any contention on the part of his mother and his wife only contributes to a bad situation.**

In Carly's case, she knows her relationship with her mother-in-law, Mona, is not going to improve, but she has learned to manage her own feelings about it. "My mother-in-law resents my husband's happiness and his monetary success," Carly complains. "At the same time, she takes all the credit for his success and continually hints that he is obligated to her. I suspect that she pushed her children to make money so that they would take care of her, although she has a husband and a nice life. I never heard of this sort of family dynamic before I married my husband. I came from another kind of family, where my parents were not expecting anything financial from their children. Mona's view is that it is payback time. Her question is not what can I do for my children, but what can my children do for me. My husband never discusses how influenced he is by his mother. He avoids confrontation with her while she continues to try to control him and intimidate him whenever she can. Sometimes they fight and he succumbs to her wishes. He simply can't handle her, that is how it has always been. When she is around, he withdraws completely.

"If my husband buys me anything, even a new vacuum cleaner, and Mona's coming to the house, I hide it. If he bought me a bracelet, she would go crazy. She would call him at the office and hint that she wanted the same one. She has no boundaries and she is confused about her son's adulthood. I feel like telling her that his priority is me now, not her.

Carly takes a deep breath, then goes on, "My way of handling this problem to invite her to visit only overnight, although they live four hours away and would like to come for several days. I hold the visits to a minimum. When Mona stays at the house, she acts as if she is royalty and I'm supposed to wait on her the entire visit. She is phony when my friends come over and acts generous and kind, which she is not. Mona is definitely not what I had in mind when I imagined a mother-in-law. Then I think about what a no-win situation it is. After all, neither of us is going to change."

Tracy has similar disputes over space and money with her mother-in-law. She takes a similar approach to Carly's and is able to distance herself. "As far as my mother-in-law goes, I don't even know she's around half the time. She doesn't fit in with my life or my values. Out of a perverse curiosity, I will invite my in-laws to come for a weekend. Anne, my mother-in-law, does not want to visit us nor does she want us to visit her. I can't believe the excuses she makes up when I do invite her. Her priority is her social life in the town where she and my father-in-law live and my husband grew up. So in a sense, our relationship works because she stays in her hometown and I stay in mine.

"What bothers me is how Anne keeps track of our money. I know that in a few years she will be asking my husband for money and he will feel guilty and say yes. It's not that I begrudge them anything, but we have commitments of our own. We have children and their education ahead of us. Just because we live well, it isn't as if we shouldn't reap the rewards of my husband's success. My mother-in-law, in all fairness, is the one who encouraged my husband to work hard and to achieve. She recognized his potential when he was just a child. For that, I appreciate her. I simply can't be with her and I don't think that will change."

Traditionally, a marriage is more than the coupling of two people. It is the joining of two families, emotionally, physically and sometimes financially. Yet, in my research, I have listened to many daughters-in-law and mothers-in-law who attempt to disregard this concept. In many cases, each woman chooses to live her life as if the mother-in-law or daughter-in-law does not exist. The high divorce rate in America may contribute to the distance between a mother-in-law and her daughter-in-law and explain the reluctance to become attached. In this way, the two women are societally driven to put up walls between each other. Yet, there are those mothers-in-law and daughters-in-law who simply are not interested in connecting on interpersonal levels. One issue in particular which is played out in many families, whether the mother-in-law and daughter-in-law are close or not, is problems concerning money.

Money, a source of disagreement between many husbands and wives, is also one of the great motivators in life. Nevertheless, it remains a complication in marriages today and affects each member of in the triangle. There are familial standards and anticipated values which come from both families of origin and which, unfortunately, rarely seem to be in sync. In-laws and money are two underlying forces in marriage. When problems arise over this, feelings of resentment and competition are evoked.

One common situation which causes disagreements is when the son and his wife have money and the son's parents have little, as is the case for Tracy. If the mother has pushed her son to succeed and her own husband is not successful, she may feel entitled to a portion of her son's financial success. A daughter-in-law may resent this assumption and feel that the co-mingling of finances with her in-laws is distasteful. When the son and daughter-in-law do support her in-laws, the daughter-in-law may feel she is sacrificing in order to enable her mother-in-law to live well. "What makes this worse," Alice Michaeli notes, "is when the in-laws have a 'depression generation mentality' and act as if they have no money. These people have lived through an ordeal and never want to feel poor or needy again. It turns out that sometimes these in-laws have stored money away for emergencies or later use, expecting to be subsidized in the present by their children."

POOR MOTHERS-IN-LAW
* The mother-in-law believes she is poor and entitled to be cared for by her son.
* The son feels that he must to fulfill this obligation.
* The daughter-in-law believes her mother-in-law covets the life the younger woman leads.
* The daughter-in-law is indignant and resentful.

Another common theme causing problems is one in which the mother-in-law has money and this makes her more attractive to her daughter-in-law. The mother-in-law might disparage her son because her husband is so successful and her son hasn't achieved this level of prosperity. The shortcomings and demands of the mother-in-law might be overlooked by the daughter-in-law for the bigger picture: money. In this situation, the tables are turned and it is the daughter-in-law who desires the mother-in-law's life. She may compare her lifestyle to her mother-in-law's lifestyle and feel that she is being cheated. Whether her mother-in-law is generous to her or not, the daughter-in-law will try to be reasonable and accommodating, while she hopes that she and her husband are remembered in the will.

"I believe that it was easier to make money years ago," Eva, a mother-in-law of twenty-five years, admits. "It was a simpler world and there was less competition. You did not have to be well-educated necessarily, but you had to have the drive. My husband has always been driven and he has been rewarded. Maybe our boys are too soft or spoiled, I don't know. The irony is that they are in the same business as their father, but the business is not what it used to be and they aren't as motivated as my husband was. My husband remains the senior partner and the boys seem like children working for their father in some respects. I imagine this bothers their wives.

"Nonetheless, my daughters-in-law look to us to take them everywhere, at every holiday, on every vacation, on weekends away. I do it because I never had daughters and I enjoy their company. Also, I do it because it gives me a chance to be with my sons. It makes us seem like a happy extended family and we are. Not for one minute, however, do I fool myself that my daughters-in-law love me for myself. My two daughters-in-law asked to be bought and we are able to buy them. All of us get a kick out of the lifestyle, but sometimes on my birthdays, as I blow out the candles, I feel my first daughter-in-law in particular, looking over my shoulder. She's waiting for the money we have to be hers, for her life to be better."

If the son and his father are in business together, the daughter-in-law may feel that her mother-in-law is reaping more rewards than she. Her mother-in-law may be controlling, because she can be. In this case, the mother-in-law's attitude is that her husband has essentially provided for her daughter-in-law and grandchildren. Some mothers-in-law will buy their daughter-in-law's affection, if the daughter-in-law is so inclined. While it may be a superficial basis for a relationship, when it succeeds, the two women bond.

CONTROL THROUGH MONEY
* The mother-in-law has more money than her son.
* The daughter-in-law can be influenced by the gifts given
  to her by her in-laws.

   In some families of wealth, deals are made between in-laws to keep
a marriage together or to pacify the daughter-in-law. J. Randy Taraborrelli,
in his recent book, *Jackie Ethel Joan*, reports that in 1957 Jacqueline Kennedy
Onassis was unhappy in her marriage to John Kennedy. Her father-in-law,
Joseph Kennedy, was determined that Jackie would not divorce John and
harm his political career. In order to appease his daughter-in-law, writes
Taraborrelli, "Joseph and Jackie actually agreed upon a trust fund in the
amount of one million dollars for any children she might have in the
future." Joseph Kennedy also promised his daughter-in-law that if she did
not have children within five years, the money would revert to her. When
Ethel learned of the trust fund and became indignant, her mother-in-law,
Rose Kennedy, suggested she discuss the matter with "Mr. Kennedy"
directly. Yet Rose Kennedy, in her role as mother-in-law, had strong feelings
about financial matters, too, and complained to Bobby about his wife
Ethel's "spending habits."
   When we apply the principle of homogamy to marriages with
money, we see that matching social characteristics, such as the same level of
lifestyle, mingling with the same people in the same places, bodes well for a
marriage. Yet there still may be discontent. "If both sets of in-laws are
pleased with the match between their children, but the children are not
happy, they might be married because of financial and social expectations
and not for love," Alice Michaeli remarks. "In this case, the money and patterns are shared and this is considered enough reason to be together."
   "My mother-in-law, Stacia, definitely exerts control through
money," says Erica, who has been a daughter-in-law for seven years. Every
year she gives us a substantial check at Christmas time. The understanding
is that it is to be used as she deems fit and that means not frivolously. Stacia
tells us she wants us to have this money while she is alive, but there are
many strings attached. At first I found this attitude of hers to be very trust-
ing and generous, but I don't think so anymore.
   "Recently, my husband, Gabe, and I found a house to buy and she
vetoed it. She disliked the place and said it needed so much work that she
withdrew the money gift. That was how we were told that she was dissatisfied. My husband simply does whatever he is told, as if he is still a small
boy. I didn't expect him to have such a wishy-washy response. I suspect
that when his father was alive, his mother exerted control over him and

was a bossy wife. I am not like that. I am interested in equality and a partnership. What I'm really interested in is not having my mother-in-law in my face, deciding where and how we should live simply because she can pay for anything. I'd rather live in a small apartment and be independent. I wish my husband saw it this way. He is brainwashed by his mother."

Money evokes strong reactions in people, as evidenced in Erica's interview, and works in unanticipated ways. For Vanessa, a mother-in-law to whom I spoke, the power she believed she had through her money was overshadowed by the money her daughter-in-law's family brought to the marriage.

"My son, Jeremy, was raised," says Vanessa, "knowing his family had money. While I wanted him to marry someone of a similar background, including education and religion, I did not expect that he would. The irony is that Jeremy married someone of great social status, surprising us all. Her parents have more money than we do and they hand it out freely. I have been accused of controlling my children through money, but my son has been bought by his in-laws.

"What happens now is that there is an ongoing competition between my son's and his wife's lifestyle and ours. If we have a party, she has a better one; if we go on a trip, she plans one. Ashley, my daughter-in-law, is continually showing me that their life is superior, and of course, this competition includes my other sons and their wives. Why doesn't my son say to his wife, these are my parents and siblings, why must you compete with them? Instead, he says nothing and has no allegiance. I cannot speak to him or to her. It is as if money is the only ingredient in their marriage and in my relationship with my son. As for Ashley, she wants no real relationship with me."

Another aspect of competition between a mother-in-law and a daughter-in-law may be over physical appearances. If a mother and her daughters are glamorous, the son might want a very different kind of wife. If looks have been overemphasized, the son might want a wife who is intellectual and not invested in her looks. If the mother-in-law is very intellectual or not concerned with her appearance, the rebellion for the son-husband may be to marry a woman who is good-looking, because she is the opposite of his mother. "When a mother-in-law has low self-esteem," psychotherapist Brenda Szulman warns, "no matter what her daughter-in-law is like or how she behaves, the mother-in-law will find fault with her." In each of these scenarios, competition will persist between a mother-in-law and a daughter-in-law.

"I'd say that the beginning of my relationship with my mother-in-law, Penny, was fairly good," Christine acknowledges. "She tried to be friendly and I tried to please her. Later on, however, she came to resent me and the lifestyle I shared with her son. Once we had a little money, she begrudged me whatever I had. If she hadn't had it in her marriage, if she hadn't gone to this restaurant or shopped at this store, why was I entitled to such things? Penny made sure my husband knew that she thought he spoiled me. Her view was that her son had forgotten her influence, how she had raised him. She didn't like that he did things in his own way. I think he did it because it infuriated her. So maybe it was really about the two of them, but she laid it all on me. She once told me that I had not put enough time in to deserve my life and that she had waited for years to live the way that I do.

"Later, Penny began to tell me how she had looked at my age and how I wasn't aging as well as she had or as she had expected that I would. It was so unfair, the comparisons and the way she would not let up. She was the one who created the distance and the competition. I would not have chosen this path for us."

Family therapist, Olga Silverstein, in her book, *The Courage to Raise Good Men*, reveals that many men are angry at their mothers and have "frequently generalized this anger to women as a class and to their wives in particular." She goes on to say that there is no pattern to this anger, but that it applies to many situations. A son can be angry that his mother was overprotective, too distant or too smothering. A case study Silverstein cites concerns a man and his wife who argue over how much time is spent with the wife's mother, compared to how little time is spent with the husband's mother. The conclusion is that although the son is not close to his mother, he hopes that his wife can be.

When a mother-in-law and her daughter-in-law are embroiled in an endless competition, such as Christine described, part of the problem is the son's history with his mother having a spill over effect. Whether the mother was close to her son during his formative years or not, she does not want to be replaced by her daughter-in-law. The competition begins when the mother-in-law becomes afraid of losing her son. She does not necessarily want to be involved with her son's wife, yet she grieves for her lost time with her son.

"The daughter-in-law replaces the mother-in-law," says Dr. Ronnie Burak. "The mother-in-law is too worried about losing her son to embrace her daughter-in-law, a relationship which the son might want to see between his mother and wife. This is complicated by the fact that daughters usually stay closer to their mothers as they get older." Although he may have no real closeness with his mother, the son-husband may be bothered when he notices that his wife is close with her mother, but not his. To make matters worse, the mother-in-law and daughter-in-law may begin to compete for the son's affection, for time with the son, for attention and to be the priority. The triangulation thus increases between the three players.

TRIANGLES EVERYWHERE
* **The daughter-in-law is distant from her mother-in-law.**
* **The mother-in-law fears losing her son to his wife.**
* **The son wishes his mother and his wife had a good relationship.**

Most mothers, as Rita's story illustrates, worry about their children's happiness. "I can't decide," admits Rita, "if Mark, my son, is a fool or thrilled with his marriage. I haven't lived with him for so long, I cannot judge. He chose this woman, Abby, to be his wife so he must know what his needs are. I just question whether she can really make my son happy. She seems like such a drain on him. What I witness is that Mark works very hard all day long and then returns home after grocery shopping and begins to cook dinner for his wife and children. What has she done all day? Doesn't she know how to fix a meal? I know that when my husband came home, dinner was ready and waiting.

"I am right around the corner and I tell my son that I will make dinner—he can even bring it home if he likes. I don't offer for Abby, I offer for Mark's sake. I do worry about him, but I don't worry about the children, because my daughter-in-law is an excellent mother. I believe that in this area, Abby is the best. I know how devoted I was to my children and I recognize that same devotion in her."

When evolution works, the daughter-in-law, by definition of her role as wife, is in the position of making decisions with her husband. She is his priority, not his mother. Yet she has her own fears and is concerned that her husband is still ruled by his mother. "A daughter-in-law also worries, like her mother-in-law, about having influence with her husband," Dr. Ronnie Burak points out. "If she feels the mother-in-law is still in charge, the daughter-in-law worries that her husband makes decisions that are not in her best interest." It is at this juncture that the daughter-in-law may attempt to keep her husband away from his mother.

AVOIDANCE
* **The daughter-in-law stays away from of her mother-in-law.**
* **The daughter-in-law worries about her mother-in-law's influence over her husband.**
* **The daughter-in-law does not want to be evaluated by her mother-in-law.**

In Clarissa's case, her husband was complicit in creating an unhealthy situation. "Jeff wasn't able to make a plan without consulting his mother," complains Clarissa. "When we got married, she moved right around the corner, to be close to her son, not to me. She would try to see him without me, but I made too much of a fuss for that to go on. I thought that he was spending too much time with her as it was. She wasn't willing to let go and admit he had a wife and that he was grown up. My mother-in-law began to invite us over every Sunday and so I made plans with friends or bought tickets to an event, anything to avoid being with her on a weekly basis.

"My mother-in-law would call at home and say, 'Put him on.' She never so much as acknowledged me. The strangest part is that I have a very nice father-in-law who says nothing. How can he stand his wife to be falling all over their son? To me, my father-in-law's behavior and attitude towards his son are much more appropriate. However, my mother-in-law won't let go. She wants Jeff for the same reasons that I do, because he is handsome, young and entertaining. But she can't have him; he's mine, not hers."

Both a mother-in-law and her daughter-in-law may be possessive of the son-husband. "A mother-in-law might be distrustful and territorial about her son, because she sees her daughter-in-law as someone foreign and therefore a threat," says Brenda Szulman. "There are loyalty issues when the daughter-in-law is introduced in the picture. Once the mother-in-law recognizes that the daughter-in-law is here to stay, she may become competitive or controlling."

Madeline's daughter-in-law is in love with her son, and Madeline respects this, although she also resents it. "I do know that Brian is completely delighted with his choice of a wife. Shannon is tender, kind, sensitive and madly in love with him. I also know that I spoiled him and she has to deal with it now. Rationally, I know that my daughter-in-law is good for my son and they are building a life together, but I'm still bothered by her. In truth, her life is nothing like mine was at her age. I was saddled with three kids and a house to keep clean. My daughter-in-law has a high paying job, which my son likes, and they have freedom without any children.

"I look at them and I wish I could turn back time. I simply don't know how they have it all and I missed out. I find myself more reclusive and depressed since my husband died and I wish I could have more time with my son. Had he married another kind of woman, he might be more available to me. Shannon is not in the least bit interested in me, but she humors me. To her, I don't really count. I would say that she is sometimes more respectful of me than my son is, but there is no feeling there, no emotion at all. If I call him and Shannon is there, I get the feeling I am intruding on them. My son does not seem to remember me anymore."

In love-based marriages, the man and woman choose one another and the parents have little or no say in their decisions. There are cultures that advocate arranged marriages, but for the most part, it is the love-based marriage that prevails. "When someone is free to marry whoever she/he wants," comments Alice Michaeli, "it causes more problems for a mother-in-law. She has very little power over her son and an extended family hasn't the standing and authority that it wields in an arranged marriage. Arranged marriages are very respectful and inclusive of the extended family, which then has a critical role in the new couples' life."

Rochelle, who has been a daughter-in-law for fourteen years, married for love. "My marriage was the opposite of an arranged marriage. My mother-in-law, Betty-Ann, would not have approved of me for one second, had she hadn't any position to say so. We have not gotten along from the start. She is a miniature version of my husband and I am tall and physically unlike her. In fact, I am totally unlike my mother-in-law in every way possible. The more I have gotten to know her, the more this has seemed true. She is completely rigid, selfish and self-indulgent and I'm flexible to a fault.

"Betty-Ann will stop at nothing to satisfy herself. She takes an inventory of her clothing. She is obsessed with her personal items and appearance. My mother will go to a hairdresser once in ten years while my mother-in-law will go three times a week. Her life revolves around herself and I think she works at a part-time job just so she can avoid me and the children. But what she does is to compare herself to me on an ongoing basis and she always comes up the winner. I tolerate all of this because my husband would be torn apart if I made a big deal of it. I put up with his mother, because it eases the tension for him."

Sarah's bad feelings toward her mother-in-law have not subsided with time and are similar to Rochelle's. Despite her negative feelings, she too has made the decision to put up with her mother-in-law for her husband's sake. "My mother-in-law will do anything for my husband's affection and always on an exclusive basis—that is, with me left out. Brad is her only son and while he is always on my side, he will never confront his mother. He says he will not fracture the relationship by confrontation. My mother-in-law has created this universe where she alienates me and reveres her son. What I realized early on in my marriage is that I have clout, because I am the wife. It is really my call and if I wanted to sever my relationship with her, even though it would upset Brad, I could. I don't do this, because I love my husband and I don't want to divide his loyalties. I know his fundamental allegiance is to me. This has to bother my mother-in-law who is always trying to be first. I have my share of power, however, which is why she has to accept me on some level."

In my research I found that sixty-five percent of the mothers-in-law felt that their daughters-in-law were responsible for the competition between them. Twenty-five percent desired to end the competitive nature of their relationships with their sons' wives and ten percent felt that their daughters-in-law's families instigated the competition between them.

Of the daughters-in-law, over fifty percent felt their mothers-in-law were to blame for creating competition between them. Forty percent held their husbands responsible for the dissension and ten percent were hopeful they could surmount the competitive impulses between themselves and their mothers-in-law.

The March/April 2000 issue of *Modern Maturity* magazine contained an article by Linda Greider titled "How Not to be a Monster-in-Law and Other Tips for the 'Other' Woman." Greider describes the behavior of "monster" mothers-in-law as those who disparage their daughters-in-law (adding that this harms a future which includes grandchildren), those who interfere with the couple's decisions and those who are rigid. She recommends that a mother-in-law establish a cordiality with her daughter-in-law's parents, that she be independent, avoid money issues and not compete or engage in power plays with the daughter-in-law.

In this chapter, we have seen how forms of competition between a mother-in-law and her daughter-in-law cause deep disturbances in the marriage. The goal is for both the mother-in-law and her daughter-in-law to behave in a mature fashion, and for the undercurrents and comparisons to cease. If a mother-in-law is not critical or intrusive and does not compete with her younger, more progressive daughter-in-law, this can happen. In return, if a daughter-in-law is more accepting of her mother-in-law's ways and does not find fault so easily with her, the two women can forge a bond. Both women have to acknowledge that they share in each other's lives as defined by their roles and must strive to achieve a comfort zone therein.

9

Holidays/Repeat Manipulations

"When my husband and I were first married," Lena recalls, "my mother-in-law expected us to show up for every holiday at her house and be there only for them. She disregarded my family completely. We happen to live far away from both sets of parents so it was always a conscious decision as to which family we would visit to celebrate. My husband's family is a much closer knit family than mine. My mother-in-law makes a big fuss over Christmas and Easter and, now that I have children, I admit it is more festive to get everyone together at my in-law's place. My mother-in-law takes pride in the celebration being perfect. However, we have to be perfect, too, and she has to be in charge.

"I also have my parents to think of. My mother doesn't demand anything of us because she claims her own mother demanded too much. So, that is how we end up being with my mother-in-law so often—she demands it. After several years of this, I am coming to the conclusion that while my mother-in-law may request our presence, I can also spend some of the holidays with my parents. We are not keeping score here, but it's that there are two sets of parents and a husband to please."

There are some mothers-in-law who do not easily tolerate resistant daughters-in-law when it comes to celebrating the holidays. Such a mother-in-law will repeatedly insist on observing the holidays in the way she wants them and on her terms. The stress created may make the holidays unbearable for the daughter-in-law. As in most mother-in-law/daughter-in-law circumstances, the son-husband is called upon to take a stand. If he defends his wife, his mother might or might not back off, but undoubtedly will become angry.

Holiday celebrations often reveal dysfunctional families at their worst. At holiday time, there seems to be a universal expectation that everyone is content and delighted to be together. "What helps to make the holidays successful," advises Antoinette Michaels, relationship expert, "is a family in which there is an emotionally healthy mother-in-law and an emotionally healthy daughter-in-law instead of competition and anger between the two women."

A daughter-in-law's response to her mother-in-law's request that she have Thanksgiving dinner at the older woman's home might be annoyance or even anger. Possibly the daughter-in-law comes from a different kind of family than her husband and she is not used to their rules or ways of doing things. Her mother-in-law will see nothing wrong with making the request, while the daughter-in-law finds it an imposition and an intrusion. This often creates conflict.

Lucia has experienced this type of conflict with her daughter-in-law. "My daughter-in-law, Neva, knows nothing about how to cook for people and how to be gracious," says Lucia. "I don't mind that she is from another culture, but I do think she can open her home for one holiday a year. Instead, she cries to my son that she is not prepared and that she doesn't know how to do it. I say, learn how. I did and most women do. I sometimes wonder how Neva was raised; maybe she doesn't want to share my son with me.

"Neva is my second daughter-in-law and the way our family works, we each take a holiday which when we host relatives. It's time for Neva to choose a holiday. My first daughter-in-law always hosts Easter dinner. I have said a few things to my son, but either he doesn't get my hints or he doesn't want to get it. What I have decided is that I shouldn't make a scene. I remember my mother-in-law and things she said that I didn't like. I won't do it that way. It will take time for me to learn Neva's ways. I've observed that her family is not warm or social and I think that is part of the problem."

A daughter-in-law's response to hosting the command performance of a holiday meal can go one of two ways. Either she accepts, perhaps even offers before it is asked of her, or she rebels.

Carrie, a daughter-in-law of three years, is reluctant to entertain her in-laws on holidays or weekends. "Before we were married, Rick and I did not see his family or mine too often. Since we have been married, Rick is always asking if we can visit his parents on a Saturday afternoon. Before we were married, we split the holidays evenly between the two families. Suddenly, it is all about his family. And now my mother-in-law is bossing me around about making an anniversary dinner for her and her friends.

"Rick sort of defends me, but he doesn't really see anything wrong with pleasing his mother. He seems to be a pushover when it comes to these things or he just chooses the path of least resistance. I don't appreciate the result. Meanwhile, I called my mother for her support and she said, stop making a fuss and just do it."

Often, the son-husband has been indoctrinated into the ways of his family for his entire life. He may not be supportive of his wife since her opposition seems curious and he doesn't quite comprehend it. A daughter-in-law may feel threatened by her mother-in-law's demands if she comes from a disengaged family where there are no rituals. The concept of hosting a holiday or family festivity is unfamiliar and probably unnerving, to her.

FAMILY WAYS
* **The daughter-in-law is baffled by her mother-in-law's treatment of the holidays.**
* **The mother-in-law demands that the daughter-in-law and son observe the holidays her way.**
* **The son-husband knows his mother's way of celebrating, while his wife is unfamiliar with the family rules.**
* **The son-husband may not always intervene.**

A mother-in-law might not purposely be contentious over holiday celebrations or any other occasions for that matter. She simply regards her requests or requirements as normal and undemanding. Regardless of how she appears to a new daughter-in-law, family get-togethers can be reinforcing for a mother-in-law. If she fits the definition of a "midlife" woman and still has her own mother-in-law to deal with, she does better in her life when family ties are positive, according to a study by Elizabeth L. Paul. In "A Longitudinal Analysis of Midlife Interpersonal Relationships and Well-being," Paul reports women in midlife find there is a "positive affect" when they feel connected to their own mothers and their grown children. If we take this finding a step further, a productive relationship between a mother-in-law and her young daughter-in-law is valuable for the mother-in-law.

Marta, a fifty-something woman, sounds apologetic when she discusses her holiday celebrations. "I confess that we do have rules about holidays," says Marta, a mother-in-law of three daughters-in-law. "My third daughter-in-law, Patricia, has been in the family for six months. Every time there is a holiday she has a problem with our plans. My first two daughters-in-law have never said a word. Each of them alternates Thanksgiving and Easter and I am in charge of Christmas. Patricia has caused great trouble, because she contests our plans. She wants her parents invited, which is difficult, although my son has asked, so I will say yes. Now she wants to host the family on Christmas Day. I told my son, Andrew, that she could have a party Christmas Eve, since Christmas Day is when the biggest traditional family celebration takes place, and he said no. Several weeks ago, Patricia and I argued about it in her kitchen and then she strongly suggested I leave. I have never been disrespected like that by anyone before.

"Andrew should have done better. He should have mediated this from the beginning. I deserved to be respected and my way of conducting the holidays should take precedence. Presently, Patricia and I are not speaking and Andrew calls me from work to check in. I plan to continue Christmas Day at our home, as we have always done."

The question of whether to celebrate a certain holiday in a specific way is one of control and dominance, explains Antoinette Michaels. "I have had clients come to me because the mother-in-law and daughter-in-law are feuding over Christmas Eve or Christmas Day. If both families celebrate Christmas Eve, for instance, then it gets complicated. The daughter-in-law might want to host it or be with her family, while her mother-in-law expects to be in charge and for everyone to be at her home. Both the mother-in-law and daughter-in-law feel entitled to have the holiday as they see fit."

These problems escalate when a mother-in-law listens to her daughter-in-law, but remains immutable in her options. Her attitude may be, *How dare you, I always planned this event.* The mother-in-law then tries to inflict guilt upon her daughter-in-law. In return, the daughter-in-law may feel a strong loyalty to her family at holiday time and will not relent. If either woman issues an ultimatum, every member of the family becomes involved. In such cases, the father-in-law often will be protective of his wife while the son-husband is protective of his own wife.

WAR
* **The mother-in-law insists the holiday be celebrated as she wants it.**
* **The daughter-in-law refuses.**
* **Both women stand their ground and their husbands are forced to take sides.**

Dr. Michaele Goodman describes holidays and vacations as "crisis points" in a many marriages. At these times, even between mothers-in-law and daughters-in-law who have established working relationships, there may be eruptions and serious misunderstandings. "Since these flare ups are unavoidable at holiday time or when the couple and the in-laws are in close proximity," says Dr. Goodman, "the couple has to learn how to deal with it and to make compromises. If such conflicts arise on a weekly or monthly basis between the mother-in-law and her daughter-in-law, then there is something wrong with how the husband deals with his mother and his wife. This may be about the son and his mother."

An extreme example of a negative situation is told by Dora. "I have never had a problem with my daughter-in-law about holidays," says Dora, "yet we have had bitter fights over summer vacations. I am very close to my son, Josh, while I find his wife, Jenny, to be cold and unfriendly. Every other weekend they come out to our vacation house at Josh's insistence. Jenny is quite unpleasant to both me and to my husband. But Josh insists they come and I can only imagine how they fight about it. She ignores us for their entire stay, every visit.

"Josh keeps thinking that these visits are fine, because they please him and I will continue to invite them, because I expect that he wants to be there. As for Jenny, who sulks and won't help in any way, not even lift a finger to set the table or to clear it, she offends me. I believe that though she wanted Josh for her husband, she did not want me as her mother-in-law. We have fights, at least once a visit, where nasty things are said. I don't see any solution in sight."

A daughter-in-law who resists her mother-in-law's overtures and wishes she was not a part of the older woman's life is unrealistic and immature. In retaliation, a mother-in-law may find herself becoming vindictive, reacting to the tension between herself and her daughter-in-law. If the son-husband placates his mother first and his wife second, the pressure builds. This often causes a wedge in the marriage, because the son is still siding with his family of origin. Holidays, vacations and special events, which occur with regularity, have to be handled gingerly, with everyone's feelings, those of the mother-in-law, daughter-in-law and son-husband, under consideration.

In the March/April 2000 publication of *More* magazine, the famed Dr. Ruth Westheimer, admonished a mother-in-law to be more careful with her daughter-in-law. She advised mothers-in-law to "examine their actions and interactions" with their daughters-in-law and to talk directly with their sons about problems with their daughters-in-law. Her view is that sons act as "go-betweens" to help keep the peace.

SONS AS GO-BETWEENS
* **The son-husband does not want to be relegated to a "go-between" role.**
* **Nonetheless, it is necessary for him to consider the feelings of both his mother and his wife.**
* **This effort insures more successful future holidays and events.**

Common sense and generosity of spirit go a long way in ameliorating these types of problems between mothers-in-law and daughters-in-law. Anna is fortunate to have a mother-in-law with both qualities. "My mother-in-law is not a take charge person, but she loves to get the entire family together several times a year," says Anna. "We have family parties and we share the holidays. When I first got married, I think my mother might have been jealous, because my in-laws are so close. She saw that I had entered their world, where people would automatically include me in family events. I looked forward to any holiday celebrations for which I was asked to plan or host, because it meant that I was included. I like this feeling. I want to be a part of the family I have married into. It has enhanced my life.

"What I have learned, however, is that with the responsibility for family events comes the backlash. For instance, if my single sister-in-law hasn't a boyfriend at the time, she gets quite nasty about participating. Sometimes my other sister-in-law tries to outdo me, so that the parties become some kind of competition. My mother-in-law is very gracious when she entertains and when she is entertained. She never stoops so low. Her view is that there are enough occasions to go around. This is how my husband was raised, by someone who has a generous spirit."

I have seen many scenarios where what transpires between mothers-in-law and daughters-in-law are a result of their family histories. If a daughter-in-law comes from a family where there has been little celebration of the holidays, she will likely be either very apathetic about participating or, at the other extreme, she will welcome the chance wholeheartedly. If a daughter-in-law comes from a family where the holidays were festive and important, she will continue this ritual with her husband. Mothers-in-law, of course, have been on the holiday circuits for years and may be more set in their ways. Yet, it might be a treat for a mother-in-law to discover that her new daughter-in-law is ambitious about hosting some holidays. It takes some of the burden off the mother-in-law and she can sit back and admire the energy her daughter-in-law puts into that special day.

What frequently happens when problems arise, however, is that the son-husband backs off. Although I have discussed in previous chapters how significant the son-husband's stance is in the mother-in-law/daughter-in-law/son-husband triangle, celebrating holidays is an area where he seems less motivated to take things seriously. Certain machinations of holiday arrangements have undeniably deeper roots than merely endangered family traditions. More than likely there are deep-seated frictions that exist between the two women which come to full fruition over holiday issues.

According to Dr. Michele Kasson, a son often wants to remove himself when it comes to holiday planning and bickering between his mother and his wife. "The son-husband is looking forward to a pleasant day off from work, surrounded by family and peace and quiet. When the mother-in-law and daughter-in-law begin to argue over the holidays, he does whatever is expedient." Most likely, the son has avoided conflict with his mother his entire life. He is not going to engage her now, especially over something he doesn't see as a high priority.

Herb Goldberg's essay, "In Harness: The Male Condition," discusses the roles that men have been forced to assume in society's script. While we have been exposed to such essays written by and about women, there is much less written by men about their societal plight and how it binds them. Goldberg makes the case that man is "oppressed by the cultural pressures that have denied him his feelings..." He points out that what stifles and stresses men are those labels they are expected to live up to. These roles encompass being a good husband, a good father and a provider. Goldberg's interviewees are so tired from trying to hold it together that a general malaise has set in, along with disappointment. It is doubtful that these men are ready and able, much less willing, to argue over where to celebrate Thanksgiving dinner.

So women, regardless of how far our liberation has taken us and the inroads made, remain the keepers of the house and the guardians of the domestic sphere. While many men are not only bored by the question of where a holiday will be celebrated, they also might not recognize the implications involved. There have been, presumably, many bones of contention between wives and mothers-in-law over time which husbands have been obliged to address. With holidays, once again, these women often compete and beg him to defend and to choose while he would rather avoid the conflict and enjoy his day off.

HUSBANDS AND HOLIDAYS
* Holidays do not represent the same amount of conflict and stress for men as they do for women.
* Men are not particularly interested in the details, and thus may not understand why these celebrations become battlefields between their wives and their mothers.

Babette's son, Jared, is a good example of a man's disinclination to address these problems. "Jared refuses to be supportive when it comes to the high holidays," Babette, a mother-in-law for nine years, tearfully relates, "and things are not improving. It used to be that his wife, Bobbie, would take the children to her mother's house for Rosh Hashanah and they would be with me for Yom Kippur. Then they moved to New

Hampshire. Since they are away from both mothers, they do Yom Kippur with friends and for Rosh Hashanah, her mother comes to visit them along with her sisters. I am deeply offended by this new schedule. Jared is not helpful and hasn't the sense to invite me, too. He has hinted to me that the reason I am not invited is that my husband and I have so many relatives living close to us. I feel rejected by my own son and, not only that, I do not get to see my grandchildren for the holiday.

"I know there is no talking to my daughter-in-law, but Jared should know better. We are a fairly religious family and for us, part of the holiday is being with each other. I have asked my husband to approach him, but he doesn't want to rock the boat. To me, Jared's inability to find a solution here reminds me of how irresponsible he was in college. By not dealing with the issue, he seems immature and unresponsive."

Maureen, a daughter-in-law of sixteen years, is unlike Babette's daughter-in-law in that she welcomes everyone to her house for the holidays. Although her mother-in-law, Harriet, felt her position was being usurped in the beginning, today she is pleased. "I won't say that there haven't been arguments between us," admits Maureen, "but I like having holiday events in my home. Even though it requires planning and I have a full-time job and two children, it also means freedom. I no longer have to listen to my sister-in-law and my mother-in-law while they push and pull about who does what and when. I simply stood up one time, after all these undercurrents, and I said, we'll do the holidays. That really stunned everyone. My husband's family is Jewish and I'm not, but I do observe the holidays with them.

"Although she seems to approve of my meals sometimes, other times, my mother-in-law has been mean about dinners I've prepared. One year I had twenty people at the table, including family and friends which I did on purpose to diffuse the tension created by my husband's family. It was hard to get the food out on time. I heard Harriet complaining to her brother and sister-in-law at the other end of the table that I couldn't serve the food while it was still hot and that every year it is lukewarm and mediocre. I know my husband overheard her, too. Afterward, while we were cleaning up, I asked him about it. He just shrugged and said, 'What do you expect from my mother?' It was at that moment that I knew that hosting the family for the holidays was for myself and my children and no matter what my mother-in-law says or does, I shouldn't let it get to me."

The daughter-in-law who hosts the holiday dinner has the upper hand in many ways. Although the mother-in-law may still be critical, she is now in her daughter-in-law's home and she cannot deny that her daughter-in-law is the one who put in the effort. "When the daughter-in-law sponsors the event," says Brenda Szulman, "she has the power. By having dinner in

her home, she is controlling it. This is on her terms and on her turf and people have to respect it. That gives her the upper hand. Often, she will invite
friends to help insulate her from the family environment."

The reverse applies as well. If a mother-in-law has the dinner in
her house, then the daughter-in-law needs to tolerate her style. As when it
was the daughter-in-law's dinner and she could invite whoever she wanted,
so can her mother-in-law do what she wants as the hostess.

HOLIDAYS AT THE DAUGHTER-IN-LAW'S
* The mother-in-law may be disapproving.
* The daughter-in-law does the work.
* She invites friends to soften family dynamics.
* She gains control.

VS

HOLIDAYS AT THE MOTHER-IN-LAW'S
* The daughter-in-law may feel uneasy.
* The mother-in-law does the work.
* She is in charge of the guest list.
* She has the control.

"During the holidays," Missy, a mother-in-law of eight years, says,
"we always have our children at our house. I have two daughters-in-law
and I see a distinction between them. I cannot really understand my second daughter-in-law, but the first one knows exactly how I do things. We
are all from the same culture and religion so I cannot quite explain why
there is all this tension surrounding the holidays and worse yet, around
vacations. Both sons will call me up and say they want to come to our
weekend house at the same time. We do not have room for the two couples plus their children. On school vacations, it gets worse. I have to allot
the first week to one son and the second to the other. When my third son
gets married, I don't know what I'll do.

"My husband has suggested that we try to buy a bigger house
and have everyone stay there at the same time. Besides the fact that we
can't afford it, my daughters-in-law do not get along well. Holiday dinners
with the two of them and their children can be very tense. My new daughter-in-law thinks the first daughter-in-law is indulged too much by my son.
The first daughter-in-law complains about the second. On holidays I
expect everyone at my table to be cordial, whatever their differences are."

A strong, matriarchal mother-in-law, as evidenced in Missy's interview, sets the rules in spite of any intrafamilial undercurrents that exist. The

concept of the matriarchal society, as Carol Tavris explains in her book, *The Mismeasure of Woman*, was one in which women ruled peacefully many centuries ago. Women were gatherers and men were hunters in some early human societies where the people in a civilization had to cooperate to survive. For this reason, women had equal status to men. In a much abbreviated life span where people lived to the ripe age of thirty, we can imagine that a mutual respect existed among family members. By the eleventh century B.C., Tavris laments, the matriarchy was over and "paradise was lost."

Soon after, society became patriarchal and women lost their status. Juanita H. Williams, in her essay, "Equality and the Family," writes that in modern times the realm of home life has been assigned to women, with the expectation of domestic "serenity" and without hope for equality. As Williams comments, in the area of child care and homemaking women were assigned the caretaker roles. If we keep these long-standing traditions in mind, it makes sense that mothers-in-law demand respect. On the other hand, the world is changing and younger women do not wish to lead convention bound lives and follow roles of the past. This belief pertains to celebrating holidays, as well, where it becomes clear that the old ways do not always apply.

Margaret Mead writes in her book, *Male and Female*, "The institution of marriage in all societies is a pattern within which the strains put by civilization on males and females alike must be resolved." Within these "strains" and anticipated norms of behavior, holidays become fertile ground for misunderstandings between a mother-in-law and her daughter-in-law. It can be very hurtful to a mother-in-law, who highly values family traditions, to find she is arguing with her daughter-in-law over the holidays. Her daughter-in-law is either disinterested in her mother-in-law's needs or has her own agenda, which has merit for her, if not her mother-in-law. Because there is almost always an imbalance in the mother-in-law/daughter-in-law relationship, someone has to be injured by this. Both women hope for family gatherings to be successful, even as they fight for their individual rights.

"I have acclimated to what is available to me." Liselle, a mother-in-law of fifteen years, explains. "I get whatever is left over on the holidays. For instance, both my daughters-in-law go to their families and my husband and I are invited. We then have to decide which daughter-in-law's family's house to go to, if we go to either. However, I am closer to and more comfortable with one daughter-in-law, Erin, than my other daughter-in-law. We know each other's rules. She is very proper, which I like because it is more like the world in which I grew up. I can count on Erin and I trust her. In this sense, she is part of our family. She's been around a long time and while we've had a few tiffs, we know each other's limits. As far as my other daughter-in-law goes, I do not approve of her lifestyle and values, but I would never say anything.

"I never believed that I'd do this, but lately my husband and I have refused both daughters-in-law's invitations for the holidays and we go our own way. Last Easter, I just turned each of them down flat. It seemed easier and less painful and it was. This doesn't mean I don't believe we all should be together, but too often it just doesn't work out. I am finally tired of trying to make it all work."

Celine is another mother-in-law who has decided, after many years of trepidation as each holiday loomed on the horizon, to pull back. "I have decided to give my daughters-in-law the easiest way out. I now let my kids do what works for them. There is enough strife in life without asking my son and their wives to tear themselves apart for me. I won't do that to anyone. Of course, it didn't begin this way. At first, I was very insistent and I told my children what my expectations about observing the holidays were. I insisted that everyone be at our home for every major holiday. No one resisted me, because I have been in charge of anything domestic for my entire marriage and my daughter and sons know how it works. I am also intuitive, however, and after several years, I recognized how my children felt and saw that there were tugs in other directions. I had to let my method of doing things go, because it was no longer working.

"I would not say that my way is obsolete, but I would admit that it doesn't apply to my children's lives and I have to respect this. I am sad, because I miss what used to be and I believed in the way I celebrated the holidays, which is a replica of how my mother celebrated. But I have let go anyway, for the children's sakes."

Of the mothers-in-law interviewed, half are intransigent when it comes to changing their holiday traditions. Approximately forty percent of the mothers-in-law have begun to compromise with their daughters-in-law and ten percent are at a standstill on the subject of holiday celebrations. Half of the daughters-in-law who were interviewed expressed a strong desire to break free of their mothers-in-law on holidays altogether and half are in search of compromises they can reach with their mothers-in-law.

Although we cannot generalize about a mother-in-law and daughter-in-law in every scenario, because each story has unique components, there are recurrent topics. For the myriad of interviewees, the subject of how holidays and to a lesser extent, vacations, are handled, holds great weight. While the husband and wife function as a team, they might not always operate together when it comes to the mother-in-law and plans for these occasions. "Just because the son-husband tries to please his mother and gets along well with his wife, does not mean that his mother and his wife will get along," Dr. Ronnie Burak warns. "The hope is that a son who does not get along with his mother will have a wife who is able to get along with her. Then the holidays are taken care of for him. What works best is when the mother-in-law takes the initiative of having a decent relationship with her daughter-in-law, because it will also improve her relationship with her son. The mother-in-law also has to respect that her son has a new primary family and let go."

LETTING GO
* **The mother-in-law realizes that the family cannot be together easily for holidays.**
* **She faces that life is changing.**
* **She lets go, for her children's sakes.**

"Originally, the holidays were shared between our two families," Darcy, a daughter-in-law of six years, explains. "My husband, Tye, and I would have part of a meal with my mother-in-law and then drive across town to my stepmother-in-law's and then finish at my mother's house, two towns away, where we would have dessert. After doing this for awhile, we were exhausted and we just gave up. My mother-in-law became hostile when I stood up for myself and told her we were changing our plans. Eventually, she has learned not to intervene—only because she saw me pulling away from her dictate. Once she had calmed down, I told her what Tye and I needed in our marriage and from her, and she listened.

"Now, during the holidays, we try to accommodate everyone, but we alternate our visiting. We tend to gravitate to my family on Christmas. What we decided was that since my in-laws are divorced, it's too complicated to please all the members on that side of the family. It wasn't just Tye's mother, but his stepmother we had to deal with, and those two women are embroiled in their own competition. My husband and I have made the decision that it is better to be with my family for holidays and an occasional Sunday dinner. We will do less formal things with my mother-in-law, like dropping by for an hour or two. We have come to an understanding."

The mother-in-law who is able to trade control for communication, as it seems Darcy's mother-in-law did, is at an advantage. While this requires trust, patience and time, the outcome is usually positive. The daughter-in-law becomes more flexible, yet is able to state and fulfill her needs. The mother-in-law also strives to be less rigid. The husband is happiest when his wife and mother are not pulling him in two different directions.

10

Resolutions/Mellowing
With the Years

"Time has calmed both of us," Monica concedes, "and, Lily, my mother-in-law, and I are no longer combative. This has taken twenty-four years and plenty of histrionics—it didn't just happen overnight. In my maturity, I have learned how to handle my mother-in-law. I have also learned how to assert myself so that my children and husband both come before my mother-in-law and my mother. In a way, Lily and my mother are very similar: demanding, expectant and aggressive. Both my husband and I had to learn how to say no to both mothers.

"I suspect that I married too young and was not equipped to cope with my mother-in-law. I was still afraid of my own mother at the time and I felt like I was caught between the expectations and demands of both these difficult women. I was fighting for my rights with my mother and my mother-in-law, two women who should have made life pleasant for me. Instead, they pushed and pulled at me. I also was trained to be a 'good girl' and felt uncomfortable arguing or causing a stir. I wanted to be involved in the mother-in-law/daughter-in-law relationship, yet at the same time, I also wanted to disappear and be free of it. What really changed matters around was when my husband saw my pain and began to seriously listen to me. Then I knew that my life counted and my mother-in-law's reign began to dissolve. That was when I saw that I could be a good daughter-in-law, for real. Once I saw how it worked and what I could and couldn't accept, I calmed down and was able to have a reasonably healthy, balanced relationship with my mother-in-law."

The recurrent theme in the mother-in-law/daughter-in-law dynamic is the daunting task of establishing a wholesome, civil relationship that may span half a century. Within this extensive, possibly fifty year connection, there is a defined beginning, middle and end to the mother-in-law/daughter-in-law relationship. It is not only a naive, young bride who may find herself in a quandary over her newly acquired family member. Despite the maturity and life experience of an older woman who becomes a daughter-in-law for the first time, she, too, may be ill-prepared for the consuming effects of marriage combined with the imposition of a difficult mother-in-law.

When a son marries early, he may be in search of a woman who will treat him the way his mother did. "Some men marry young, in search of the same emotional security as they had at home," Dr. Michelle Kasson explains. "This sets up a competition between the mother-in-law and daughter-in-law since they each have the same relationship with the son. Ideally, as years pass, family relationships mature. The mother-in-law who felt competitive toward her daughter-in-law initially, now relaxes. Once the mother-in-law accepts this change in status, the two women have a chance to be close."

Raising a son in our culture is one of the most challenging tasks expected of mothers. Olga Silverstein remarks in her essay, "Mothers and Sons," that mothers have perpetuated the myth that sons are encouraged to don armor in order to face the world as men. She notes "the paradoxical role of women in mothering sons," and describes the mother as "nurturing, caring, responsive, self-sacrificing." Men, by contrast, are raised to be detached, independent, aggressive and free. Even now, at the dawn of the twenty-first century, this remains our established social structure. The daughter-in-law/wife, in some ways, has not achieved a great deal more ground than her mother-in-law when it comes to dealing with the men in her life, her husband and her son(s). Most women, however, learn as they go along, becoming the wiser for the experience.

Mother-in-law and daughter-in-law alike, regardless of their age differences, share certain roles as women in a patriarchal society. It is ironic that a daughter-in-law who has been critical of her mother-in-law for years, blaming the older woman for her husband's shortcomings, eventually finds herself raising her own sons and utilizing similar methods.

"I think back to the girls my son dated and I don't think I ever liked any of them," Veronica admits. "No one seemed wonderful, no one seemed good enough, so maybe it was my problem. Then my son decided on Gabrielle and she has been his wife for sixteen years. She was very determined and there was no way he was going to escape her once she'd set her sights on him. In some ways, I admired her for that, but I also disliked it. She is a very bright and capable wife. She makes my son feel important, which he needs. The best part is, I'll never have to worry about him again, because she takes good care of him. Either I'm losing my sense of humor or Gabrielle is getting one, because things are slowly improving between us.

"I know what she goes through, raising three sons, and no matter how times have changed and how women say they are able to handle a job and a family, some things never change. I know what her responsibilities are, as a mother raising sons. I identify with her, because I raised boys as well. Gabrielle knows that and we look at each other and agree, it isn't easy. When I go to her house, I l always notice her wedding album on the coffee table. Who would have dared to tell a young bride all she will experience as a wife and mother? I now feel a great solidarity with Gabrielle, because we have experienced so much that is the same. That's why we have to keep together, no matter what our differences were at first."

We need only to look at Tipper's and Al Gore's wedding picture to see what an innocent bride of twenty-one was like in 1970. In *Inventing Al Gore* author Bill Turque writes of Tipper's first meeting with her future mother-in-law, Pauline Gore, as an intimidating and formidable affair. After all, Al Gore's parents had high hopes for their son's political career. Pauline Gore, who, Turque indicates, was as much the senator as her husband, was determined that no one get in the way of this ambition. By contrast, former First Lady Barbara Bush writes in her memoir that her daughter-in-law, Laura Bush, wife of her son George, "is a very special person" and considers her excellent company. Tipper Gore and Laura Bush became daughters-in-law to different, but equally strong women.

As the years have passed, we can assume, as in so many mother-in-law and daughter-in-law situations, Tipper Gore and Laura Bush came to understand their mothers-in-law. For political wives whose husbands follow family traditions of service to their countries, mothers-in-law who have stood in similar positions have set certain precedents, despite the changing times. The Kennedy family women are described by author J. Randy Taraborrelli in *Jackie Ethel Joan* as "Kennedy wives." This included Rose, the matriarch, and her daughters-in-law, Jackie, Ethel and Joan. All four women "often influenced the course of events" and functioned as public relations links with their husbands' constituencies.

Joseph Kennedy was fascinated with his daughter-in-law, Jackie, but, Taraborrelli indicates, Rose was less smitten with her. Once Jackie became the first lady, she garnered the most attention of all the Kennedy women. While Rose might have resented her daughter-in-law's charm and status, according to Doris Kearns Goodwin in her book, *The Fitzgeralds and the Kennedys: An American Saga*, she could not have influenced her. Jacqueline Kennedy was too unlike the Kennedy clan to ever be fully invited in by them or to assimilate completely. Any mutual acceptance between mother-in-law and daughter-in-law in this case was a kind of compromise. One wonders if these two "Kennedy women" were ever united, even when John Kennedy died and they were bound by loss and grief.

The circumstances of life may prompt a mother-in-law and her daughter-in-law to form a practical connection. This might occur when the daughter-in-law is unexpectedly widowed and mourns along with her mother-in-law. When a daughter-in-law loses her mother, she may, as a result, become closer to her mother-in-law or perhaps the mother-in-law loses a sibling and so does her daughter-in-law, uniting them in a mutual sorrow. In the worst of all possible circumstances, a child/grandchild becomes ill or dies and the mother-in-law and daughter-in-law are locked together in unspeakable grief. In the face of a tragedy, both women may come to recognize that their petty battles and power struggles are virtually meaningless. Mother-in-law and daughter-in-law may seek each other out in a time of crisis and misfortune.

THE BONDS OF LOSS
* **The mother-in-law grieves for a beloved family member who has died.**
* **The daughter-in-law grieves also.**
* **The women are bound together in sadness and loss.**

Dalia, who was widowed at the age of thirty-three, struggled to find a comfortable rapport with her mother-in-law despite their common tragedy. "There is no question that Janie, my mother-in-law, was there for me as I was for her. We had gone through a terrible ordeal together. Still, there had been so much stress caused by my husband's illness and this affected my mother-in-law and me. Sometimes things were strained between us. I had three young daughters and I was overwhelmed by caring for them and coping with my husband's illness. His mother and I hung in together, because we were hoping for his recovery. After two years, we knew he wouldn't make it. Janie and I had to get through all of that together, too. And we did. We were there for each other, sharing our horrific loss. She knew, though, that she could never replace her son, but I was a young woman who could remarry. I hadn't died, but a part of me had. At first, I felt as if she looked to me to be a martyr. I knew, however, especially after I had seen the face of death, that I would not be that. I intended to grab hold of life, wherever I could.

"Years later, I have a satisfying relationship with my mother-in-law. I have remarried and Janie accepts this. She has arrived at some sort of peace with her son's death and she agrees it is good for my girls that I have remarried. Sometimes at night I remember what it was like, those days when Todd was fighting for his life and his mother and I stood at his bedside, helpless. Then I feel love for her and I have this sense of duty to her, because she was and is my first mother-in-law and we will always share that bond."

Other difficult circumstances affect the mother-in-law/daughter-in-law relationship in a positive way. For Rollie, a change of heart toward her mother-in-law occurred after the older woman survived cancer. "My mother-in-law, Marie, came to live with us after her surgery," Rollie explains, "because she was a widow and I couldn't stand for her to be alone to recuperate. We had never really gotten along and I'm sure she saw things she didn't like about me and probably sensed how I felt about her. However, this situation was bigger than our fights and it was time to overlook our differences.

"That was all well and good, but my husband and I live in a small home and I gave her my daughter's room since she was away at college. It was still a very confined situation and the room was crammed full of my daughter's things. Despite all this, my mother-in-law was extremely grateful. Also, I feel I have made my husband very happy. He has assumed financial support of his mother, too, which would have infuriated me before she became ill. I know how hard he works and how hard I work and I would have fought him on it. I also know Marie wasn't left with much money when she was widowed. When you are alone and sick, money is the one thing about which you need to feel secure. Basically, I have let bygones be bygones. She is staying with us indefinitely—something I would not have predicted would ever happen, but it is working out fine."

When the mother-in-law is not as powerful as she once was, physically or emotionally, the daughter-in-law will often change her attitude and become more caring. If a mother-in-law cannot carry on with the same vehemence toward her daughter-in-law and is, in fact, fighting for her health, a daughter-in-law will not engage her in disputes. The realities of aging change both women. "Just as our mothers become weaker, so do our mothers-in-law," Dr. Michaele Goodman notes. "This evokes another kind of response for the daughter-in-law. Seeing a woman age and perhaps become ill has tremendous impact on the younger woman and the reality that life is finite sets in." A mother-in-law who is frail or who has a physical impairment will usually invoke her daughter-in-law's sympathy.

OLDER, FRAILER MOTHERS-IN-LAW
* **When a mother-in-law loses her health and becomes ill, the daughter-in-law sees her in another light.**
* **Whatever acrimony transpired between the two women may dissipate.**
* **The daughter-in-law may care for her mother-in-law.**

There are certain other situations which offer the mother-in-law and daughter-in-law a chance at becoming close, even after a rocky history. "If the daughter-in-law becomes motherless at some point in her marriage," Brenda Szulman, psychotherapist, explains, "the daughter-in-law might then look at her mother-in-law differently. If a daughter-in-law becomes estranged from her mother, her mother-in-law could eventually become a mother figure to her." In return, over time the mother-in-law often comes to appreciate how her daughter-in-law has balanced her marriage, career and children and has proven herself to her mother-in-law. What the mother-in-law once criticized, she might come to admire.

"I was hard Zoe, on my daughter-in-law," confesses Marion, "because she was married to my only son. For ages, no matter what she did, it wasn't right and it wasn't enough. My daughter-in-law knew how difficult my son could be and I'm sure she blamed me for how I raised him. Zoe accused me of giving her mixed messages, like *Why don't you return to work, you both need the money* versus *How could you contemplate returning to work and abandoning these children?* I look back and I see that I have not been easy on her. We simply did not get along and the times I spent alone with her, without my son or my grandchildren, were uncomfortable.

"Then I was widowed and I became more needy. After fifty years of marriage, I was sad and I watched myself become a lonely old woman. I have always dreaded being alone in the world and now I am. I can read my daughter-in-law's face when she comes to visit and I know how I have shrunk from life. Today, I give Zoe credit that I would not have before. I see my daughter-in-law as strong and focused, as someone who will share her time with me and who has feelings for others. I know she would not send me off to a nursing home or care facility. I count on her to keep me here, because she understands that I want to remain in my home as long as I am able. I do regret how hard I was on her in the past."

"Often, we encourage our parents and in-laws to move to a warmer climate and we ship them off to Florida or Arizona," Alice Michaeli, sociologist, points out. "Then the mother-in-law and daughter-in-law do not have as much interaction as they would if they lived close to each other. In some ways, this eliminates the tension of face-to-face communication." In terms of keeping in touch, a savvy mother-in-law might take a computer course and learn how to E-mail her children and grandchildren on a daily basis. While this works out well if a mother-in-law is happy to live in a new community, far from old friends and family members, for those mothers-in-law who do not find the idea appealing, the obligation to care for them as they grow older often falls on the daughters-in-law's shoulders.

Priscilla's mother-in-law's illness represented an opportunity for her and her husband. "I thought that when my mother-in-law, Maude, had a stroke it would be the end of my marriage. This happened over a year ago. My husband said she had to stay with us, because there was no one else to care for her. It was the first time that I hated where we lived, because it was her hometown, too. Her two daughters live thousands of miles away and that is why we became obligated to care for her. Maude came to live with us and we fixed up our guest room for her. For months, I was very angry about this. In fact, I was furious because our lives were being changed by her. She was fine as a mother-in-law, although I had always kept my distance. I never sensed a lack of communication and her company was fine. But this was something else entirely, having her live with us. On top of being sick, my mother-in-law, who keenly felt her limitations, became depressed. She became so numb from all of her medication, she could barely communicate. That was what got my attention and made me feel terrible. I found myself reading to her and trying to bring her out of her depression. My husband was very grateful to me and that encouraged me. I began to forget what went on before her stroke and I could only take pity on her. In a strange way, my mother-in-law's condition has given me direction and made me more compassionate."

DAUGHTER-IN-LAW AS CAREGIVER
* **A mother's serious illness forces her son to take her into his home.**
* **The daughter-in-law accepts the role of caretaker.**
* **The husband is grateful to his wife for her efforts.**

The ultimate test of the mother-in-law/daughter-in-law connection comes when the mother-in-law is gravely ill and it becomes the daughter-in-law's responsibility to care for her. Strangely enough, this shift in familial duty could be for the best, according to Dr. Ronnie Burak. "When the mother-in-law is older and needs care, it is a way to bring the mother-in-law and daughter-in-law closer together. However, this depends on both the history of the two women before the mother-in-law fell ill and what type of care is required of the daughter-in-law. If a mother-in-law is incapacitated, this may be too much of a burden for a daughter-in-law to take on. Most importantly, the husband and wife should not fight over his mother's situation." Though it is not always the case, the two women will usually become closer when the daughter-in-law is caring for her mother-in-law. By this time, the mother-in-law will hopefully let go of judgements and criticisms and appreciate her daughter-in-law's effort. At the same time, the daughter-in-law will have gained perspective and won't take things her mother-in-law does and says personally. Open communication between husband and wife is essential in to ease burdensome decisions and tasks related to the mother-in-law's care.

GAINING PERSPECTIVE
* **A daughter-in-law who cares for her ill mother-in-law should set limits.**
* **She should not take her mother-in-law's complaints or depression personally.**
* **Communication between husband and wife is key.**

"Once my mother-in-law moved in with us, I saw where my husband got all of his negative traits—not that I hadn't suspected all along," Suzanna begins. "Before then, I never had the opportunity to see my mother-in-law in her own home, instead visiting with her at restaurants or other relatives' homes. So I had had no idea how she acted in a domestic setting. I saw pretty quickly that my husband gives orders, because his mother always gives orders. I began to look at my husband and say to myself, *He's exactly like his mother, always telling me what to do.* To make matters worse, my husband and his mother don't even get along.

"By this time my mother-in-law was very ill, so I tried to let the smaller issues go. But I still fought over the bigger ones. For instance, my husband, who has a controlling personality, would tell me I couldn't go to a meeting at night. Then his mother would echo his sentiment. Once she opened her mouth, my husband would disagree with her and tell me to go to the meeting. That was how he reacted to her. Meanwhile, this was all happening while she was confined to a wheelchair. Frankly, I had no intentions of listening to either of them anyway.

"What I do respond to in my mother-in-law is her emotional neediness. That was how we achieved some kind of peace between us. The old games and disagreements of the past began to recede and I was able to have sympathy for her and to see some of the humor in my situation. What I really learned is how women age, because if my mother-in-law is this old, then I am also gaining in years. Dealing with her aging and her illness has made me more contemplative and more considerate. This circle of life I see before me makes me more introspective and pushes me to do the right thing."

The problems in many mother-in-law/daughter-in-law relationships reflect similar issues that arise between mothers and daughters. Many times a daughter-in-law's response to her mother-in-law will be an extension of her response to her own mother. Nancy Friday writes in her book, *My Mother My Self,* that a daughter eventually "accepts that mother didn't have to be perfect." Friday recommends we daughters, "give up our resentment that she (our mother) wasn't ideal so that we can take in what she was good at." Once this happens, the daughters' lives will be uplifted, according to Friday. If we take this concept and apply it to our mothers-in-law, it becomes apparent that daughters-in-law who achieve a certain serenity with their mothers-in-law are the winners. Daughters-in-law might come to see, in time, that their mothers-in-law's intentions were always sincere or that the good the women projected outweighed the bad.

IMPERFECT MOTHERS-IN-LAW
* The daughter-in-law appreciates what her mother-in-law has taught her.
* The daughter-in-law recognizes her mother-in-law's intentions and accepts her imperfections.
* She is old enough to handle two mother figures.

Over time, mothers-in-law like Bernice, come to recognize their own and their son's imperfections. "I no longer find fault with my daughter-in-law, Kendra, because I have come to admit my son's shortcomings," Bernice tells us. "It took me fifteen years to be able to reach this conclusion. My son has not been able to keep a job and this causes tremendous pressure for my daughter-in-law. Money is tight and this makes her unhappy. Kendra has stuck it out and she has carried him, much as I would have, through the toughest times. How can I be hard on her, when she saved my son?

"I must seem unfriendly to her. She sees how busy I am with my daughters and their children. One daughter is on welfare and obviously she needs the most help of all with her kids and her work schedule. We are close, because in our family mothers help their daughters. I have a sense that Kendra needs me now, maybe she needed me all along. I regret I wasn't there earlier, when things started to sour with my son. I should have praised her more and told her she was a good daughter-in-law and a good wife. I know my son couldn't be without her. I'm ready to let her into the fold, if it isn't too late."

For a mother-in-law who was afraid that her son would not be protected without her support or that her connection to him would be usurped by her daughter-in-law, it may take many years for her to give credit to her daughter-in-law. If the son is troubled or has career setbacks and his wife is supportive, the mother-in-law will most likely come to recognize her value as a wife. There is proof that the couple, in hardships and in happy times, work hard to stay together. Any choices and mistakes the son has made with his wife belong to the marriage and are off-limits to the mother-in-law. Eventually, the mother-in-law will see the substance and worth of both the marriage and her daughter-in-law.

HUMBLE MOTHERS-IN-LAW
* **The son-husband has matured with his wife beside him.**
* **His wife has stuck it out through thick and thin.**
* **The mother-in-law recognizes the daughter-in-law's devotion to her son and becomes supportive of the younger woman.**
* **The two women reach an understanding.**

The idea that people change over the years as they mature holds true. "People get wiser," Antoinette Michaels points out. "What is important at the age of twenty is not as important at forty. By the age of fifty-five and older, there are fewer unnecessary issues bothering people. Often, both the mother-in-law and daughter-in-law give up some of their efforts to gain control. The two women then rise above their own egos and this diminishes the conflicts between them."

Nancy, after eighteen years of marriage, has come to the conclusion that Ida, her mother-in-law, deserves to be a part of the family. "I spent all these years pushing her away. I think I associated anything my husband did wrong as something he had learned from his mother and as a rejection of me. I was young and I really took offense. I disliked the examples that my mother-in-law had set for her children. So I stepped aside while my husband and his mother battled it out, but I was always on his side and he knew it. I did not want to get into the middle of their flights and I didn't let my mother-in-law get into ours. I was too pragmatic to play the game or so I thought. Now I know that if you are a daughter-in-law, you are a part of whatever goes on in the family. It's inevitable.

"We are all older now and once I learned that I have power, because I am the wife, I became secure. I stopped *trying* to be loving and kind to my mother-in-law and just became loving and kind to her. I stopped caring if Ida blackened my husband's mood and what kind of pathology was between them. I stopped filling in for him when my husband tried to escape her visits. I used to think, *I'm not the one she wants, she wants her son.* Now I'm not so sure. Her husband is very ill and she counts on me. We get along—I see her good points. She sees mine, too, and we don't worry about the rest. We are family, after all this time."

The process of aging ties into the gradual peace that comes to mothers-in-laws and their daughters-in-law. The daughter-in-law is no longer an insecure young bride nor a young mother. Her self-esteem and sense of confidence have improved and she knows where she stands in her marriage. In cases where the daughter-in-law and her husband perceived his mother as an enemy and were united against her, these feelings dissipate and eventually cease. Now that the mother-in-law is widowed or her husband is in a nursing home leaving her ill and alone, the daughter-in-law shows compassion for her mother-in-law, who then, in turn, reaches out to her son and his wife. An effort is made by both parties. Grown grandchildren who are attentive to their grandmothers also help to fill the void in these women's lives. There is compassion from the family toward this ailing, aging and, perhaps, lonely woman. For those mothers-in-law and daughters-in-law who were quarreling for years, the war is finally over.

"The problems I had with Tammie, my daughter-in-law," Bridget concedes, "were because of my son and grandchildren. I was too invested in how they were doing to go easy on Tammie. I suppose I was vying for attention when she came along and she got back at me through the children. My son tried to be a kind of referee and to placate us both, but that didn't work. I think we had to work it out our way, which was loud and vicious at times and not very flattering to either of us. Some nasty things were said and done. It isn't as if we ever blended together, like some Kodak advertisement.

"My son and Tammie have been through a great deal together and this has brought them closer. After ten years or so, I saw them disconnect from me and it frightened me. I didn't want to grow old with my son alienated from me. I am a widow and recently my sister died. Then I stopped wanting to be a negative topic of conversation in their marriage. So I told them this and they were astonished. Together, we have come to some agreement."

As is evident from Bridget's comments, expectations and attitudes alter as we become older. A mother-in-law who was ready and able to fight it out with her daughter-in-law in the early stages of the marriage, recognizes the dangers of this behavior as she grows older. When we ask ourselves the question, *What makes people change?*, the answer is life's circumstances. As a daughter-in-law becomes a seasoned mother and an older woman, her mother-in-law is not as intimidating to her as she once was. At the same time, her mother-in-law may not be interested in continuing the conflicts that exist between them. By now, she may be widowed, divorced or ill. "Even the most argumentative of women become mellower as they age," Dr. Michaele Goodman remarks. "They do not have it in them anymore. Philosophically, people get tired of fighting the same battles." Once the fighting stops, tranquility and acceptance often replace past issues. There is more time and energy for other aspects of life once bitter arguments between mothers-in-law and daughters-in-law cease.

EXPECTATIONS SHIFT

* **The grandchildren are grown, whether the mother-in-law agreed or not on how they were raised.**
* **Both women are entering new phases of their lives.**
* **Their experiences change their perspectives.**
* **Neither mother-in-law nor daughter-in-law wishes to be combative anymore.**

The benefits of aging are documented by author Joan Borysenko in her book, *A Woman's Book of Life*. For women, once the years as a mother have ended, the future now provides a new beginning. "Modern women enter the previously uncharted, unnamed midlife years, a time of life that used to be synonymous with old age," with many opportunities available to them, Borysenko asserts. An older woman who has fulfilled her obligations as wife, mother, mother-in-law and grandmother, now has the option to try something new and not altogether predictable. Borysenko describes this older woman as someone who is a "peace-keeper" but prepared to be a "warrior for justice." These women, many of whom are mothers-in-law, are improving with age and are at last able to celebrate the qualities that they have had throughout their lives. As author Natalie Angier views aging women in her book, *Woman: An Intimate Geography*, "the elder female is somebody we have always known. She is there in the corner of the female unconscious, quiet, fierce, loving, obliterating."

Maturity has helped Lillian become a caring and thoughtful mother-in-law. "I have been a mother-in-law for seven years," Lillian tells us, "and a daughter-in-law for thirty-five years. There have been uncomfortable feelings between my daughter-in-law and me on occasion, but they have passed. I try my best to make ours into an open and friendly relationship. What I wish is that I was more involved in her life and my son's life. This has to come from my daughter-in-law, because I know from my own experience as a daughter-in-law, the wife is the one who sets up the social life and any extended family life. Mostly she and I discuss her three children and I love to hear how they are doing.

"I have taken what I learned from my mother-in-law and mother and tried to give this knowledge to my daughter-in-law. Today I am in my mid fifties and I feel stronger and wiser than ever before. My mother-in-law has lived with me for twenty-five years, ever since my husband put an addition on our house and gave the space to his mother. When my husband died, I knew that she would stay and that it would be the two of us living together.

"It was after I lost a child and a husband, that my mother-in-law, a widow for thirty-five years, and I truly came together. We had both had happiness and sadness in our lives. We've come to understand each other. I hope my daughter-in-law can be open to what I have to offer. Our relationship has been difficult so far. She is polite, but distant. It could take years and life experience for her to see what I am striving for. I know I wasn't ready for my mother-in-law in the very beginning. I tell my daughter-in-law that I approve of her mothering and her part-time work, because I have always worked. Gradually, I think things will improve."

When we combine the knowledge of how women strengthen with age with the complicated relationships that exist between mothers-in-law and daughters-in-law, we see how time often works its magic on refining and improving the interactions and feelings between the two groups of women. In the final analysis, in spite of their many mixed feelings, these women need each other.

POSSIBLE PATH FOR THE TWO WOMEN
* **A daughter-in-law is uncertain she wants to let her mother-in-law into her life.**
* **A mother-in-law is uncertain her daughter-in-law is deserving.**
* **Both women search for fulfillment and independence.**
* **Many times, a daughter-in-law nurses her mother-in-law in the final years.**
* **Both women age, mature and come to understand each other.**

Cynthia is an example of a woman who has achieved great growth and maturity over the years. "I was married so young, at eighteen," Cynthia, a mother-in-law and daughter-in-law, muses. "In retrospect, I realize I was only a kid. I did not know that my mother-in-law was not comfortable with us as a couple and my husband was clueless. She wanted to be the matriarch and not only was that not what I had in mind, but I didn't understand her role in the family. I played at being a wife and daughter-in-law but I really didn't know what I was doing. That was fifty years ago. Since my mother-in-law died only five years ago, it was a lifetime that we spent together. We learned from one another. The times were not the same, but taking care of children was not that dissimilar. After the first ten or twelve years, my mother-in-law and I learned to get along. She began to appreciate me and we stopped the ridiculous tugs of war. Because of this reversal in our relationship, I was determined to be a good mother-in-law from the start. I decided I wasn't going to make my daughter-in-law prove herself to me.

"Time is a great healer and whatever went wrong at first with my relationship with my mother-in-law is long forgotten. For the last eight years of her life, she lived with us and I was happy to take care of her. I have friends who say the worst nightmare in the world is caring for your mother-in-law when she is dying, but it wasn't that way. My daughter-in-law has had a firsthand look at what happens to women. We outlive our husbands, we become tough after we have been told to be weak and then we age, first gracefully, then horribly, then we die. Men seem to fade as they get older whereas women get older and stronger. Meanwhile, my daughter-in-law is young and I don't say too much. I just let her know I want to be connected to her in some way."

There are many possible combinations of mothers-in-law/daughters-in-law today, be it a vital mother-in-law who is seventy with a newly wed forty-year-old daughter-in-law, to a daughter-in-law who is twenty and has not only a young mother-in-law to contend with, but her mother-in-law's mother-in-law, a grandmother-in-law. In any of these scenarios, it is unlikely that the women want an ongoing hostility, particularly the women who have reached maturity. Even if the two women get off to a bad start, a truce is always possible and something to work toward. Both daughters-in-law and mothers-in-law can then begin to start their relationship on a new, more fulfilling path.

The battles between mothers-in-law and their daughters-in-law can actually harm the marriages. What is necessary for a cease fire is for one of the women, or both, to ask why is this going on and why continue. "Over the years, I have become more sympathetic," Evelyn, a daughter-in-law, tells us. "I have pity for my mother-in-law, because she is enfeebled. She has two daughters, but she is not close to either of them. She was only close to her sons and one of them died. Then my husband became her only son. Her mentality is that the man gets the bigger piece of meat. Since I come from a family of girls, her way of thinking really irritates me. Then I say to myself, what is the big deal? There have been so many incidents and ongoing fights. I'm sure that my mother-in-law feels that I never gave enough to her as a daughter-in-law, but I'm not really sure what those requirements were. Every time we had a family get-together, we invited her. Now, I find I have a soft spot for her, because she is older and sickly. Her one effort recently, asking my husband and me to come visit for a weekend, because she was feeling better, meant so much to me. I decided that I don't want to hold grudges. Who knows how much time is left for her and I don't want to make any more mistakes. One day I'll be in her shoes and I already can project what will be reasonable and what will seem cruel."

Witnessing the process of dying makes it almost impossible for people not to soften their hearts. "It is very hard not to open a door when faced with a dying mother-in-law," Dr. Michaele Goodman comments.

"Illness and approaching death give both women the chance to try one last time and to feel good about each other. Whatever battle of wills has persisted, they are finally laid to rest. The mother-in-law and daughter-in-law are able to let go and any suffering one inflicted upon the other is forgiven."

"Right before my mother-in-law died," Tabitha recalls, "she told me that I'd been good to her. This was coming from a woman who had nothing nice to say about anyone, a woman who I had loathed in my twenties, tolerated in my thirties and nursed in my forties. I suppose I was flattered; I was definitely touched. I realize now that while I always said my mother-in-law had little impact on my life, she actually did. She was there, very much in my husband's life and I was acutely aware of it and how it affected me. I am grateful for how she raised her sons. Over all, she was beneficial in my life. And I will not forget that I was there, holding her hand, when she died."

Epilogue

In viewing the mother-in-law/daughter-in-law relationship on the threshold of the twenty-first century, we see that age-old problems will continue and new problems will arise. However, the triangle formed by mother-in-law/daughter-in-law/son-husband remains a constant in our changing society. As women from across the country came forward candidly to share their tales, I realized that what is significant is how modern themes have made an impact on the conventional roles of mother-in-law and daughter-in-law. The narratives throughout the book substantiate the fact that divorce, custody battles, remarriage, interracial marriage, interfaith marriage, wives' commitments to careers, finances and longevity influence how the relationship between the two women functions.

Betty Friedan wrote of the joylessness of being a wife and homemaker almost thirty years ago, in *The Feminine Mystique*. Yet even today, many mothers-in-law remain dedicated to the concept of home and family. What we see from the multitude of women I interviewed is that mothers-in-law today must coexist, happily if possible, with a new breed of daughters-in-law, who often challenge the "traditional" mother-in-law/daughter-in-law bond. There are mothers-in-law who have evolved, too, becoming more independent and less available to their families. What has not been created yet, however, for either role, is a new and revolutionary replacement for the traditional relationship.

The concept of family values, those of togetherness, loyalty and stability, still rank high on the list of priorities in most families today. In

Marriages and Families, edited by Mary LaManna and Agnes Reidmann, we are reminded of the concept of families wanting to perpetuate themselves as a group. It is the personal versus the communal goals of the family that become so striking. A daughter-in-law most commonly seeks the individual orientation of her husband's family and may resist the group orientation.

Notwithstanding many daughters-in-law who desire autonomy, there are mothers-in-law and daughters-in-law who are more open with each other than in the past. This openness manifests itself in more honest, possibly more demanding, relationships. In many cases, the stereotypical mother-in-law of yesteryear, a woman who commanded the respect of her daughter-in-law and son, a matriarch within the patriarchy who grew old caring for and running her extended family, no longer abounds in great numbers. This iconic figure has been replaced, in many cases, by mothers-in-law who have established their own careers and have sought their destinies in the workplace. Hence the "norm" is shaken. Possibly, there no longer is a "norm." This new style also applies to those mothers-in-law who are not working, but who travel the globe or move to create a life of their own, free of the classic obligations of the mother-in-law. There in lies the empty nest syndrome in reverse, created by the free-spirited, nimble bodied mothers-in-law of the new millennium.

I found that daughters-in-law do appreciate mothers-in-law who offer satisfying connections. This kind of mother-in-law knows that boundaries are beneficial in creating good relationships and that both women will benefit from sharing their lives with each other. In some cases, the two women may treat each other with respect, but are not attached in any meaningful way. There is neither antagonism nor is there a great deal of interaction or bonding.

A daughter-in-law who hasn't the historical respect for her mother-in-law and is not one to keep her feelings to herself, is a product of our times. How can we expect a woman who has gone beyond her mother's generation educationally, and maybe beyond her husband's accomplishments in the work world, to follow the lead of the traditional, fifties model daughter-in-law? Her values may not mesh with her mother-in-law's and the generation gap is wide, yet certain expectations may still prevail. The mother-in-law might come to admit this breadwinning daughter-in-law is an asset to the marriage. The modern daughter-in-law may come to value some of the traditional concepts of life in the extended family that she once denigrated.

Above all, let us remember that there are many mothers-in-law who approve of their daughters-in-law and provide support without imposing on their lives. In fact, such mothers-in-law enrich the younger women's lives. What I found notable in my research, also, was that a large number of mothers-in-law, despite their differences with their daughters-in-law, consider them to be good mothers to their grandchildren.

Let us bear in mind that in many cases, the son-husband also must learn he needs to communicate with his wife and mother. This is key. With his assistance, the relationship is able to move forward decisively, with enlightened self-awareness on the part of both women.

As Thomas More reminds us in his book, *Soul Mates*, each family member needs to look at the larger picture, that of the rewards of belonging to a family. "It's often a struggle for family members to forge a new imagination of what they are, especially as various members go through their individual rites of passage and life transitions. But if they have the courage to imagine themselves continually as family, while remaining loyal to their traditions, they will be caring for the family soul."

In the intensely personal, penetrating narratives that I have presented in this book, a myriad of both mothers-in-law and daughters-in-law have expressed profound disappointment, frustration, distance and rivalry. But ultimately for many, a mutuality develops, a joining together, which benefits and enriches the lives of both women. To gain this end, compromise is necessary on the part of both mothers-in-law and daughters-in-law. New attitudes and appreciation of the divergent roles of women are needed for the mother-in-law/daughter-in-law relationship to become more flexible, honest and giving.

Mother-in-law/Daughter-in-law Questionnaire

One hundred and fifty women responded to this survey. The results follow.

MOTHERS-IN-LAW

1. Please state your age.

48-52	10%
53-58	20%
59-65	11%
66-72	28%
73-80	30%
81-85	1%

2. At what age did you become a mother-in-law?

36-45	1%
46-52	67%
53-58	20%
59-65	12%

3. How many children do you have?

1	16%
2	44%
3	30%
4	9%
5 or more	1%

4. Do you get along with your daughter(s)-in-law?

Yes	30%
Fairly well	30%
No	20%
Very Poorly	20%

5. Is your daughter-in-law close to her mother?

Very Close	31%
Close	34%
Not Close	25%
Not Applicable	10%

6. Did you have a close relationship with your mother-in-law?

Very Close	10%
Close	33%
Fairly Close	14%
Not Close	33%
Poor	10%

7. Do you think your daughter-in-law is a good mother?

Yes	40%
No	10%
Fair	30%
Not Applicable	20%

8. If applicable, how many grandchildren do you have?

1	16%
2	40%
3	30%
4 or more	14%

9. Do you believe your daughter-in-law is a good wife to your son?

Yes	40%
No	30%
Fair	30%

10. What do you admire most about your daughter-in-law?

Organizational Skills	40%
Mothering	40%
Energy	20%

11. If applicable, does your daughter-in-law encourage her children to spend time with you and to develop a close relationship?

Yes	45%
No	25%
Sometimes	30%

12. Do you host family dinners and encourage family get-togethers?

Yes	55%
No	20%
Sometimes	25%

13. If applicable, does your daughter get along well with your daughter-in-law?

Yes	30%
No	30%
Sometimes	40%

14. Did you approve of your son's choice when he married his wife?

Yes	40%
No	25%
After Time	35%

15. Has your son divorced
    and remarried, thus
    giving you at least two
    daughters-in-law for
    this son?

    Yes   40%
    No   60%

16. What do you value most
    about your role as a
    mother-in-law?

    Having Grandchildren   40%
    Seeing Son Happy   30%
    Getting To Know   30%
    Daughter-In-Law

DAUGHTERS-IN-LAW

1. Please state your age.

   25-29   9%
   30-34   33%
   35-39   11%
   40-44   10%
   45-49   24%
   50-54   13%

4. How many children do you
   have?

   0   31%
   1   21%
   2   21%
   3   19%
   4 or more   8%

2. At what age did you become
   a daughter-in-law?

   20-24   37%
   25-29   44%
   30-34   8%
   35-39   6%
   40-44   5%

5. Do you get along with your
   mother-in-law?

   Very Well   8%
   Yes   55%
   Fair   23%
   No   10%
   Very Poorly   4%

3. How many years have you
   been married?

   Less than 5   25%
   5-9   18%
   10-14   30%
   15-19   9%
   20-24   5%
   25-29   11%
   30-34   2%

6. Are you close with your
   own mother?

   Very Close   33%
   Close   47%
   Fairly Close   12%
   Not Close   4%
   Not Applicable   4%

7. If you have children from a previous marriage, how does your mother-in-law treat them?

Kindly	40%
Indifferently	40%
Not Very Kindly	20%

8. If your husband has sisters, how do they treat you?

Inclusive	30%
Exclusive	43%
Indifferent	27%

9. If applicable, is your mother-in-law close to her daughter(s)?

Yes	60%
No	20%
Somewhat	20%

10. If applicable, do you think your mother-in-law feels you are a good mother?

Yes	47%
No	22%
At Times	31%

11. Do you believe that your mother-in-law feels you are a good wife?

Yes	67%
Maybe	21%
No	12%

12. Has your relationship with your mother-in-law changed since your children were born?

Yes	58%
No	22%
Somewhat	20%

13. Has your husband been involved in the interactions between you and your mother-in-law?

Yes	71%
No	12%
On Occasion	17%

14. What do you admire most about your mother-in-law?

Generosity	30%
Tenacity	15%
Dedication To Family	55%

15. Do you encourage your children to spend time with your mother-in-law and to be close?

Yes	65%
No	16%
On Occasion	19%

16. Do you ever feel that you are excluded from your mother-in-law's and/or sister-in-law's plans?

Excluded	63%
Not Excluded	10%
Sometimes	27%

References

Angier, Natalie. *Woman: An Intimate Geography*. New York: Anchor Books, 2000.

Bateson, Mary Catherine. *Composing a Life*. New York: Plume, 1990.

Borysenko, Joan. *A Woman's Book of Life: Biology, Psychology and Spirituality of the Feminine Life Cycle*. New York: Berkeley Publishing Group, 1998.

Bush, Barbara. *Barbara Bush: A Memoir*. New York: St. Martin's Press, 1994.

Chodorow, Nancy. "Family Structure And Feminine Personality." In *Women, Culture and Society*, edited by Rosaldo and Lamphere. Chicago: University of Chicago Press, 1999.

Daniels, Pamela. "Dreams vs Drift in Women's Careers: The Question of Generativity." In *Psychology of Women: Selected Readings*, edited by Juanita H. Williams. New York: W. W. Norton, 1985.

Davidson, James. "Outside the Church." *Commonweal*, September 1999.

Fales-Hill, Susan. "My Life in Black and White." *Vogue*, June 2000.

Faludi, Susan. *Stiffed: The Betrayal of the American Man*. New York: William Morrow, 1999.

Friday, Nancy. *My Mother My Self: The Daughter's Search for Identity*. New York: Delacorte, 1977.

Friedan, Betty. *The Feminine Mystique*. New York: Dell Publishing, 1973.

Gilligan, Carol. *In a Different Voice: Psychological Theory and Women's Development*. Cambridge, MA: Harvard University Press, 1982.

_____. "Woman's Place in a Man's Life Cycle." In *Psychology of Women: Selected Readings*, edited by Juanita H. Williams. New York: W. W. Norton, 1985.

Glenn, Evelyn Nakano. "From Servitude to Service Work: Historical Continuities in the Racial Division of Paid Reproductive Labor." In *Feminist Frontiers*, edited by Richardson, compiled by Taylor and Whittier. New York: McGraw Hill, 1996.

Goffman, Erving. *The Presentation of Self in Everyday Life*. New York: Anchor, 1959.

Goldberg, Herb. "In Harness: The Male Condition." In *The Norton Reader*, edited by Peterson, Brereton and Hartman. New York: W. W. Norton, 1996.

Goodwin, Doris Kearns. *The Fitzgeralds and the Kennedys: An American Saga*. New York: Simon & Schuster, 1987.

Greer, Germaine. *The Female Eunuch*. New York: McGraw-Hill, 1971.

Greider, Linda. "How Not to be a Monster-in-Law and Other Tips for the 'Other' Woman." *Modern Maturity*, March/April, 2000.

Hite, Shere. *The Hite Report on the Family: Growing up under Patriarchy*. New York: Grove Press, 1994.

_____. *Women and Love: A Cultural Revolution in Progress*. New York: Alfred A. Knopf, 1987.

Kleiman, Gerald L., Myrna Weissman. "Depressions Among Women." In *The Mental Health of Women*. London: Academic Press, Ltd., 1980.

LaManna, Mary A. and Agnes Riedmann. *Marriages and Families*. Belmont, CA: Wadsworth Publishing Co., 1999.

Lerner, Harriet G. *The Dance of Anger: A Woman's Guide to Changing the Patterns of Intimate Relationships*. New York: HarperCollins, 1997.

Martinez, Ruben. "The Next Chapter." *New York Times Sunday Magazine*, 16 July 2000.

Mead, Margaret. *Male and Female: A Study of the Sexes in a Changing World.* NY: William Morrow, 1949.

Moore, Thomas. *Soul Mates: Honoring the Mysteries of Love and Relationship.* New York: Harper Perennial Library, 1994.

Ojita, Mirta. "Best of Friends, Worlds Apart." *New York Times,* 5 June 2000.

Paul, Elizabeth. "A Longitudinal Analysis of Midlife Interpersonal Relationships and Well-being." In *Multiple Paths of Midlife Development,* edited by Lachman, Margie and Jacquelyn Boone James. Chicago: *University of Chicago Press,* 1997.

Robinson, B. A. "Facts About Inter-faith Marriages." Internet, www.religioustolerance.org, March 1999.

Rossi, Alice. "The Bio-social Side of Parenthood." In *Psychology of Women: Selected Readings,* edited by Juanita H. Williams. New York: W. W. Norton, 1985.

Shapiro, Stephen A. *Manhood: A New Definition.* New York: Penguin Putnam, 1985.

Sheehy, Gail. *New Passages: Mapping Your Life Across Time.* New York: Ballantine Books, 1996.

_____. *Understanding Men's Passages: Discovering the New Map of Men's Lives.* New York: Ballantine Books, 1999.

Silverstein, Olga and Beth Rashbaum. *The Courage to Raise Good Men.* New York: Penguin, 1994.

Silverstein, Olga. "Mothers and Sons." In *The Invisible Web: Gender Patterns in Family Relationships,* edited by Walters, Carter, Papp and Silverstein. New York: Guilford Press, 1988.

Singer, David, ed. *American Jewish Year Book.* Vol.98. New York: American Jewish Committee, 1998.

Stengel, Richard. "Let Us Now Praise Social Climbing." *New York Times,* 16 July 2000.

Taraborrelli, J. Randy. *Jackie Ethel Joan: Women of Camelot.* New York: Warner Books, 2000.

Tavris, Carol. *The Mismeasure of Woman: Why Women are Not the Better Sex, the Inferior Sex or the Opposite Sex.* New York: Touchstone Books, 1993.

Temmerman, Fennella. "Letters to Columbia." Internet, www.aifw.org/aif/journies/columbia.htm.

Turque, Bill. *Inventing Al Gore.* New York: Houghton Mifflin Co., 2000.

Walters, Marianne. "Caught in the Muddle." In *The Invisible Web: Gender Patterns in Family Relationships,* edited by Walters, Carter, Papp and Silverstein. New York: Guilford Press, 1988.

Walters, Carter, Papp and Silverstein. *The Invisible Web: Gender Patterns in Family Relationships.* New York: Guilford Press, 1988.

Westheimer, Dr. Ruth. *More,* March/April 2000.

Williams, Juanita H. "Equality and the Family." In *Psychology of Women: Selected Readings,* edited by Juanita H. Williams. New York: W. W. Norton, 1985.

Williams, Juanita H. "The Importance of Marriage." In *Psychology of Women: Selected Readings,* edited by Juanita H. Williams. New York: W. W. Norton, 1985.

Yamato, Gloria. "Something About the Subject Makes it Hard to Name." In *Feminist Frontiers,* edited by Richardson, Taylor and Whittier. New York: McGraw Hill, 1996.